KING of HEISTS

KING of HEISTS

THE SENSATIONAL BANK ROBBERY OF 1878 THAT SHOCKED AMERICA

J. NORTH CONWAY

The Lyons Press
Guilford, Connecticut
An imprint of The Globe Pequot Press

To buy books in quantity for corporate use
or incentives, call **(800) 962–0973**
or e-mail **premiums@GlobePequot.com.**

The Lyons Press is an imprint of The Globe Pequot Press.

Text designer: Libby Kingsbury
Layout artist: Kim Burdick

Library of Congress Cataloging-in-Publication Data is available on file.

ISBN 978-1-59921-538-9

Printed in the United States of America

10 9 8 7 6 5 4 3 2

THIS BOOK IS DEDICATED TO MY WIFE, JULIA.

Contents

INTRODUCTION

The greatest bank robbery in American history took place in October of 1878, when thieves broke into the Manhattan Savings Institution at Bleecker Street and Broadway and stole nearly $3 million in cash and securities. Based on economic calculations conducted through the Economic History Service, the Manhattan bank heist amounts to approximately $50 million by today's currency standards. This far surpasses the 1950 Brink's armored car robbery in Boston, Massachusetts, that netted thieves approximately $3 million (approximately $21 million today), or the great train robbery in London, England, in 1963, where thieves made off with $4 million (about $22 million today). Neither of these twentieth-century bank heists can compare to the Manhattan bank robbery of 1878, and no bank robbery since has equaled it.

According to bank examiners, the exact amount the robbers stole was $2,747,700, nearly $2.5 million of which was in stocks and bonds. It was an incredible amount of money by nineteenth-century standards. The New York Times hailed it as ". . . the most sensational in the history of bank robberies in this country."

The robbery was planned down to the minutest detail by criminal mastermind George L. Leslie, dubbed "the King of Bank Robbers" by New York City police, newspaper reporters, and underworld figures. According to police reports, Leslie was responsible for more than 80 percent of all the bank robberies in the country from 1869 through 1878. Despite his reputation, Leslie was never apprehended and never spent a day of his life in jail.

What made the robbery of the Manhattan Savings Institution more incredible than just the amount taken in the heist was that the bank itself was one of the largest and most imposing in the world. The Manhattan Savings Institution was not just a bank; it was also a depository for the money, jewelry, securities, and other valuables of some of the most prominent, wealthy citizens of New York City. The building was a ponderous labyrinth of bolts, locks, and steel doors, making it an almost impregnable fortress. Using George L. Leslie's intricate plans, which took him three years to devise, his gang was able to pull off the almost impossible feat of cleaning out the *Titanic* of American financial institutions.

This book narrates the incredible double life of George L. Leslie leading up to the Manhattan Savings Institution robbery. Leslie arrived in New York City in 1869. The son of a prosperous Cincinnati brewer, a graduate of the University of Cincinnati, and a successful architect, he ingratiated himself with many of New York City's social, cultural, and financial elite, choosing a life of crime as his means to fame and fortune. Known as a ladies' man, Leslie engaged in a slew of romantic liaisons with several of the wives of his criminal cohorts. Ultimately, it was Leslie's roving eye—not his criminal behavior or the robbery of the Manhattan Savings Institution—that led to his downfall.

It took Leslie three years to plan the robbery. He began by posing as a customer and depositing a substantial sum of his own money in the bank. This allowed him to frequent the building whenever he wanted. He then carefully surveyed the premises until every inch of it was familiar to him, using his training and talent as an architect to build a replica of the bank in an abandoned warehouse. Leslie rehearsed the well-planned robbery with his handpicked gang for months, right down to the split-second timing.

Leslie found a bank vault fabricator and learned how to duplicate the combination of the Manhattan bank vault. He bribed a night watchman and was able to break into the bank whenever he liked in order to try his various vault combinations. Leslie worked tirelessly to find the secret to the vault's tumblers until he finally cracked the combination. The Manhattan Savings Institution was his for the taking. All in all, Leslie broke into the Manhattan Savings Institution three times before his gang actually robbed it.

One of the largest investigations in New York City police annals began immediately following the heist, and slowly, one by one, the men who robbed the Manhattan Savings Institution were tracked down and brought to justice—all except George Leslie. A different fate lay in store for him.

This story about George Leslie and the greatest bank robbery in American history is set in a period of great economic and social contrast—the opulent lifestyle of the wealthy alongside that of the poor and working class during the notorious "Gilded Age" in New York City— which echoes our current times. The phrase *The Gilded Age* was coined by Mark Twain, and served as the title of one of his books, published in 1873. According to Twain, the Gilded Age was a period of great wealth, greed, and poverty, and New York City—where much of this story takes place—was the hub.

The Gilded Age was also a period of tremendous industrial growth and invention. With dramatic increases in the production of iron, oil, and steel, great fortunes were made by enterprising businessmen like Andrew Carnegie, John D. Rockefeller, Jay Gould, James Fisk Jr., and Cornelius Vanderbilt. Dubbed *robber barons* by historian Matthew Josephson, these great business leaders and industrialists were able to accumulate great wealth through often ruthless and sometimes illegal business practices. According to national economic trends of the period, 1 percent of the population owned 99 percent of the wealth during the Gilded Age. Unfortunately, the Gilded Age was also a period marked by massive immigration, unemployment, dire poverty, unsanitary tenement housing, and violent crime. George Leslie was part of this complex era in our country's history, although he did not amass his fortune through business or industry; he simply stole it.

King of Heists is set against the historic backdrop of New York City, intertwined with a host of memorable real-life Gilded Age characters, including Fredericka "Marm" Mandelbaum, the greatest "fence" in the country, and her reign in New York City as queen of the criminals; John D. Rockefeller, president of Standard Oil; Cornelius Vanderbilt, American steamship and railroad builder; Andrew Carnegie, steel magnate; Jay Gould, owner of much of the country's means of communications, including Western Union; and John Roebling and his quest to build the greatest bridge in the world—the Brooklyn Bridge.

This story is about financial wizard "Jubilee" Jim Fisk, owner of the largest brokerage house in New York City and the man responsible for the "Black Friday" stock market crash in 1869; Boss Tweed, corrupt leader of New York City's political machine; Samuel Tilden, the man who lost the most-disputed presidential election in the United States in 1876; President Ulysses S. Grant, and corrupt officials in his administration; Josie Mansfield, New York City showgirl and Fisk's mistress; and Thomas Nast, the political cartoonist who helped bring down Boss Tweed and his cronies. It is about the gangs of criminals who robbed banks, ran whorehouses, gambling dens, barrooms, and saloons, and carried out any and all sorts of criminal offenses. It is about the dichotomy between the rich and the poor, the powerful and powerless, the haves and have-nots.

But mostly, *King of Heists* is about three of the greatest bank robberies in America during this era: the robbery of the Ocean National Bank in 1869; the Northampton Bank robbery in 1876; and the Manhattan Savings Institution heist in 1878, each a record-setting robbery and each carried out under the direction of George Leslie.

Many contemporary economists and pundits have dubbed our current era "The New Gilded Age." With the recent collapse of the financial and housing markets sending the American economy into a dismal recession, the comparison to this previous age seems complete. David Francis in the March 6, 2006, edition of *The Christian Science Monitor* wrote, "The richest 1 percent of Americans now get about 15 percent of total U.S. income, close to the 18 percent the same small group had in 1913. In a way, the days of the robber barons, the tycoons, and the Gilded Age are back . . ." Harvard economist Benjamin Friedman, writing about contemporary times, said, "Inequality by some measures is very high by historical standards."

Currently many corporate CEOs are being paid exorbitant salaries. According to one recent report, the CEO of one major oil company was paid a salary of $55 million a year, while the poverty level in America is $18,000 for a family of four. Recent national economic trends indicate that 43 percent of the nation's 37 million poor people are in deep poverty. Home foreclosures are at an all-time high, hundreds of thousands of people remain out of work, and retirement funds have been lost in the collapse of the financial markets.

We are living today in a period of unparalleled greed and an expanding entrepreneurial era, contemporary economic times uniquely similar to the Gilded Age of the late 1800s. The parallels are astounding, and extend even to politics, and the contested presidential election between Samuel Tilden and Rutherford B. Hayes, which many American voters maintained was stolen by Hayes—similar to public sentiment regarding President George W. Bush's "stolen election" in 2000.

I have made every attempt to not portray Leslie as heroic in any way. Nor have I tried to cast aspersions upon any of the multitude of characters that inhabit this book, rich or poor. I am not trying to judge them, nor am I trying to tell the reader to judge them. I have simply tried to tell you as good a story about George Leslie as I could possibly tell. I have modeled this book, as I have modeled almost every one of my books, after one of my favorite authors, John Dos Passos. He is the author of the *U.S.A.* trilogy, made up of *The 42nd Parallel* (1930), *Nineteen Nineteen* (1932), and *The Big Money* (1936).

Dos Passos used an assortment of techniques in writing these books, including providing the reader with actual newspaper clippings, songs, radio broadcasts, and a degree of what is referred to as *fictional realism* in order to tell his stories. I have attempted to do the same. Wherever I have included quotation marks, these represent the actual words of the person speaking. In other places I have used strictly a chronological narrative. In many instances, I have provided the reader with actual newspaper headlines, news stories, and actual quotes relating to some aspect of the story as it unfolded. I have provided these in order to paint a vast and lively landscape of society and culture during this period in American history.

Some of this story seems hard to believe, but I assure the reader it is all true, as all of the actual newspaper clippings will attest. Even the story about the "cheese and crackers" bank robbers and murders is true. Two notorious criminals were apprehended because a grocery store clerk found their behavior highly suspicious: They came into his general store and bought cheese and crackers just before a bank was robbed and the cashier murdered. The store clerk reported to police that he knew the two men were the culprits because they didn't bother to have the cheese and crackers wrapped up. (Indisputable evidence, if you ask me.) However absurd it may all seem, it is nonetheless true, as are all of the astounding exploits of George Leslie, Marm Mandelbaum, and a host of other real-life characters that inhabit this book. Thank you for your attention.

KING of
HEISTS

1

DELMONICO'S—NEW YORK CITY, 1869

What is the chief end of man?—to get rich. In what way?—dishonestly if we can; honestly if we must.

—MARK TWAIN, AMERICAN HUMORIST AND
AUTHOR (*THE GILDED AGE*, 1873)

Some things never change.

Good looks, nice clothes, and fine manners will take you far, and George Leslie knew that these and other qualities he possessed would take him exactly where he wanted to go. Life had been pretty much a la carte for twenty-seven-year-old George Leslie. He could afford to pick and choose what he wanted depending upon his appetite. Now, he was hungry for a tasty slice of New York City, with a side of easy money.

In 1869, Leslie had just arrived in New York City from Cincinnati. Most of his possessions were still in transit. He set up residency, at least for the time being, at the exclusive Fifth Avenue Hotel. He only knew a handful of people in New York, and one of them was civil engineer John Roebling. Not long after settling in, Roebling invited him to dinner at the exclusive Delmonico's restaurant.

—⚊—

The war was never far from George Leslie's mind. How could it be? The bloodiest conflict in the country's history had come to an end just four years ago, and the wounds were still fresh, for both North and South. Close to three and a half million men had fought in the Civil War, and nearly 700,000, both Union and Confederate troops, had died. A million more were maimed or wounded. Although George Leslie wasn't one of them, it wasn't luck that had saved him.

The specter of the war he had *not* fought in plagued him, followed him everywhere, weighing him down like a great albatross hung around his neck. It drove him from his comfortable home in Cincinnati and his successful architectural business, even from the woman he was once engaged to marry. It followed him everywhere, even to New York City, where Leslie hoped to lose himself in the anonymity of the great burgeoning metropolis. But the ghosts of the war were everywhere, a constant reminder for him— not of what he *had* done during the war, but of what he hadn't.

On every New York City street corner he saw them: tragic young men and boys, begging on the streets, wearing their tattered Union army coats, some sporting medals hanging from faded ribbons on their lapels, a constant reminder of his own imperfection. Their gaunt faces and hollow eyes were grim souvenirs of the horror of the past conflagration. Some wore black patches where an eye had once been, or had a folded coat sleeve tacked to their shoulder where there had once been an arm. Some hobbled on makeshift crutches to support themselves, a leg missing, a foot gone. Others were mere shells of their former selves, lying in the gutter holding out tin cups. Their bodies, minds, and hearts were scarred forever. These horrific casualties proliferated the city's landscape, bearing witness for all to see of the costs of this Great War to preserve the Union. Leslie could not escape them, not even on the busy, crowded streets of New York City.

The Civil War had taken a terrible toll on the country's psyche as well as its people. Men and women, fathers and sons, brothers and sisters, women and children—all had suffered through the four bloodiest years in American history. Even four years after the war's end, the deep wounds inflicted on the country and its people had not healed.

Leslie's home state, Ohio, had provided a quarter-million able-bodied men as soldiers and military officers during the war; only the states of New York and Pennsylvania had provided more troops. His own hometown of

Cincinnati had been a major source of supplies and troops for the Union Army. Several leading generals hailed from the Buckeye State, including President Ulysses S. Grant, William Sherman, and Phil Sheridan. Grant, the "Hero of Appomattox," born in Point Pleasant, Ohio (not far from where Leslie had grown up), had been elected President of the United States in a landslide victory in 1868. At the outset of the war in 1861, thousands of young men from Cincinnati had flocked to military service, but Leslie wasn't one of them. His father had seen to that, buying Leslie's way out of the draft.

Even tucked away at the University of Cincinnati, where he had studied architecture and graduated as an honors student, Leslie wasn't able to escape the scandal that swirled around him. In 1863, at the height of the war, George Leslie was twenty-one years old, a prime candidate for the draft. Hundreds of young men from his hometown were either being drafted to fight in the Union cause or signing up to serve. The Union Conscription Act of 1863, drastically unpopular and a source of riots across the country, called for all able-bodied males between the ages of twenty and forty-five to be drafted into military service. However, it included a provision that allowed wealthy men to pay $300 to buy their way out of service, or to hire a substitute soldier to go in their place.

Leslie's father had paid the $300 outright for George's release from military service—and George had been paying for it ever since. It was a perfectly legal but a highly unpopular course of action, and one that many did not forget after the war ended. Wealthy young men like George Leslie could not have been thought less of; they were considered worse than deserters. Although deserting during wartime was punishable by death, people could at least understand it. The horrors of war could make a young man do just about anything. At the very least, being a deserter meant a man had at least served, at least faced the enemy, even if he chose to run away . . . whereas young men like Leslie were thought to have run away before the first shot had even been fired.

After the war was over, Leslie found himself in the unpopular position of facing ridicule and scorn from many in Cincinnati despite his lofty social standing. There was open hostility toward him, and he was ostracized by many Cincinnati families and former friends who had served or lost someone dear in battle. Their resentment overwhelmed him.

He wanted to start over.

After graduating from the University of Cincinnati, Leslie had been engaged to marry a fragile, beautiful young woman who came from a prosperous Cincinnati family. She was a shy, quiet young woman who wrote poetry, read books, pressed flowers for a hobby, and taught Sunday school. Her father had made a fortune during the war, supplying shovels to the Union Army. After the war, his business continued to flourish when he was contracted to provide shovels for the building of the country's transcontinental railroad. They had their whole life before them.

Her father was a Lincoln Republican and his brother served as a major general during the war. The brother was best known for ordering the raid that became famous as the Great Locomotive Chase. The Chase, sometimes known as Andrews's Raid, was a Union military raid in northern Georgia in 1862. Twenty-two volunteers from Ohio regiments stole a Confederate train, trying to disrupt rail service that ran from Atlanta, Georgia, to Chattanooga, Tennessee. They hoped to burn bridges and dynamite train tunnels along the way. After infiltrating Confederate lines and hijacking a train, they were pursued by other locomotives before finally being captured and imprisoned. Several of them were executed as spies. Some managed to escape back to their regiment. Several of the surviving members of Andrews's Raiders became the first recipients of the Medal of Honor.

It was with a certain degree of trepidation that her father gave his blessing for his daughter's marriage to Leslie. Leslie did, after all, come from a well-to-do family. His father was a successful brewer in Toledo, Ohio. He was well educated, independently wealthy, and ran his own successful architectural firm in Cincinnati. Still, despite his many attributes, there were reservations, mostly because Leslie had bought his way out of the draft. Ohioans did not look kindly on men who paid their way out of the army—not when so many of their young men had died while trying to preserve the Union. Her father was somewhat inclined to overlook it, for the most part, although there remained a nagging doubt about the character of his soon-to-be son-in-law.

Everything was going as planned and would have culminated in a grand wedding and reception sometime in May of 1867, if it were not for the return of Jacob Parrot, a former suitor. At the outbreak of the war, Parrot had volunteered as a private in the 33rd Ohio Infantry, and had also volunteered to take part in the daring train raid in Georgia. He had been one of the lucky ones. He and fourteen others managed to escape, but only six, including Parrot, reached their regiment safely. In 1863, Jacob Parrot became the first recipient of the Union War Department's Medal of Honor. He was a hero, and his return to Cincinnati spelled an end to George Leslie's upcoming nuptials. Within months of Parrot's return, the engagement was broken off and Leslie was banished from his fiancée's household. She ended up marrying Parrot, the war hero.

Leslie knew he could never escape his past transgressions—at least, not while living in Cincinnati. After the death of both his parents in 1867, he sold the family home, closed his architectural firm, packed up everything, and fled to the anonymity that he believed New York City would afford him.

Leslie was twenty-seven years old when he arrived in New York City in the winter of 1869. New York was a bustling metropolis, bursting at the seams with opportunities. Fortunes were being made in oil, banking, railroads, and communications. Important and exciting things were happening. Leslie wanted to shake off his old life and become part of it all. He was not interested in reestablishing his architectural career. For reasons that were not clear to him at the time, he had set his sights on becoming something and someone entirely different. This much he did know: Whatever he ended up pursuing, he wanted no part of his past interfering with his future there in New York City. And he knew he wanted a chance to make what he called "easy money." For George Leslie, there was no easier way of making money than stealing it.

All the respectable things of the world—position, education, and wealth—didn't mean a thing to him anymore. They had all come easily to him and had ultimately gotten him nowhere. What he wanted now was what he'd never had in his life—mystery and adventure. He could never have found them in Cincinnati, and decided he would look for them in New York City.

—⁓—

Delmonico's smelled of charcoal and smoke. The aroma of sizzling beef and boiling potatoes filled up the dining room. A thick cloud of cigar smoke hung like an incoming storm cloud over the noisy patrons. There was the clink of wineglasses and the clatter of plates and silverware. A steady din of modulated conversation was sporadically interrupted by the occasional shriek of laughter. Waiters dressed in white waistcoats and equally white gloves moved like choreographed dancers through the noisy, smoke-filled restaurant, balancing trays filled with food and expensive bottles of wine.

The prices of the famed cuisine at Delmonico's restaurant were sufficiently high to discourage anyone but the very wealthy from patronizing it. It was New York City's most renowned culinary spot. Located in a converted mansion at the corner of Fifth Avenue and Fourteenth Street, a block from Union Square, it was the most luxurious restaurant in the city. It had a café and an elaborate dining room on the first floor. Upstairs was a spacious and lavish ballroom and a score of private dining rooms where many select social functions and private dinners were held. It catered to the city's wealthy upper classes, indulging every culinary whim of its affluent patrons.

The restaurant was started by Giovanni and Pietro Delmonico (John and Peter) in 1837 and soon became known as the country's first fine dining establishment. After Giovanni's death, his son, Lorenzo, joined his uncle in managing the operation. After moving its location several times throughout the city, Delmonico's moved to a refurbished Union Square mansion in 1862. It was the first four-star restaurant in the country, and a gathering place for most of New York City's fashionable elite, from politicians (including the infamous Boss Tweed and his archrival Samuel Tilden) and writers (such as Mark Twain and Ambrose Pierce) to wealthy businessmen, including Wall Street speculator "Jubilee" Jim Fisk and international banker, August Belmont.

It was one of the first stops on George Leslie's New York City itinerary.

—ᴍ—

. . . members of the Delmonico family of restaurateurs . . . were found at their . . . rendezvous of gastronomes on Fifth Avenue . . . A steady stream of celebrities—social, plutocratic, artistic, journalistic, legal and every other shade of professional gentlemen . . . poured through the door of the café, a salon of almost Saracenic splendor and sauntered in and out . . . all over the beautiful building . . . There is now no restaurant in Paris, or London or Vienna which can compete with our Delmonico's in the excellence and variety of its fare . . .

—*New York Tribune* (1869)

—🕮—

Leslie had been the sharpshooting champion of the University of Cincinnati, but the recognition meant very little to him. He had never truly cared for guns. He was not a Union sharpshooter during the war, which might have earned him some modicum of respect and admiration. If he had been, he could have justifiably placed his medals for bravery or sharpshooting, if he had earned them, right next to his university sharpshooting trophy. Then all of it might have meant something.

It was his father's idea for him to join the rifle club at school, and with the help of a private tutor (hired by his father), George learned to shoot both pistols and rifles expertly. Despite all the drudgery of it and the lack of any meaningful recognition, it produced a certain undeniable inner confidence, knowing he could shoot the lights out of anything or anyone, at practically any reasonable distance, with either hand, if he needed to. This skill might have served him well if he had been in the Wild West, but he wasn't. He had lived in Cincinnati, and now, New York City, and it was 1869. Things were more civilized, at least among the more respectable denizens of the great metropolis—or at least they appeared to be. Leslie had little reason to use this acquired skill. Perhaps it was the mere knowledge of this hidden talent that gave him a sense of superiority.

George Leslie was a tall, handsome man—lean, fit, and muscular. Some might have called him rugged were it not for his exquisite taste in clothes. He wore the finest suits money could buy. Since coming to New York, he had purchased several frock coats, vests, and trousers from Brooks Brothers, where everyone who was anyone bought their apparel. He was clean-shaven, with a cleft in his strong chin. His complexion was clear and genial, his wide brown eyes, sincere and bright. With his dashing good looks and dress, impeccable manners, and outgoing personality, Leslie had very little trouble ingratiating himself with New York City's social elite.

There was an apparent air of superiority that emanated from him. It was not the expensive clothes he wore, or his education, or his personal wealth that gave off this initial impression to others. It was something about the way he cocked his head back and to one side, appearing to look down his nose through his spectacles that made him appear judgmental, if not downright superior. He had started wearing glasses after graduating because the close, meticulous work at his drafting table had taken a toll on his otherwise perfect eyesight. He might not have had good eyesight, but George knew he had vision. He saw everything, including his future, clear as a bell.

His propensity to cock his head and, with a penetrating stare through his glasses, appear to weigh someone's every word made him appear to be judging whether the speaker truly had anything worthwhile to say. This was unnerving for some, who likely misconstrued it as arrogance or conceit. It wasn't. It was an overt mannerism that was initially unnerving but was soon forgotten and forgiven within the continuum of Leslie's all-encompassing persona of exquisite charm, astonishing good looks, and impeccable manners. There wasn't the slightest bit of etiquette that escaped him, from the gentlemanly habit of bowing slightly when introduced, to waiting until everyone else was seated before seating himself. He lit cigarettes and cigars for companions and guests, and poured wine for tasting. He opened doors and held chairs for ladies, and he would rise from his seat when anyone (except, of course, the help) joined his company. He was gracious and charming to everyone he came in contact with.

Leslie was a voracious reader and could converse easily on almost every subject, from current affairs to history. He had brought a dozen crates of his favorite books from Cincinnati, along with four crates of his best furniture, six chests of fine china and silverware, and ten trunks of clothes and other personal provisions. He had packed and shipped only a single photograph of his parents, and none of himself. Everything was in transit, due to arrive shortly at Penn Central train station, having been shipped from Cincinnati. He took up temporary residency at the exclusive Fifth Avenue Hotel, renting a suite to accommodate his soon-to-arrive belongings.

—⟫—

At Delmonico's that evening, Leslie unfolded his napkin and placed it carefully on his lap. He had ordered the classic Delmonico steak, a twenty-ounce boneless rib eye cooked to perfection, baked oysters with bacon, tomato, and hollandaise, and a glass of Cabernet. He surveyed the lush dining room with its ornate oak furniture and tiger-wood tables, the marble and carpeted floors, the frescoed walls, the glimmering silver chandeliers, and the stained-glass windows. He took an admiring and careful inventory of the table set before him. The linen tablecloths glistened with engraved glassware, crystal stemware, porcelain service, Haviland china, and hand-painted Limoges orchid plates. Although the plates didn't match, the patterns complemented each other in a distinct Delmonico's tradition.

An array of silverware was spread out before him, nontraditionally, from the right of the plate, rather than the left—polished forks for dinner, salad, sardine, fish, and dessert courses. These weapons of class distinction were made of delicately etched sterling, and Leslie used each and every one with deft accomplishment. George Leslie was nothing if not precise, paying special attention to the small and intricate cut-glass salt and pepper shakers with their sterling silver caps. The minuscule shakers could fit into the palm of his hand.

John Roebling was seated nearby. The eminent engineer was tall, over six feet. He was well proportioned, his chest broad and his frame muscular. He had a long face with a broad forehead and a curved, longish nose with flaring nostrils. He had bushy eyebrows, and his thick, dark beard was longer than what was typical for the day. He had a huge down-curling mustache and luxuriant muttonchop whiskers. Confident and poised, Roebling cut a dashing figure. His eyes, dark and squinting, darted to and fro with enthusiasm as he spoke. His face had the stamp of authority.

Leslie knew Roebling by reputation. New to the city and without many social contacts, Leslie drew on his architectural background to make acquaintances. Roebling had ties to Leslie's hometown of Cincinnati, having built the Cincinnati Suspension Bridge, a landmark since its completion in 1866. The 1,057-foot main span of the Cincinnati Bridge was, at the time of its completion, the longest in the world. It was also the first suspension bridge to employ both vertical suspenders and diagonal stays crossing from either tower to support it. It was an engineering marvel that Roebling intended to improve upon in his next big project, the building of the Brooklyn Bridge, which he projected would far surpass the Cincinnati Suspension Bridge in length, making it an unparalleled engineering feat.

Roebling had recently been named chief engineer for the building of the Brooklyn Bridge. The plans he submitted for building the enormous structure called for a crossing between the city of Brooklyn and lower Manhattan. It was viewed as a solution to the overpopulation of the city, which in 1869, was made up of only the borough of Manhattan. Roebling claimed that when he completed the proposed Brooklyn Bridge, it would not only be the greatest bridge ever built in America—it would also be the greatest engineering achievement of the century. According to Roebling, the great towers he planned to build to support the bridge would be worthy of being designated as national monuments. Leslie had no reason to doubt him. Roebling's conversation seldom strayed from his relentless talk of his much-heralded project. He invited Leslie down to the wharf along the East River to view the proposed site for himself. It was the last thing in the world Leslie was interested in doing, here in majestic and mysterious New York City. Still, charming as ever, he graciously accepted the invitation.

John Roebling had first proposed building a suspension bridge over the East River in 1855, as an alternative to the slow and cumbersome Atlantic Avenue–Fulton Street Ferry. He was by then the wealthy owner of a successful wire-rope company and already a famous bridge engineer. He had worked out every detail of the planned bridge, from its proposed gigantic stone towers to its mighty steel cables. His plan was initially met with skepticism by New York and Brooklyn politicians, but Roebling countered the opposition with some political clout of his own. He enlisted the support of William Kingsley, a Brooklyn businessman with vast political connections, and the publisher of the highly influential newspaper, the *Brooklyn Daily Eagle.*

Kingsley then solicited the cooperation of Henry Murphy, a New York state senator and the former mayor of Brooklyn. Murphy crafted a legislative bill that he submitted to the New York State Legislature that would permit a private company to build a bridge connecting the two cities of Manhattan and Brooklyn. By 1867, a group of prominent political and businessmen had formed the New York Bridge Company, whose sole purpose was to build and maintain a bridge across the East River. The Brooklyn council pledged $3 million of the capital stock, while the city of New York subscribed to half that amount, $1.5 million. The New York Bridge Company was allowed to fix toll rates for pedestrians and vehicles for which they would receive a profit of 15 percent per year.

To convince those who still doubted the necessity of the bridge, Roebling predicted that the projected population and business growth in the cities of New York and Brooklyn would require the construction of even more bridges in the future. In addition to the Brooklyn Bridge, Roebling proposed building additional bridges, including the Williamsburg and

Queensboro bridges. In 1869, the New York City Council and the Army Corps of Engineers approved Roebling's plan to build the much-touted Brooklyn Bridge.

Roebling had come to America from Prussia in 1831, where he led a group of friends to Saxonburg, Pennsylvania. There they established a successful farming community. He went on to invent wire cable to replace the hemp ropes used in towing. The success of his wire business led him to ultimately buy a three-acre tract of land in Trenton, New Jersey, where he established his first wire-manufacturing factory. His first contract was to build a bridge over the Monongahela River. It was completed in 1846. But the bridge that ultimately established Roebling's reputation as a master bridge builder was the suspension bridge he constructed over Niagara Falls, finished in 1855. This was followed by the construction of the Cincinnati Bridge over the Ohio River, and, finally, to his beloved Brooklyn Bridge proposal.

But Roebling was not the only one whose dreams were coming true. George Leslie's dream of establishing himself in New York high society was coming to fruition as well. While Roebling prattled on about the bridge, Leslie surveyed his surroundings, feeling smugly confident and self-satisfied, immersed in Delmonico's atmosphere of gaiety, surrounded by the city's social elite, knowing full well how easily he fit in. The conversations swirling around him were glib and flattering, sometimes subtly sexual, and always profoundly engrossing. He had finally arrived.

—⟋⟋⟍—

After the Civil War, New York City had become the hub of commerce and industry in the United States. It was home to many of the country's wealthiest families—the Astors, Carnegies, Vanderbilts, and Rockefellers—and, accordingly, home to the largest banking and financial institutions as well. It was one of the world's largest cities, with a population of a million and a half people. But along with its opportunities and opulence, New York also had a darker side. It was one of the poorest and most corrupt metropolitan centers in the world. The city was riddled with waterfront slums and overflowing with poor immigrant families who were crowded into filthy tenement housing, trying desperately to survive in an environment of hunger, poverty, ignorance, and crime. Although the city's movers and shakers who lived in the lap of luxury in upper Manhattan were aware of the woes of the immigrant population, they were kept at a comfortable distance. New York's financial and social elite were content to let the police and crime lords reign over this ugly part of city life.

For New York City and the rest of the country, it was the beginning of the Gilded Age, an era in American history marked by lavish wealth, greed, corruption, and a socioeconomic divide between the haves and have-nots greater than had ever been experienced before. *The Gilded Age* was a term coined by the country's preeminent humorist, Mark Twain. In their novel, *The Gilded Age: A Tale of Today* (1873), Twain and his co-author, Charles Dudley Warner, ridiculed the excess of the country's rich, painting a portrait of an American society steeped in corruption and scandal. According to Twain and Warner, America was divided not into the North and South, but into the ultra-rich and the devastatingly poor—a society that placed no limits on luxuries for the rich, with no hope in sight for the poor immigrants who flooded into urban areas like New York City looking to fulfill the American Dream.

Twain summed up this period in American history (1870–1900) simply enough: "What is the chief end of man?—to get rich. In what way?—dishonestly if we can; honestly if we must."

It was an era of great industry and invention. The Standard Oil Company was incorporated by John D. Rockefeller. Andrew Carnegie founded Carnegie Steel, which would later become U.S. Steel. Companies as varied as the Sherwin-Williams Paint Company, Pillsbury, B. F. Goodrich, and Liggett & Myers Tobacco Company were created. The telephone was invented by Alexander Graham Bell. Thomas Edison invented the phonograph and the lightbulb, and established Edison Electric Light Company, which became General Electric. Central Park in New York City was completed, and the Brooklyn Bridge was built.

With the dramatic increase in the production of iron, oil, and steel during this period, vast fortunes were made by businessmen like Rockefeller, Vanderbilt, Carnegie, and others. Their great wealth supported their opulent lifestyles, the likes of which had never been seen in the country before. Families such as the Vanderbilts and Astors built mansions in New York and luxurious summer homes in places such as Newport, Rhode Island, emulating European aristocracy. They lived like royalty, pursuing hobbies such as sailing, horse breeding and racing, fox hunting, and polo. They spent excessive sums of money on furnishing their homes with stunning European art and exquisite furniture. The Vanderbilts' Hyde Park mansion, built in 1898, was considered the most palatial mansion ever built in the United States.

Vernon Louis Parrington, a Washington University professor and winner of the 1928 Pulitzer Prize in history for his work, *Main Currents in American Thought,* said of the era, "Exploitation was the business of the times." Still others would condemn the period as one that lacked an ethical or moral compass. Historian Matthew Josephson reinforced Parrington's opinion, noting that America in the Gilded Age was formed by the "exploitation of many by the few." It was Josephson who coined the term *robber barons* to depict the likes of Rockefeller, Vanderbilt, Carnegie, J. P. Morgan, and others—men who amassed their great fortunes at the expense of the poor and lowly, through illegal means and ruthless business practices.

The vast corruption and greed that proliferated throughout America during the Gilded Age reached all the way to the highest office in the land. During Ulysses S. Grant's presidency (1869–1877), Grant and most of his cabinet were tainted by a series of spectacular scandals that rocked the country. The Credit Mobilier affair was perhaps the worst, an intricate scheme involving the building of the transcontinental railway. Building the railroad was considered one of the principal American engineering feats of the nineteenth century. Ceremonially completed in the spring of 1869, it served as an integral network for American commerce and travel, connecting the eastern and western halves of the country. The railroad was financed with substantial amounts of money provided by the government. The board of directors of the Union Pacific Railroad formed a fake company called Credit Mobilier of America, awarding themselves huge construction contracts and funneling millions of dollars into the pockets of the directors and their friends. Congressmen, members of Grant's cabinet, and even his vice president, Schuyler Colfax, were caught up in the scandal. Many accepted bribes in exchange for not investigating the scheme. Colfax accepted railroad stock as a bribe, and his involvement in the scandal led to the end of his political career.

Along with the great strides in industrialization during the Gilded Age, the country was also experiencing a tremendous growth in population, with thousands of immigrants flocking to urban areas such as New York City. Many came carrying all they owned on their backs, looking for work and their piece of the American Dream. What they found instead was poverty, sickness, crime, and open hostility. The population of the United States had reached nearly 50 million people, of which almost 7 million were immigrants. Slums and dilapidated tenements spread across city landscapes, creating neighborhoods that teemed with crime and filth. Most Americans, the "many" that Josephson alluded to, labored in sheer poverty.

During the dubiously named Gilded Age, New York City was *the* most corrupt metropolitan area in the world. Politicians were easily and readily bribed, graft was an accepted political procedure, the police force was on the take, and crime, at the hands of hundreds of disparate gangs, ran the city. Few if any politicians or law enforcement officials tried to control the corruption. According to one report, New York City during this era harbored more than 30,000 known criminals, ranging from murderers to pickpockets, 20,000 prostitutes, 3,000 drinking houses, and 2,000 illegal gambling operations.

This was the New York City George Leslie discovered when he arrived. It was everything he expected it would be, and more.

—w—

As they finished their meal at Delmonico's, Leslie picked up the tiny crystal salt and pepper shakers that had been set on the table. He studied them for an instant, admiring the way the miniature cut glass reflected the light from the overhead chandeliers, turning it into a prism of rainbow colors. He cupped both shakers in the palm of his hand and shook them briefly like someone might shake a pair of ivory dice. He slid his hand into the pocket of his waistcoat and let them fall into his pocket; when he withdrew his hand, he held his gold pocket watch. He flipped it open to check the time. Leslie did not look around to see if anyone had noticed what he'd done. It didn't matter; Roebling was oblivious.

Leslie didn't need salt and pepper shakers regardless of how ornate and precious they might have been. He could afford to buy dozens of them if he'd wished. It wasn't that he needed them or even wanted them; it was simply that he could get away with it. That was the thrill for him. Taking what wasn't his in plain sight, right under everyone's noses—that's what drove him. And if anyone had asked, he would simply reply that he'd accidentally dropped the shakers into his coat pocket when he'd reached for his watch., Who wouldn't believe him? His watch alone was a hundred times more valuable than the crystal salt and pepper shakers. Leslie smiled to himself. They would understand—the fat and flattered, the rich and respectable. He wasn't any different than they were. Granted, they stole on a much grander scale—stole what they wanted, whether land or businesses. Stole whatever they could get their hands on in plain view. Stole even what they didn't need, just to have more. Respectability had its benefits. They were only salt and pepper shakers, but they were a start. Soon, he imagined, he too would steal on a grander scale just like the rich and powerful did. And he would do it in ways they could never imagine. Sometimes he thought of himself as a madman, disguised as a rational human being.

—⁓—

Roebling pointed across the crowded dining room to where a short, rotund man with reddish hair and a generous mustache sat entertaining a beautiful young woman and a rather dour-looking younger gentleman. The portly gentleman was shamelessly animated, waving his arms over his head, engaged in some humorous account that seemed to delight the young woman even as it annoyed the younger man sitting close beside her.

Roebling had promised to introduce Leslie to some of the city's finest and most important citizens. Little did he suspect that he was about to meet one of the city's *most* flamboyant and successful financiers, Jubilee Jim Fisk. Roebling led the way with Leslie following close behind. The salt and pepper shakers clinked in the pocket of his waistcoat as he crossed the floor, politely dodging harried waiters.

2

JUBILEE JIM

The blonde, bustling and rollicking James Fisk, Jr. . . . came bounding into the Wall Street circus like a star acrobat, fresh, exuberant, glittering with spangles, and turning double-summersets, apparently as much for his own amusement as for that of a large circle of spectators. He is first, last and always a man of theatrical effects, of grand transformations, and blue fire . . .

–W. W. FOWLER, WALL STREET STOCKBROKER (1869)

Meeting Jubilee Jim Fisk, one of New York City's most successful financiers, was a high spot of the evening for George Leslie. Fisk was, in his own milieu, everything Leslie aspired to become. He was the best at what he did, and he had grown fabulously wealthy doing it. How could Leslie not be attracted to such a man? He had all the attributes Leslie desired, except one. Leslie had no intention of becoming another New York City Wall Street speculator. He had his eye on Wall Street, but for entirely different reasons.

Fisk—the flamboyant thirty-six-year-old Wall Street speculator, owner of the Erie Railway Company, the Narragansett, Fall River, and Bristol steamship lines, and impresario of the newly refurbished Grand Opera House at West Twenty-third Street and Eighth Avenue—did not bring corporate looting and corruption to New York City. It was already in full swing when he arrived in 1866. Fisk merely turned it into a fine art.

Jubilee Jim was short and rotund, weighing close to 300 pounds, homely but with expressive features. He had sagging jowls and a full handlebar mustache, expertly waxed to almost dangerous fine points at the ends. He sported abundant muttonchop whiskers that showcased his wide-set, protuberant eyes and reddish-yellow hair, parted smartly down the center of his head and ending in two smartly waxed curls along his temples. His fingers flashed with a wide assortment of gold and diamond rings, and his tie pin was a solid diamond the size of a silver dollar. He was uproariously merry and good-tempered, laughing loudly at his own off-color jokes behind a constant cloud of cigar smoke that caused a chronic cough behind his bushy red mustache. He was physically clumsy and awkward, and never cared for physical exercise of any sort. "I'm like one of our Erie locomotives. I always have a tender behind. I never rode on horseback an hour in my life without having to take my meals from a mantelpiece for three days afterward," Fisk once said of himself.

He spoke without grace or manners. Although he had a tinny, high voice, his gregarious nature and often sunny disposition made it tolerable to listeners. Whether intentionally to throw off an unsuspecting audience and make them think he was indeed the hayseed hick from Vermont they imagined he was, or to guilelessly express his true nature and blustering excitement, Fisk tortured and mangled the English language, often filling his statements with outrageous, often incomprehensible, but always colorful language. He admitted to making up some phrases on his own, while he confessed he had picked up others in the backwaters of his home state of rural Vermont, or at the circus where he had worked for many of his formative teen years as a barker. Whatever the case, he was apt to infuse his speech with the likes of "Honesty is worth two in the bush," thereby mangling two well-known proverbs. Or he might utter the likes of "It went where the woodbine twineth" if referring to some missed opportunity to make money. "It is better to have lost and won than never to have played at all," was another example of his colorfully scrambled diction. Even when occasionally called on it, Fisk would attribute his language to some vague confusion, confessing he was like "Bedlam in a breeze."

Besides being known for his financial acumen, the animated, extremely extroverted Jubilee Jim was widely known throughout New York's high society for his loud and outlandish dress. He had recently bought the rank of colonel from New York's Ninth Regiment militia and had purchased expensive and extravagant uniforms for them, all heavily festooned with gold braid. He had a special uniform made for himself as well that included a two-thousand-dollar, diamond-studded jacket with a black velvet robe and mink collar, along with a gold, jeweled sword. His uniform was reported to have been as gorgeous as a Mexican general's regimental attire. The running joke was that his tailor must have had to tie two tape measures together in order to determine Fisk's enormous girth.

—⁓—

Leslie bowed slightly as if being introduced to royalty while graciously shaking Fisk's hand in a hearty, congratulatory way. As in everything he did, Leslie's gesture was deliberate and rehearsed. It was not done solely for Fisk and his guests. He had practiced his outward behavior as if preparing for a part in a play, and perhaps George Leslie did indeed see himself as the leading man in some lavish production of his own creation. He would spend hours standing before the full-length mirror in his hotel room, practicing his bow, his handshake, and his intriguing smile.

Each bow had its purpose—always to show respect, of course, but also to indicate his level of admiration and respect for the person he was being introduced to. A slight bow, more of a tip of his head than anything else, was reserved for those he was not enamored of. A more pronounced bow, bending slightly at his waist with his shoulders thrust a bit forward, was used for those he was interested in becoming acquainted with but had yet to discover why or how. The last bow in his repertoire, a full-blown flourishing bow at the waist, was strictly reserved for the cream of the crop, and Jubilee Jim Fisk was surely one of New York City's finest.

Leslie also took great pains to practice his handshake by using a pincushion and standing in front the mirror. The faint, barely recognizable handshake, limp in nature, was once again reserved for the general populace. It was a handshake that said, "Yes, I am required to do this, but I have no interest in continuing any relationship with you." The indents in the pincushion would be hardly noticeable. His second handshake, reserved for those he was inclined toward knowing better, was a tighter, firmer handshake—not overly aggressive, but sincere and memorable, one that was sure to let the person know that he was indeed pleased to be in his or her company and would like to continue the relationship. The pincushion would show the clear definition of his palm and fingers. Lastly, reserved, once again, for the cream of the crop, like Fisk and others whom he greatly admired or in some way wished to emulate, he had practiced a hearty, lasting, congratulatory, and overly animated handshake that clearly conveyed his great admiration and respect. In this case, the pincushion he practiced on would show the effect of his crushing grip.

For the ladies he was introduced to, he had developed a single sweeping gesture that he had practiced endlessly to perfection. This and only this modus operandi applied to every woman, young or old, rich or poor, beautiful or homely. He would bow with great enthusiasm, as if greeting a long-lost friend, cup the woman's hand gently in his, as if not so much holding her hand as balancing it delicately on his own, and with the slightest brush of his lips, he would kiss her hand and then gently remove his own, leaving the woman's hand floating in space. The kiss was always brief and appropriate but tinged with a certain sense of mystery. Rising up from his bow and from kissing the woman's hand in this gentlemanly way, he would maintain deep and penetrating eye contact with the woman, as if judging her response to his ovation. It usually sent hearts aflutter, exactly the reaction he was looking for.

His smile too was practiced to perfection, often many times before going out in public. A slight parting of his lips beneath his dark trimmed mustache was reserved for the general public. A broader, more expansive grin, where he bared his pearly white teeth, was awarded to those he would like to get to know better. And a wide, open-mouthed smile that stretched lines in his cheeks—sometimes referred to as smiling from ear to ear— was saved for royalty like Jubilee Jim. Being introduced to Fisk at Delmonico's, Leslie pulled out all the stops. Smiling ear to ear, he bowed deeply and shook Fisk's hand heartily.

Leslie was introduced as a successful architect from Cincinnati, the son of a wealthy Toledo beer magnate. Even before being introduced to the other two people dining with Fisk, Ned Stokes and Josie Mansfield, Leslie congratulated Fisk on his new theatrical venture, the Grand Opera House. Leslie noted that Pike's Opera House—which had been refurbished by Fisk and renamed the Grand Opera House—had been built by a Cincinnati man, Samuel N. Pike. Leslie lavished praise on Fisk for what he had accomplished, making the opera house the most majestic theatrical venue in the entire city. Fisk was not beyond flattery when it came to the theater, and he beamed with pride upon hearing Leslie's unsolicited assessment of the place. His plump cheeks grew rosy red with delight. Fisk immediately offered Leslie free tickets to his newest production, an extravagant musical performance called *The Twelve Temptations*.

—ᴍ—

In 1868, Fisk and Jay Gould, his dour partner at the Erie Railroad, bought the former Pike's Opera House at West Twenty-third Street and Eighth Avenue. The former owner, Samuel N. Pike, had lost a considerable amount of money trying to produce operas at the huge, four-story, 2,600-seat theater. Pike was more than happy to sell it to Fisk for the previously unheard-of amount of more than $800,000. The building was to serve not only as a theatrical venue, but also as the corporate headquarters for the Erie Railway, with extravagantly renovated offices to be located on the top three floors. The theater was completely refurbished at a cost of close to $300,000, and renamed the Grand Opera House. A great spiral staircase was installed in the lobby of the main building. The walls and ceilings of the theater portion were lavishly frescoed and the windows were draped with luxurious red silk curtains. Lush red carpeting was installed throughout the lobby, and gilded banisters and doorways adorned every room. A huge bronze bust of Shakespeare greeted theatergoers as they entered the lobby.

Although often claiming that the Erie Railway enterprise was too destitute to pay its directors substantial dividends from their investments, Fisk's offices on the second floor were even more palatial than the theater below. Two huge oak doors opened onto a vast hallway upstairs. Outside Fisk's office stood two uniformed guards assigned the task of opening and closing the huge bronze gate that protected Fisk inside his inner sanctum. He sat in a raised, gold-trimmed chair, more throne than chair, behind a massive oak desk, which was on most occasions devoid of any paperwork. Whatever Erie-related business Fisk attended to, he kept in his head and nowhere else.

The ceiling was painted with a gilded crimson emblem with the word ERIE in the center, hovering over Fisk's huge desk and throne-like chair.

Bright red silk curtains hung from every window, and the walls were adorned with an array of gilded mirrors. The floor was covered with wall-to-wall plush gold carpeting, on top of which were laid a series of expensive Persian rugs. A huge marble washstand was built in one corner of the vast ornate room. On the tops of various tables throughout the room were beautifully hand-painted porcelain bowls adorned with an array of frolicking nymphs in questionable and appropriately seductive positions. Fisk had spared no expense in making his second-floor office a spectacular den of luxury and splendor.

The considerable suite of sumptuous offices above the Opera House became the scene of nightly revelry, gambling, and other assorted vices. For Erie stockholders it remained a questionable extravagance and one that led to countless lurid rumors of theater showgirls romping half-naked through Fisk's palatial office, drunk on champagne, stuffed with Delmonico oysters, and engaged in debauchery the likes of which could only be compared to Roman orgies of old. Fisk never denied cast members from his shows the chance to visit his upstairs offices and simply shrugged off criticism of his rumored shocking behavior.

Fisk was bound and determined to make the Grand Opera House a financial success, at any price. Everything he had touched had turned to gold, and there was no reason to assume that his foray into the entertainment business would be any different. He ingeniously worked at making the endeavor a moneymaker, relying heavily on his background as a circus barker to attract audiences to his theater. He advertised special train rates for people wanting to attend one of the opera house performances. He assembled gaudy and costly lamppost signage where he advertised the Grand Opera House shows in ornate glass panels. On the opposite and less-conspicuous side of the signs he blandly advertised Erie Railway business, including train timetables. Fisk also made available free private theater boxes to select theatergoers, often plying them with free champagne and other assorted luxuries, all at the expense of the railroad. He attempted to lure crowds to the theater by lowering admission rates to fifty cents.

Following a series of less-than-spectacular shows, including a succession of maudlin melodramas, Fisk produced his first major theatrical success—the gaudy song-and-dance show called *The Twelve Temptations*. The production was staged at the huge cost of $75,000. It included a bloated cast of more than two hundred actors and actresses, and among other innovative, if not extravagant props, a real water fountain. The show featured a rip-snorting cancan number, complete with an array of questionably clad, leggy and buxom, ravishingly beautiful dancers, alternating blondes and brunettes in an extraordinary chorus line of singers and dancers. *The Twelve Temptations* played to packed houses week after week, and each week, Fisk added a new innovation, boosting his chorus line from fifty beautiful showgirls to more than a hundred.

—∞—

THE DEMON CAN-CAN
Received Nightly with Wild Enthusiasm

TERPSICHOREAN AEROSTATICS
—The Mystery Still Unsolved

THE EGYPCIAN [sic] BALLET
—The Most Novel of Novelties

THE GRAND TRANSFORMATION SCENE
The Wonder of Wonders

100 BEAUTIFUL YOUNG LADIES
Contains Nothing Objectionable

—Advertisement for *The Twelve Temptations*
(appearing in the *New York Tribune,* 1869)

—∞—

Before Leslie had a chance to say another word, Fisk thrust two tickets to the show into Leslie's hand. He then introduced Leslie to his dinner guests. Leslie took Josie Mansfield's extended hand and cupped it gently, kissed it quickly, and took his hand away, looking deeply into the beautiful young woman's eyes as he stepped back. Mansfield was voluptuous in a black silk dress, red velvet jacket, and hat, with a mini veil covering her forehead. Around her long, slim neck she wore a string of pearls and gold bracelets on each wrist. From her ears dangled two noticeably large diamond earrings. And on every other finger on both of her hands she wore an assortment of gold, emerald, diamond, and ruby rings of varying sizes and styles. Her large, dark, oval-shaped eyes gave her a slightly Asian appearance. Her hair was a mass of purple-black curls, and her skin was smooth and pale. Her mouth was wide and expressive, her lips full and alluring. She was splendidly pear-shaped and moved with girlish ease and dexterity. As he gazed into her otherwise dark blue eyes, Leslie noticed one small defect—a speck of brown in one eye that in no way detracted from her otherwise flawless beauty.

When Mansfield smiled at Leslie, her whole face lit up, merely adding to her already striking good looks. It was a sweet, innocent smile, but one, like Leslie's own gentlemanly attributes, calculated to obtain undefined results from the person she was kind enough to bestow it upon.

Fisk had rescued the stunningly beautiful former San Francisco showgirl from dire poverty and had adorned her with expensive jewelry, gowns, and furs. He had even purchased a magnificent four-story brownstone at 359 West Twenty-third Street, down the street from the Grand Opera House and his Erie Railway offices. Fisk spent a small fortune decorating the place for his twenty-two-year-old mistress, supplying her with a cook, butler, and chambermaid—even a coach and horses. Nothing was too much for his paramour. Fisk went on to buy a dozen houses along Twenty-third Street, setting himself up in one of them halfway between his work and Mansfield.

Mansfield originally came from Boston. Her family had moved to San Francisco when she was young. She was reportedly involved in several sordid affairs in California, all of which she was able to successfully conceal from practically everyone, including Fisk. When Fisk met her, she had merely been a leggy showgirl. The Grand Opera House was to be a showcase for Mansfield's dubious acting talents, but Fisk later thought better of that idea. He did not want his mistress on display to the world; instead, she was relegated to a life of idle luxury. Coming from an ambiguous if not disreputable working-class background, Mansfield was not accustomed to simply doing nothing. She had no hobbies, didn't like reading, and was not otherwise engaged in feminine activities like sewing, painting, or even socializing. She had become bored, hungry for something new and exciting, something or someone to quench her manipulative thirst. She found it in ways that Fisk, the otherwise astute businessman, failed to recognize.

—⁘—

Before meeting Jim Fisk, Helen Josephine Mansfield had been an unemployed actress. She owned nothing except the dress she wore. Behind on her rent and facing eviction from the dirty flophouse she had been living in, she was being hounded by bill collectors of every shape and size. She often had to disguise herself in order to elude them.

By 1869, things had changed dramatically. As Fisk's mistress, she was living on a scale that had once been unimaginable to her. Through Fisk's amorous generosity she had acquired the four-story brownstone on Twenty-third Street that she owned outright. Her majestic home was furnished with expensive furniture, antiques, paintings, chandeliers, fine china, and silverware. She had a stunning collection of the most expensive gowns, furs, and jewelry worth more than $100,000 and worthy of any Fifth Avenue socialite. Along with servants and her own private carriage and coachman, she had a private box at the Grand Opera House, an entire club car reserved for her on any of the Erie Railway lines, and a private berth in any number of Fisk's steamships. She owed everything to Jim Fisk and his generosity, but still, she had a restless heart and a roving eye that included both men and women. And surely this would include the handsome, gentlemanly George Leslie.

—⁘—

Jim Fisk was married in 1854 at the age of nineteen to Lucy Moore, just fifteen at the time, from Springfield, Massachusetts. He bought her a four-story mansion in the fashionable Chester Square in Boston, where he kept her out of sight and mind while he immersed himself in his businesses in New York. A solitary yet comfortable arrangement for his wife, it was one that Lucy herself preferred. A shy, retiring young woman, Lucy Fisk disliked the hustle and bustle of New York City. The sedate pace of Boston was more to her liking, and besides, she wasn't sure she could tolerate her husband's rough-and-tumble public antics. Although an odd arrangement, it was a separation of her choosing, and one that preserved their marital bliss. Not especially keen on being alone in the huge mansion he had bought for her, Lucy Fisk brought in childhood friend Fanny Harrod to live with her. The two became inseparable companions—some even rumored lovers.

This, like his wife Lucy's romantic involvement with another woman, was another matter Jubilee Jim Fisk failed to recognize. With Lucy stashed away in Boston, Fisk was able to devote his time to his many businesses. The arrangement also allowed him to publicly squire a succession of New York City showgirls around the city—until he fell under the spell of the young, beautiful Josie Mansfield, sarcastically referred to behind Fisk's back as "The Cleopatra of Twenty-third Street."

Although Fisk did not remain faithful to his wife, he did remain dutiful, visiting her in Boston every few weeks, and spending summer vacations and holidays with her. He remained married to her until his violent and untimely death in 1872.

—⁂—

Leslie shook hands limply with Ned Stokes, seated next to Josie Mansfield at the table in Delmonico's. Although Stokes appeared unusually anxious for some reason, he was certainly fashionably dressed, wearing an elegant topcoat, dark trousers with gold piping, and immaculately shined riding boots.

Edward Stiles Stokes was a Wall Street acquaintance of Jim Fisk's. The twenty-eight-year-old was a social gadfly, a sportsman, and a splendid fashion plate who wore even more diamonds and jewelry than Fisk himself, although his jewelry was often in hock in order to finance his extravagant lifestyle. Stokes had a lithe but athletic physique. He was classically handsome, with straight, jet-black hair brushed back over his ears and mustache. It was rumored that Stokes spent upwards of two hours a day tending to his grooming. Addicted to gambling, especially betting on racehorses, he followed the racing season from one track to another, traveling from New York to Rhode Island and even Florida to bet on the ponies.

Born in Philadelphia, Stokes moved to New York with his family in 1860. His father was a wealthy produce wholesaler. Stokes married young and well. His wife, Helen Southwick, was the daughter of a rich furniture magnate. He and Helen had a six-year-old daughter whom Stokes didn't see much of, given his propensity for gambling and certain other disreputable activities.

During the Civil War, Stokes, like Leslie, had bought his way out of the draft. He made a small profit in the New York produce business during the war, selling to the military. He also managed to make a financial killing in the oil business. Using money he had borrowed from his parents, he constructed an oil refinery in Brooklyn. When the refinery was nearly destroyed in a fire and the oil business went belly-up, Stokes was forced to file for bankruptcy.

Although intent on reestablishing himself in the oil industry, his attraction to racetracks, betting parlors, showgirls, and saloons limited his business pursuits. With money from his (and his wife's) parents, Stokes was able to continue living in luxury with his family at their fashionable home along Fifth Avenue and Twenty-sixth Street.

It was Jim Fisk who gave Stokes his big break. Seeing the possibility for big profits in oil refining, Fisk formed a company with Stokes and provided the money to rebuild Stokes's original Brooklyn-based refinery. With Fisk as president of the new company and Stokes as treasurer, the rebuilt refinery prospered. Under normal circumstances, the profits would have wiped out all of Stokes's back debts—were it not for the fact that Stokes was able to incur new debts faster than he could realize profits from the oil refinery business.

Fisk took a liking to the erratic Stokes and introduced him to Josie Mansfield. Among other things, Stokes began spending an inordinate amount of time at the Grand Opera House, which featured an elegant saloon. Stokes would often call on Mansfield to join him for drinks when Fisk was otherwise occupied with his complicated business dealings. Soon, Stokes and Mansfield became inseparable, not only socially but privately as well. Mansfield's romantic entanglement with the handsome and unreliable Stokes went on right under Jubilee Jim's rather bulbous nose.

—⚏—

It was no simple accomplishment to put one over on Jubilee Jim Fisk; despite being one of the most astute financial wheelers and dealers, he was nonetheless a fool for love when it came to Josie Mansfield.

No one would have suspected that beneath the facade of his flamboyant and jovial demeanor, Jubilee Jim was one of the country's shrewdest and most arrogant and ruthless business tycoons. Born in Bennington, Vermont, in 1834 on April Fools' Day, he ran away from home when he was sixteen years old and joined a traveling circus, Van Amburgh & Co.'s Mammoth Circus & Menagerie, where he plied his trade as a midway hawker, cajoling customers into trying their skill at a variety of midway games. After trying his hand at any number of jobs, from being a hotel waiter to pedaling goods door to door, he settled in Boston where he became a salesman for the Jordan Marsh dry-goods company. Through his hard work and shrewd business acumen he was able to earn a share in the company. During the Civil War, Fisk had no compunction about smuggling Southern cotton through Union blockades and dealing in Confederate bonds, selling them in the European marketplace. During Reconstruction, Fisk continued his endeavors in the cotton business and managed to amass a small fortune.

He left Boston in 1864 and moved to New York, where he became a stockbroker for financier Daniel Drew. Drew was an independent stockbroker and sat on the board of directors of the Erie Railroad, where he engaged in a vicious battle for control of the railroad with his archenemy and fellow robber baron, Cornelius Vanderbilt. Drew and Fisk, along with Jay Gould, conspired against Vanderbilt, issuing fraudulent stock to keep Vanderbilt from grabbing control of the railroad. It worked. Vanderbilt sustained heavy financial losses and gave up control of the Erie Railroad to them.

The Erie Railroad connected New York City to Lake Erie and eventually to Chicago, and was the focal point of Wall Street stock manipulations, graft, greed, and deceit following the Civil War. When the fraudulent Erie Railroad stocks came due, Fisk refused to honor his contracts and left thousands of investors penniless and ruined. Fisk unashamedly used stockholder funds to bribe judges and other public officials, including the notoriously corrupt Boss Tweed. Fisk ultimately betrayed his benefactor, Daniel Drew, joining forces with Jay Gould to manipulate stock prices in order to gain complete control. The scheme caused Drew to sustain massive financial losses. Through their well-planned corporate raid, Fisk and Gould obtained control of the Erie Railroad and became lifelong business partners. Fisk's net worth at this time was reportedly $11 million.

But the best of their financial shenanigans was yet to come. On "Black Friday," September 24, 1869, Fisk and Gould tried to corner the market on gold, throwing the New York Stock Exchange into a panic. Fisk and Gould bought as much gold as they could, forcing the price through the roof; it eventually reached more than thirty dollars an ounce over what it had been. When it reached its highest point, Fisk and Gould began selling. Their plan was thwarted when President Grant's administration ordered the sale of $4,000,000 in government gold.

When the government gold hit the market, the stock market panicked and the price of gold plummeted. Investors raced madly to sell off their holdings in gold, but it was too late. Unlike Fisk and Gould, who had sold off their gold before the price fell, other investors were ruined. Most investors took out loans to buy gold. When the price fell they had no money to pay back the loans. But Fisk and Gould made a colossal profit estimated at nearly $12 million. Both men went into hiding to avoid angry and ruined creditors, but soon reemerged into the public spotlight with their coffers overflowing from the financial devastation caused by Black Friday.

It was only a few short months from the time Leslie was first introduced to Fisk at Delmonico's that Fisk set his infamous gold scheme into motion. Ironically, Fisk later tried to coax Leslie into investing in gold, slyly telling him that he had it on good authority that the price of gold was going to go through the roof and that the government would not be issuing any government gold into the marketplace. It was a bit of insider information, Fisk told him, that he was passing on to a select number of friends. It would be a chance to make a small fortune, he advised Leslie—but Leslie did not take the bait. Leslie had other plans for his money and they didn't include investing.

—⁓—

Fisk took an immediate liking to the gentlemanly George Leslie after their brief encounter at Delmonico's. Josie Mansfield did as well. Fisk subsequently sent Leslie an invitation to join him at a private party to be held at 79 Clinton Street, the home of Marm Mandelbaum. The invitation intrigued Leslie. He had heard of Fredericka Mandelbaum from friends, and was well aware that she was known as the biggest fence in the city.

Whatever Jim Fisk was doing associating with the likes of her was beyond him, but Leslie was more than happy to attend. Perhaps Mandelbaum could open a few of the doors that Leslie was hoping to step through. Since he had abandoned all thought of plying his trade as an architect, and since he didn't really know what he wanted to do with the rest of his newfound life New York City, he thought meeting Marm Mandelbaum might be a step in the right direction since he had come to New York City, intent on beginning a new career—a life of crime.

—ɯ—

In 1869, New York City was made up of five separate boroughs. It was not until a new charter was adopted in 1898 that the five boroughs were incorporated into a single metropolis. Brooklyn and Queens made up the western portion of Long Island, while Staten Island and Manhattan remained on their own land mass. The Bronx, to the north, remained attached to the New York State mainland.

The New York City that George Leslie encountered was populated by four sociological groups: the rich, the political machine, criminals, and the poor. The wealthy robber barons were represented by the likes of soon-to-be Standard Oil president John D. Rockefeller; American steamship and railroad builder, Cornelius Vanderbilt, who when he died left an estate of almost $100 million; Andrew Carnegie, whose Carnegie Steel produced more steel than all of England; Jay Gould, who controlled most of the communications of the country through his ownership and control of Western Union and several other telegraph companies; and, of course, financial wizard and master manipulator Jubilee Jim Fisk. It was estimated that between these robber barons, their pyramid of wealth led to 1 percent of the American population possessing more collective wealth than the rest of the entire country.

If the New York City rich were represented by the Rockefellers, Vanderbilts, Carnegies, Goulds, and Fisks, among others, then the political machine in New York City in 1869 was personified by Tammany Hall and its flamboyant leader, William M. "Boss" Tweed. Founded in 1789 for patriotic and fraternal purposes, Tammany Hall united the city's Democratic Party and the Society of St. Tammany. The fabric of city politics was woven through the mayor's office, the Democratic Party, and the social club organization. At the head of this intricate political machine was Boss Tweed, who had started out as a bookkeeper and volunteer fireman and was later elected alderman. He progressed through various municipal positions, secured control of the seventh ward in the City's Lower East Side, and became the first "Boss of New York" when he was crowned the grand sachem of Tammany Hall in 1863.

By 1869, Tweed was so powerful and had placed so many of his cronies in political positions throughout the city—known as the "Tweed Ring"—he was able to control practically everything, including the city treasury. It is estimated that between 1865 and 1871, Boss Tweed and his gang stole between $30 million and $200 million from the city. Even the likes of Rockefeller, Vanderbilt, Carnegie, and others curried Tweed's favor.

So did the criminal strata of the city, represented by a series of loosely knit gangs, each exporting their own criminal specialty: Johnny Dobbs's gang; Tom "Shang" Draper's gang, who worked out of Draper's Sixth Avenue saloon; Johnny "The Mick" Walsh's gang in the Bowery; and, most famously, Marm Mandelbaum and her associates.

The city's poor were crowded into what was the most miserable of New York City's slums, an area called Five Points. Located in the Sixth Ward, the neighborhood was named for the five points created by the intersection of Anthony, Cross, Mulberry, Orange, and Water Streets. Although predominantly Irish, many other racial and ethnic factions also inhabited the area, including Germans, French, English, and African-Americans. More than 3,500 people populated this tiny, crime-filled half-mile area. Garbage was thrown out of tenement windows onto the streets, often piled so high that it surged over the tops of the boots of passersby. Chamber pots were emptied in the streets, producing vast lakes of human excrement that permeated the air with a vile stench.

Dressed in rags and carrying all they owned, the half-starved and sickly immigrants gravitated to the cheap housing available in Five Points. Whole families moved into dilapidated tenements with names like Jacob's Ladder, Gates of Hell, and Mulberry Bend. It was rare to have a single room for a family. Others without families lived in boardinghouses, which often consisted of a series of grimy, dirt-floor spaces where throngs of immigrants shared a single room, often sleeping on straw mattresses. They were charged inflated rates, and if unable to pay, many of their possessions would be confiscated in lieu of payment.

Surviving in this environment of dire poverty meant that all members of the family had to find ways to earn a living, by whatever means possible. Some were forced to resort to a life of crime or prostitution in order to survive. Alcoholism was rampant, and frequently children, orphaned or simply abandoned, were left to fend for themselves, roaming the streets and joining criminal gangs, destined to a life of misery. During this time, nearly 75 percent of poor children under the age of two died each year. Disease, typhus, and cholera epidemics killed many of these poor immigrants and their children. Still others died from poor nutrition and unsanitary conditions. One of the city's newspapers described it as a "loathsome den of murderers, thieves, abandoned women, ruined children, filth, drunkenness . . ."

The most famous description of this symbol of mayhem, violence, and urban despair came from English novelist and social reformer Charles Dickens. On his visit to New York City in 1842, Dickens described it as: "Ruined houses open to the street, whence, through wide gaps in the walls, other ruins loom upon the eye, as though the world of vice and misery had nothing else to show: hideous tenements which take their name from robbery and murder; all that is loathsome, drooping, and decayed is here."

Besides the poverty and filth of places like Five Points, New York City also boasted the country's most violent criminal gangs. The gangs included thugs, murderers, loan sharks, pickpockets, gamblers, fences, bank robbers, and an assortment of other criminal types, engaged in every conceivable crime or vice. Five Points was home to nearly 300 saloons and more than 600 bordellos. Prostitutes plied their trade openly in many of the city's poorest sections.

Five Points was not the only cesspool of poverty, violence, and vice. The entire city was rampant with these filthy, crowded slums. The Fourth Ward, located to the south of Five Points along the waterfront of the Lower East Side, had twenty tenements, each housing more than two hundred families. During a single one-year period during the early 1870s, it averaged nearly twenty-five deaths per tenement.

There was also the Tenderloin district located on the west side of midtown Manhattan, between Fifth and Seventh Avenues, where hundreds of bordellos were openly in operation despite a large police presence. Most, if not all, of the police officers assigned to the Tenderloin district took bribes to look the other way. Tourists, sightseers, drunks, prostitutes, and known murderers and criminals mingled side by side with police officers in this section of the city.

The Bowery, another crime-infested section, had the dubious honor of being New York City's official red-light district. An ethnically and racially varied region, it was a well-known shopping district by day and by night, a vice-laden den of sex, gambling, bars, saloons, and all-night dance halls. Many of these were owned by political bosses who used criminal gangs to bring in the votes during election time and to cause trouble within opposing political parties.

All of these notorious New York City slums and crime dens hovered just beneath the surface of high society, those living in the lap of luxury along Broadway and other high-rent districts of the city—including the Fifth Avenue Hotel where George Leslie had recently established his residency.

For George Leslie, these two disparate worlds presented a golden opportunity. He decided he would make his fortune right here, in the middle of this mélange of good and evil.

3

THE LITTLE JOKER

A tool is but the extension of a man's hand, and a machine is but a complex tool. And he that invents a machine augments the power of a man and the well-being of mankind.

—HENRY WARD BEECHER, PRESBYTERIAN MINISTER
AND AUTHOR (1869)

It wasn't losing the money that bothered Leslie, although the two hundred dollars that had been in his wallet was a lot of money by anyone's standards. And it wasn't losing his personal papers that were also in the wallet; he could always replace them. It was the little, round metal plate—the prototype of his invention—that was irreplaceable. He had been working on it for three years and had yet to test it out. Somewhere in one of his many notebooks he had sketches of it. But these notebooks, along with the rest of his possessions, were still in transit, coming by train from Cincinnati to New York. Losing this small mechanical device would be a major setback for him. Among his many other talents, George Leslie had an uncanny mechanical ability. His invention, a little tin wheel that he had sarcastically dubbed "the little joker," might take a year or more to duplicate. It had been stolen when someone picked his pocket at the train station.

Leslie had left Delmonico's restaurant feeling on top of the world. He had met the infamous Jubilee Jim Fisk; he'd received free tickets to the Grand Opera House performance of the sold-out show, *The Twelve Temptations*; and he'd also received a personal invitation by Fisk to attend the next dinner party at Marm Mandelbaum's. Fredericka "Marm" Mandelbaum, acknowledged by almost everyone as "The Queen of the Underworld," was also known for throwing some of the most lavish parties in the city, where she entertained many of New York's wealthiest socialites, including businessmen, lawyers, judges, and politicians. Word was that you really hadn't made it in New York City if you hadn't been to one of Marm's exclusive soirees. She was definitely someone Leslie wanted to meet.

More important, he had made the acquaintance of the beautiful and seductive Josie Mansfield, and although theirs had only been a brief introduction, Leslie was sure he would meet her again, in more intimate surroundings. If Leslie had any weak spot in his character—and he had so few, since he didn't smoke, drink, or gamble—it was women. He couldn't resist them, and very few could resist falling under the spell of his good looks and endless charm.

He had sensed he would be hearing more from Mansfield, and he was right. Later that week he received a note from Mansfield, written in her own hand on a small, scented floral card, and delivered by private messenger to his room at the Fifth Avenue Hotel. It was a personal invitation to be a guest of hers in her own private theater box at the Grand Opera House for the performance of *The Twelve Temptations*. Jim Fisk, she explained in the note, would be in Washington, D.C., for the week, attending to some pressing business. (Fisk and his partner, Jay Gould, were on the verge of setting in motion their elaborate scheme to corner the gold market.) Leslie readily accepted her invitation.

Fisk's elaborate production of *The Twelve Temptations* at the Grand Opera House on Twenty-third Street was not New York's first Broadway musical. That honor belonged to impresario William Wheatley's *The Black Crook*, the first American musical presented at Niblo's Garden in 1866. Located on Broadway and Prince Street, Niblo's Garden Theater was built in 1840 and was known for producing a variety of musical shows and melodramas. Wheatley, a popular actor himself, leased the theater and took charge of all its productions, including *The Black Crook*, his greatest accomplishment. Wheatley combined drama, dance, and full orchestration, and the show caused a sensation. The Broadway musical was born. The show ran for over a year and earned approximately $1 million.

Reporting on Wheatley's show, Mark Twain wrote, "Beautiful bare-legged girls hanging in flower baskets; others stretched in groups on great sea shells; others clustered around fluted columns; others in all possible attitudes; girls—nothing but a wilderness of girls—stacked up, pile on pile . . ."

Everything would have been fine if his wallet hadn't been stolen. Leslie would have to report it to the police—for all the good it would do. There were hundreds of cases of stolen wallets reported each day. The city streets were lined with pickpockets, ready to take advantage of unsuspecting tourists. Leslie had just become one of them. But for him, the loss of his invention, "the little joker," was a major setback.

—⁊⁊⁊—

Along with being a time of great industrialization in the country, 1869 was also a time of great inventions, both large and small. Thomas Edison created his first invention, the electric vote counter, which could instantly record votes. It was intended to be used in congressional elections, but members of the United States House of Representatives rejected it. He also invented the stock ticker that year, an electrical mechanism that would keep investors updated on their stock-market dealings.

Ives McGaffey invented the first vacuum cleaner, a "sweeping machine" that cleaned rugs. Inventor Sylvester H. Roper built the first steam-powered motorcycle. The first typewriter was invented and patented by Christopher Sholes, Samuel Soule, and Carlos Glidden. In George Leslie's home state of Ohio, W. F. Semple invented chewing gum.

All of these inventions in some way revolutionized life in America. Not to be outdone by any of these extraordinary devices, George Leslie also tried his capable hand at inventing. His invention would also revolutionize a certain aspect of American life, specifically banking—more specifically, bank robbing. If he was correct, Leslie was certain that his "little joker" would turn bank robbing into a modern science, no longer requiring holdups, guns, dynamite, or any other previously used, time-consuming apparatus.

—⚉—

In 1862, Linus Yale Jr. invented the modern combination lock. Almost everyone believed that the new combination locks were burglarproof. What they hadn't counted on was something as inventive as George Leslie's little joker. It was a simple device: a small tin wheel with a wire attached to it that would fit inside the combination knob of any bank safe. All anyone had to do was take off the dial knob of a bank lock and place the little joker on the inside of the dial. Then, after carefully replacing the knob, it could be left there undetected. When bank officials opened the vault the next day during regular business hours, Leslie's little joker, still concealed under the safe's knob, would record where the tumblers stopped by making a series of deep cuts in the tin wheel. The deepest cuts in the wheel would show the actual numbers of the combination. Although it wouldn't record the exact order of the numbers in the combination, it would only be a matter of trying several different combinations before the safe would open. Leslie was sure of it.

A bank robber could then sneak back into the bank, remove the knob, and examine the marks in the tin plate. All the robber had to do was figure out the exact order in which the stops were used. Using the device *did* require a robber to break into a bank twice—once to place the contraption inside the dial of the vault, and a second time to retrieve it—and not many robbers had the aptitude or patience to perform such a tricky endeavor. It would take a very special kind of person to accomplish the undertaking, someone with brains, patience, and nerves of steel. George Leslie saw himself as that person.

The little joker eliminated the need to use dynamite to blow open a vault. Robbers often blew up more than just the vault door when pulling off a bank heist. Hundreds of times robbers used too much dynamite and ended up blowing up all the cash, securities, and other valuables inside— or worse, injuring themselves. And of course, the blast from using dynamite drew attention and caused panic, leading to many failed robbery attempts.

The little joker also eliminated the need for long and laborious safecracking techniques used by many robbers—turning the dial this way and that, listening with a stethoscope to determine the right sequence of combination clicks. Safecracking took hours and it wasn't foolproof. Leslie was sure that his device was the safest, most effective way of robbing a bank. No bank vault would be safe from it.

The most popular method of safecracking was to simply steal the entire safe and move it to a place where it could be taken apart in a leisurely fashion. However, banks and other financial institutions were now investing in huge, complex steel vaults, so moving a safe was no longer an option. Most robbers were forced to use one of four techniques: lock manipulation to determine the combination, screwing the vault, drilling it, or blowing up the vault using either gunpowder or dynamite. None of these methods were expedient.

Lock manipulation required skill and time. The robber would try a series of possible combinations, listening to the tumblers through a stethoscope to determine the exact location where the tumblers stopped. The process could take an inordinate amount of time, and depending upon the number of tumbler stops, it would require the robber to try hundreds, if not thousands, of possible combinations.

Screwing the vault required the robber to drill a hole into the door plate and then tap a thread through it where a heavy machine bolt would be inserted and used to slowly unscrew the door bolts. This was also time-consuming, depending on the thickness of the door. It also required the robber to use dozens of drill bits that would be chewed up in the process.

Drilling required the robber to have access to engineering drawings of the vault's bolt mechanism, and then locating a point on the safe door to drill through. A screwdriver was then shoved through the opening and maneuvered to free the bolts. This process bypassed the vault's combination lock completely. It was also a lengthy process, and without the vault's engineering schematic showing the exact workings of the lock, there was no way of telling where the correct spot was to begin drilling.

Finally, bank robbers could resort to using either gunpowder or dynamite to blow up the safe. Although faster than any of the other three methods, it was fraught with danger. Too little gunpowder and the lock would not be blown. Too much dynamite, and not only would the vault door be blown off its hinges, but the contents of the safe could also be blown to smithereens. In the worst-case scenario, the robbers could blow themselves up as well. The explosion caused by using either gunpowder or dynamite always attracted attention.

But these methods were all a bank robber had to work with, except for the mythical device that some robbers had unsuccessfully tried to create. It would let the robber know exactly what the vault combination was so that the vault could be opened quickly, safely, and without drawing attention to the crime. Many criminals had tried to perfect such a device but none had succeeded; that is, not until George Leslie put his mind to it.

—⁓—

What makes a person turn to a life of crime? What factors determine criminal behavior? Nature or nurture? Genes or environment? Despite centuries of study and thousands of reports, no one knows for sure why any one person becomes a criminal. Surely the reasons behind George Leslie's decision to choose bank robbing as a profession remain a mystery.

Before leaving Cincinnati, Leslie had told friends he wanted to make "easy money" in New York City. It was difficult for anyone to figure out what this cryptic message meant. Leslie had no intention of resuming his architectural career, and, although he admired people like Jubilee Jim Fisk for their cunning and daring on Wall Street, Leslie had no interest in becoming a Wall Street investor.

Coming to New York City, leaving behind old friends and family (his mother and father had both died, and he had no siblings), shedding the baggage of his past, he was free to become anything he wanted. Given his obsession with perfecting his little joker even before moving lock, stock, and barrel to New York, it seems apparent that he had decided to re-create himself in a way no one would have ever suspected. In his quest for easy money, Leslie had set his sights on a life of crime. Although he hadn't told anyone, he had planned it all out. He intended to make his fortune by becoming a bank robber—but not just any old run-of-the-mill bank robber. He intended on becoming the king of thieves—more famous and even richer than Jesse James. Leslie had an obsession with the cowboy outlaw and was an avid reader of the pulp westerns that hailed the exploits of the James Gang and other notorious bandits.

Jesse and Frank James had joined forces with Cole Younger and his gang after the Civil War. In 1868 the James-Younger Gang robbed a bank in Kentucky, making off with thousands of dollars. James and his brother later robbed a county savings bank in Missouri, where Jesse shot and killed a bank teller that he mistakenly believed was a Union officer who had killed one of his friends during the war. The tabloid newspapers and pulp magazines were quick to immortalize Jesse James, building up his legend with scores of books and newspaper articles.

Even though George Leslie idolized Jesse James (Marm Mandelbaum later nicknamed him "Western" because of his fixation on western outlaws like Jesse James), he wanted no part of six-guns or killings. His bank robberies would be works of art. But Leslie was at a distinct disadvantage when it came to fulfilling his dream. He knew nothing about robbing banks, and he didn't know anyone who had ever robbed one. Leslie had no association with anyone remotely connected with the criminal world. The world of crime was as alien to George Leslie as his New York City surroundings. But somehow Leslie knew that his good looks and manners, along with his sharp mind—the same qualities that had helped him with his entrée into the world of New York high society—would also help him find a way to acquaint himself with members of the criminal elite. It was, as far as Leslie was concerned, just a matter of time.

Besides, if ever there was a place to begin a criminal career, New York City was it. A would-be bank robber like Leslie couldn't have been better situated. The wealthiest men and women in the country made New York City their home, which meant that they kept their money, jewels, stocks, and other valuables in banks. There seemed to be a bank on every corner of New York. There had to be millions of dollars just sitting there, waiting for the right kind of bank robber to come along and make a withdrawal. George Leslie intended to be that robber.

—⚊—

SAVINGS BANK ROBBERY

There was another savings bank robbery in this city yesterday. The victimized institution was the Dime Savings Bank of the Eastern District. The loss was comparatively trifling for a bank robbery, only eight thousand dollars, and the depositors will not suffer. But these frequent robberies are likely to impair public confidence in Savings Banks as trustworthy institutions. The trouble seems to be that there are too many savings banks in the city, some of which do not transact business enough to pay for the employment of people enough to keep a proper watch upon the premises.

—*Brooklyn Daily Eagle* (1869)

—⁓ᴍ⁓—

The first recorded bank robbery in America took place in the summer of 1798 in Philadelphia, Pennsylvania. Not a shot was fired nor was the bank vault blown. The robber simply unlocked the vault and stole the money. Approximately $163,000 (roughly $1.9 million based on today's monetary standard) —an enormous amount of money for the period—was stolen from the vault at the Bank of Pennsylvania located at Carpenters' Hall in Philadelphia. There was no sign of forced entry reported, either into the building where the money was being kept or the vault where it was stored. Authorities surmised it had been an inside job, and suspected blacksmith Patrick Lyons. Lyons had been working on changing the fittings and locks on the two iron vault doors for the Bank of Pennsylvania, and disappeared right after the robbery. Lyons was apprehended a short time later in Lewiston, Delaware. Despite professing his innocence, Lyons spent three months in jail. Two outside watchmen who worked the night of the robbery were also arrested and held.

It did turn out to be an inside job, but Lyons had nothing to do with it. The perpetrator was actually Isaac Davis, one of the bank employee's customers. Davis had visited Patrick Lyons's shop shortly before the robbery to have a copy of the vault key made claiming he needed an extra key for his work. Lyons found nothing suspicious about the request. A bank teller named Thomas Cunningham hid in the bank after it closed and let Davis in. Davis easily unlocked the vault with his copy of the key, and the two men slipped away with the loot. It appeared to be the perfect crime. But not for long.

Cunningham died shortly after the heist from yellow fever, which had reached epidemic proportions in the city at the time. Davis, not having enough sense to leave the city himself, decided that the best way to dispose of the stolen loot was to deposit it in various banks throughout the city, including the very same bank he had robbed—the Bank of Pennsylvania at Carpenters' Hall.

The authorities were quick to notice Davis's sudden newfound wealth and confronted him. With no logical explanation of how he had come by his new fortune, Davis confessed to the crime, explaining that Lyons had had nothing to do with the robbery. Davis agreed to return all the money in exchange for a full pardon, which was granted to him by the governor. All of the money was returned and Davis never spent a day in jail, although he was banished from the city.

Patrick Lyons's fate was not as cut-and-dried. Despite Davis's full confession and the return of all the money, the authorities maintained that Lyons was still a suspect in the heist because he'd knowingly made a copy of the vault key for Davis. Lyons languished in jail for several weeks despite the capture of Davis. Later, Lyons would sue the bank and local law enforcement officials, winning a verdict of $12,000 for false imprisonment. Lyons later wrote a book detailing his imprisonment and ultimate vindication.

—⁂—

If the first recorded bank robbery in the United States was a bungled affair from top to bottom, the first bank robbery in New York City was less than enigmatic. In March of 1831, Edward Smith slipped into the City Bank on Wall Street and hid inside. After the bank closed, Smith used a set of duplicate keys to unlock the vault and stole $245,000. Smith was caught by authorities shortly after the heist, drawing suspicion as Isaac Davis had with his lavish spending. He was arrested, convicted, and spent five years in New York City's Sing Sing Prison.

—⁂—

The day after his dinner at Delomico's, George Leslie arrived early at the Erie Railroad Depot, located at the foot of Chambers Street and Pavonia Ferry, to make arrangements for his trunks to be picked up and sent to the Fifth Avenue Hotel. The grand hotel, located at 200 Fifth Avenue, was the unofficial headquarters for New York City's upper echelon who defined New York City's political, social, and economic life. Guests and visitors to the block-long gleaming white marble hotel included a Who's Who of national and international celebrities, among them the Prince of Wales, who stayed there in early 1860; Prince Napoleon; *New York Tribune* editor, Horace Greeley; William "Boss" Tweed; financier Jay Gould; iron ore magnate Peter Cooper, who founded the Cooper Union for the Advancement of Science and Art; celebrated author Mark Twain; poet William Cullen Bryant; district attorney Samuel Tilden; eighteenth President of the United States, Ulysses S. Grant, who was reportedly first proposed as the next president in a plan hatched at the hotel by prominent New York City Republicans; and even Charles Sherwood Stratton, better known as one of P. T. Barnum's human curiosities, the midget extraordinaire, Tom Thumb.

The hotel was built in 1859 by Amos R. Eno, a wealthy capitalist who lived at nearby 32 Fifth Avenue. When it first opened amid great fanfare, the luxuriously extravagant hotel was not given much chance of success. Initially nicknamed "Eno's Folly," the Fifth Avenue Hotel soon became the most prominent lodging in the city.

Despite being one of the most lavish hotels in Gotham, the prices were affordable. Each room, like Leslie's own, came fully furnished, with a host of amenities including a fireplace and four meals a day—the fourth being a late-night supper for those whose appetites were not extinguished during a night of otherwise gala enterprise. The cost was a mere $2.50 per day, well within George Leslie's comfortable means.

—⁂—

It was American satirist and author Washington Irving who first referred to New York City as "Gotham" in his 1807 publication of the pamphlet *Salmagundi; Or The Whim-Whams and Opinions of Launcelot Langstaff, Esq. and Others*. Irving lambasted and lampooned the culture, politics, and morays of "the renowned and ancient city of Gotham," the first recorded use of the word to describe New York. Irving's allusion came from a Middle Ages reference to the English village of Gotham, whose inhabitants were legendary for their stupidity.

—⁂—

Outside the Erie Railroad station Leslie had commandeered three ample carriages to accommodate his many belongings. Leslie spared no expense, whether in the ultimate care in transporting his luggage or in his visible demonstration of social standing by renting two fully equipped, top-of-the-line Brewster brougham carriages—by today's standards, the Rolls-Royce of coaches—and a smaller White Chapel wagon. Leslie rented the carriages from Brewster's warehouse on Broad Street, where master carriage maker James Brewster, known as the "Carriage Builder for the American Gentleman," had his fleet on display.

Jubilee Jim Fisk was renowned for traveling through the city in a variety of Brewster's most expensive carriages, pulled by four matched white horses. Coachmen who rode along with him always jumped out to spread a red carpet between his carriage and the doorstep wherever he went. Any man of worth was marked by the bearing of his carriages, and Jim Fisk kept his six smart Brewster carriages, each one different and adorned with Fisk's personal and lavish imprint, in his stables that were located on Twenty-fourth Street, behind the Grand Opera House. His lightweight phaeton was used for quick jaunts through the city, and was festooned with flags posted at each of the four corners: a Stars and Stripes, a New York state flag, an Erie Railroad banner, and a Ninth Regiment bunting. The carriage was lined with plush golden fabric and well-appointed cushions specially made to provide Fisk with added comfort.

Fisk had over a dozen horses, an equal mixture of black and white that were cared for by a staff of stablemen who fed and groomed them, making sure they were ready at a moment's notice should Fisk decide to go on one of his many excursions through the city, which he was wont to do, often with Josie Mansfield beside him, or, on occasion, a few chorus girls as willing passengers. He kept a trunk of ice at the ready in each of the carriages to cool the bottles of champagne and platters of oysters he often enjoyed during his delightful forays through the streets of New York.

Although Leslie's three carriages had none of these special amenities, being Brewsters, they still provided him with the sort of public display of wealth and stature that he wished to portray.

—ɯ—

As Leslie approached his rented, beautifully adorned horse-drawn carriages, his eyes were diverted to the legless beggar in front of him, holding out a tin cup. Pale and sickly, the man was wearing a tattered Union Army uniform and was braced against the cold granite wall of the train station— a reflection of so many young men who had come home from the Civil War, broken and scarred. The sight of the legless veteran conjured up in Leslie the disgrace that had haunted him ever since his father had bought his way out of the war. He was filled with a sense of shame, mingled with pity. He stopped, took out his wallet, and counted out several dollar bills, placing them into the beggar's tin cup. In one way or another, Leslie would be paying for his father's well-intentioned deed for the rest of his life. Leslie turned quickly and kept apace with the crowd, leaving before the beggar could utter a thank-you. His generosity did not go unnoticed.

Standing in the harsh sunlight along the street amid the hectic combustion of the New York City boulevard, Leslie felt a tug on the corner of his frock coat. When he looked down, he saw a small, beautiful child, a little girl of about eight or nine, dressed in rags and covered with soot, her blond hair a snarled mess. She was staring up at him with sad blue eyes and holding out what looked to be a withered apple in the palm of her hand. The little girl asked for two pennies for the withered apple.

The girl's pathetic state overwhelmed him. Again he reached into his wallet, took out a crisp new dollar bill, and handed it to the child. Her face brightened into a broad smile of astonishment. She could hardly speak as Leslie handed her the dollar and took the withered apple from her palm. He turned to go. Suddenly, a boy moved swiftly out of the crowd, bumping into him. He was older but no better off than the girl. He took the little girl by the hand, snatching the dollar bill from her, explaining the little girl was his sister. He berated her for begging on the street. The boy offered to give back the generous amount Leslie had given her for the apple, but Leslie declined. He headed straightaway to one of his rented carriages, where porters were beginning to load in his many trunks and boxes. Leslie placed the small apple into the pocket of his coat and climbed into one of the half-filled carriages without looking back. If he had, he might have seen the wry, knowing smile that crossed the lips of the boy as he and his sister melted back into crowd.

Leslie would not discover his missing wallet until much later that evening. Everything was gone—the tickets to the Grand Opera House, two hundred dollars, and his prized little joker. He went directly to police head-quarters on Mulberry Street to report the robbery.

—⁓—

Police captain Stephen Killalee served as Jim Fisk's conduit to the city's needy, responsible for providing fuel in the form of coal or wood, baskets of food, provisions, flour, milk, or medicine—whatever was necessary for the poor, unfortunate, and downtrodden.

Despite his reputation as a ruthless Wall Street financier, Fisk was privately generous when it came to dispensing charity to the poor and out-of-work. The fifteen-dollar fee he received for each of his Erie Railroad Company shareholders was summarily, at his instruction, distributed to the needy, many of whom would gather daily outside the Grand Opera House, looking for handouts. His trusted private secretary, John Comer, who handled all of his business affairs and then some, was told to let anyone with a hard-luck story into the offices and to provide them with whatever handout—food, money, clothing, fuel—might be available at the time. Larger contributions to the poor and other various and sundry matters were specifically handled by Captain Killalee. Fisk's generosity earned him the title "The Prince of Erie," and the Grand Opera House the nickname "Erie Castle."

Killalee wasn't optimistic about getting Leslie's wallet back. The New York City police department had twenty designated police detectives working the crime-ridden streets of the busy metropolis. The detectives, called "shadows," were broken into squads, each with their own specialties—burglaries, robbery, vice, and pickpockets. The detectives made themselves conversant in each class of crime they were responsible for, familiarizing themselves with the known culprits and the way each crime was carried out. Detectives were assigned to infiltrate saloons and gatherings where a majority of these crimes were reported to have been committed and to arrest, detain, or drive off any known criminals. One of the squads, directly under Captain Killalee's command, was responsible for rooting out pickpockets and shoplifters. A photo gallery of known criminals, divided into categories of crime, was available at the Mulberry Street Police headquarters, where victims could peruse the photos in hopes of identifying the perpetrator.

Leslie was shocked to see the faces of so many young boys and girls in the pickpocket gallery at the police station. According to Killalee, the city was infested with "street rats"—orphaned or abandoned children without any formal education who lived on the streets and slept in alleyways, vacant buildings, and warehouses, plying their trade on unsuspecting victims. Some worked, if they could, at menial jobs, sweeping sidewalks or selling newspapers, but mostly they survived by scavenging or turning to a life of crime. The Bowery along the East River waterfront, with its saloons, hotels, post offices, banks, and congested railway stations, was known as "pickpockets' paradise." Train stations were fertile territory for young pickpockets, providing a virtual playground of unsuspecting tourists.

Although the exact number of child pickpockets roaming the New York City streets was debated, police chief George Matsell had estimated that somewhere between 5,000 to 10,000 children lived on the streets. A majority of them were engaged in some crime or vice. According to Chief Matsell, "[C]rime among boys and girls has become organized, as it never was previously." Street children were a sad and tragic fact of life in almost every industrialized city during the burgeoning Gilded Age. These were difficult times according to one of the detectives, assigned to cover the street-rat population. The economic depression of the late 1860s had only added to the problem. "The bad times have driven a small army into our streets," the police officer said.

According to a report issued by the Children's Aid Society—an organization started in New York City in 1853 by Presbyterian minister Charles Loring Brace, to help the poor and homeless—street children ". . . gnawed away at the foundations of society undisturbed. In a country which identified geographic mobility and physical movement as freedom, the street kids represented the logical nightmare—the replacement of community, familial and even spiritual bonds with the rootless individualism of the nomad."

Harper's Weekly claimed that the street children were the breeding grounds for more criminal activity. "Those who have once adopted the semi-savage and wandering mode of life in early youth seldom abandon it," according to *Harper's*.

A look through the photo gallery didn't produce any results for Leslie; he'd reached a dead end. Killalee suggested that Leslie talk with one of the county sheriffs, Peter O'Brien, who had close ties to the Tammany Ring.

Before being appointed sheriff, O'Brien had worked directly for Boss Tweed. It was worth a try, since O'Brien had contacts with some unsavory characters who might have information about Leslie's stolen wallet. Killalee advised him that it might cost him, but Leslie didn't care; he was more concerned about his little joker.

Leslie met with O'Brien and expressed his desire to get the wallet back. He told him he wasn't concerned about the money that was in it as much as some of the personal papers. He would be willing to pay for its safe return. O'Brien was a wiry fellow with a long, dour face and thin, bloodless lips. When he spoke his mouth never moved, his words slipping out in a monotone from behind a row of yellow and crooked teeth. Leslie told him he needed the wallet back before his dinner at Marm Mandelbaum's. O'Brien's eyes lit up when he heard that Leslie was somehow *in* with Marm. O'Brien agreed to help and said he'd contact Leslie if he learned anything. When Leslie told him he was staying at the exclusive Fifth Avenue Hotel, O'Brien's eyes lit up again. He assured him he would make it a top priority to locate the missing wallet.

Two years later, Leslie would recall his brief meeting with Sheriff O'Brien. It was O'Brien and the new county bookkeeper, M. J. O'Rourke, who would testify against Boss Tweed. Both O'Brien and O'Rourke, considered two low-level city officials with a grudge against the Tweed Ring, provided *The New York Times* with reams of documentation that detailed the vast corruption at the 52 Chambers Street courthouse, along with other city projects. The newspaper published a series of articles in 1871, which, combined with the scathing political cartoons of Thomas Nast that appeared in *Harper's Weekly*, led to the downfall of Boss Tweed and his gang of cronies at Tammany Hall. Sheriff O'Brien had believed Tweed was not paying him enough money for his troubles and decided to pass along incriminating documents to the state committee that was investigating Tweed. O'Rourke joined him in exposing Tweed's courthouse corruption.

—⚬—

The knock at the door startled Leslie; he wasn't expecting anyone. He had so few acquaintances in New York. Leslie called out but no one answered. He went to the door and opened it. No one was there. On the floor just outside his door was his wallet. Leslie checked inside. As he'd suspected, all the money was gone, but everything else was there—and most important, the little joker had been returned to him intact. Leslie breathed a sigh of relief.

His next stop was Marm Mandelbaum's dinner party, but before that, knowing that Jubilee Jim was still out of town, he paid a visit to Josie Mansfield at her brownstone. The Cleopatra of Twenty-third Street greeted him warmly, opening more than her arms to the distinguished charmer from the Midwest.

4

MARM

With the facilities that the police possess of raising the curtain for a peep behind the scenes of ordinary life, it is practically impossible for the nefarious operations of this woman and her pupils—persons who are constantly under surveillance—should be unknown to the police.

—NEW YORK CITY DISTRICT ATTORNEY PETER B. OLNEY, FOLLOWING
THE ARREST OF MARM MANDELBAUM (1884)

Fredericka Mandelbaum, often called "Marm" or "Mother Mandelbaum," stood five foot three and weighed nearly three hundred pounds. She had beady black eyes, protruding cheeks, black curly hair always hidden beneath an ill-fitting bonnet, and thin lips set in a perpetual frown. Since 1854 she had been the acknowledged "Queen of Fences," earning the New York press's nickname of "Ma Crime."

It was estimated by authorities that during the heyday of her fencing operations, Mandelbaum handled approximately $10 million worth of stolen merchandise. She ran a school on Grand Street where young boys and girls were taught the fine art of professional pickpocketing, along with more advanced studies in burglary and confidence schemes. She was able to conceal this operation by claiming the school was actually a charitable organization aimed at rescuing and protecting poor, unfortunate orphaned street children. Mandelbaum kept track of the massive amounts of stolen goods she received from heists all over the eastern seaboard through an intricate network of warehouses situated throughout the seedier parts of the city. Using bribes and payoffs to police and politicians, notably Boss Tweed and his Tammany Hall Ring, she was able to avoid prosecution. She secured the services of the most brilliant and crooked criminal attorneys of the day, William Howe and Abraham Hummel, and kept their firm on a $10,000-a-year retainer. Howe and Hummel prided themselves on representing what one journalist referred to as "the upper crust of the lower order."

William F. Howe was a shady Boston-born trial lawyer and Abraham Hummel a former law clerk turned lawyer. Together, they made up one of the most successful criminal legal teams in the country. Howe had handled more than five hundred murder trials in the course of his career, winning a majority of them. Howe was known for his profligate dress, often wearing colorful silk vests and an abundance of jewelry including garish stickpins in his ties and an assortment of glittering jeweled rings. Hummel, a dour little man who wore thick spectacles, practiced civil law. He was also the brains behind the firm's lucrative blackmail scam that represented chorus girls and thwarted lovers, often bullying married men with exposure and well-off young bachelors with suits for breach of promise of marriage.

Howe's legal expertise was no more legendary than when he was able to persuade a jury that his client, Ella Nelson, was not guilty of first-degree murder because, although she did have a pistol in her hand at the time of the murder, her trigger finger had slipped, causing the gun to go off. More amazing was the fact that Howe convinced the jury that Nelson's trigger finger had slipped not just once, but six times in a row. Howe and Hummel kept no files and vigorously pursued newspaper coverage of their many cases. Both the legal community and law enforcement officials were appalled by their flagrant abuse of the law. Still, they remained the most successful legal team in New York City history.

Criminals of every ilk flocked to Mandelbaum in droves because they understood she could fence any stolen loot. She once boasted of selling a herd of stolen sheep, no questions asked, for a reasonable price. Although there was no honor among thieves, Mandelbaum had the reputation of being fair and honest even among the most despicable of criminals. She would often lend out the services of her high-priced lawyers if one of her operatives was arrested and landed in jail. It wasn't an altruistic gesture on her behalf; she needed her cadre of criminals out on the streets, robbing and stealing in order to stay in business. *The New York Times* called her "the most successful fence in the history of New York." By 1869 Mandelbaum had progressed from merely fencing stolen merchandise to helping finance major bank robberies.

Despite her notorious reputation, she was also known for her generous and lavish dinner parties and dances, where she entertained many of the city's social elite, including wealthy businessmen, lawyers, judges, authors, politicians, and even police officers. Intermingled among many of the city's most upstanding and notable guests were some of the most infamous criminals in New York City. Mandelbaum had but one rule when it came to her hooligan guests: Hands off! None of her legitimate guests were to be robbed, roughed up, or solicited in any way—at least not during the party. If you hadn't been invited to one of Marm Mandelbaum's celebrated parties, you just hadn't made it in New York.

Not long after the return of his stolen wallet, having finally settled into his suite at the hotel—all of his many books, clothes, and other possessions neatly organized and stored—Leslie was more than ready to make it in New York City. He had been invited to one of Mandelbaum's parties by Jubilee Jim Fisk, and he was well on his way. Predictable and punctual to a fault, and not a fan of surprises, Leslie didn't realize that he was actually on his way to the surprise of his life. No one on earth knew what Leslie had up his sleeve—what he had planned for the rest of his life—up and until then. But now, someone else knew, and he hadn't even met her yet.

—⁂—

The developments in the Mother Mandelbaum case are likely to prove somewhat torrid for the police unless the usual hushing up process is managed again. There are five or six million people scattered over the United States who know that Mother Mandelbaum was a notorious receiver of stolen goods from thieves and burglars. Thousands of citizens in New York knew where her houses were and her name was familiar to everyone. She waxed rich and is asserted on reliable authority to be worth more than half a million dollars at the present moment. Despite all these facts, the police of New York were never able to catch Mother Mandelbaum. Any citizen could go to her place and see her in the act of carrying on her trade, and yet 2,500 policemen, the extensive detective bureau and the vast machinery of the force was utterly unable to arrest her so that the district attorney sent for an outside detective and had the woman hauled up in court without much difficulty. This is [the] curious and by no means unusual state of affairs in New York. If this should be proved, as threatened, that the police are actually in collusion with Mother Mandelbaum, the effect will not amount to much. It is no longer a matter of question that the force here is in anything but a pure and unsullied condition. Meanwhile, it is very curious to observe the intense excitement in police circles over Mother Mandelbaum's threatened confession. "The finest" is perturbed.

—Brooklyn Daily Eagle (1884)

—ɯ—

Mandelbaum and her husband, Wolfe, both German Jews, immigrated to America in 1849. They were part of the first wave of German immigrants to reach American shores, with nearly 1.5 million arriving between 1845 and 1864. Many of them fled the potato rot that had all but destroyed German farming. Some fled to America after the failure of the 1848 revolutions that spread across Europe.

The Mandelbaums were well off when they came to America, and had enough money to buy a home and a dry-goods and haberdashery store at 79 Clinton Street on the corner of Rivington Street. Rivington, located between the Bowery and Pitt Street in the Lower East Side, had a sizable Jewish community. It was known as *Kleindeutschland,* or Little Germany. The Lower East Side in Manhattan was bordered by Houston Street to the north and the East River to the south.

A near-solid wall of tenements lined the streets, most home to some type of store on the ground floor. A majority were grocery or clothing stores. Racks of fabric and clothes were on display outside the apparel stores, while wooden barrels of pickled herring and cucumbers adorned the sidewalks in front of the grocery and dry-goods stores. The stores were in constant competition with the pushcart merchants, whose array of carts stood side by side from one end of the street to the other, selling everything from the exotic to the mundane, all at reduced prices. And if the price for something wasn't low enough, the pushcart merchants were more than willing to haggle over the cost. The street was overflowing with the most affluent of bargain hunters who could well afford to buy top of the line but could not bring themselves to pass up a bargain. Horses drawing wagons laden down with goods and supplies and carriages filled with finely dressed uptown shoppers and their coachmen clip-clopped slowly down the busy, narrow cobblestone street. Noisy children from the neighborhood darted in and out of traffic and around and under the stream of pushcarts. Thrifty shoppers bartered loudly over goods and merchandise with merchants and peddlers.

The first-floor storefront of the Mandelbaums' three-story building on Clinton Street was stocked with the usual array of dry goods. This is where Marm's husband, Wolfe, and son Julius attended to customers, haggling over this and that. In the back of the building on the top floor was a series of lavishly decorated living rooms filled with rare antiques, fine furniture, expensive carpets and drapes, costly silverware and glassware, and high-priced pieces of art—all of it stolen merchandise. This extravagantly adorned part of the building was where Mandelbaum held her frequent parties. She worked with all of the many underworld gangs that roamed the city, fencing the stolen goods these hoodlums managed to get their hands on. She and the gangs she fenced merchandise for were all indebted to Boss Tweed and his Tammany Hall Ring for protection from the authorities. Graft and bribes to Tweed, himself a frequent guest at Mandelbaum's parties, kept the police and prosecution at bay.

Their business at the haberdashery and dry-goods store was good, but not good enough for Marm's liking. This is what led to her career as a fence. Marm, who had always been the brains behind their legitimate dealings, remained the boss of her new illegitimate sideline, applying her natural business acumen to her fencing enterprise. Tough and tightfisted, she paid her criminal lot a mere 10 percent of the value on any stolen merchandise. But if she was cheap when it came to buying the stolen merchandise brought to her, she was generous and kind to the men and women who brought her the stolen goods, often buying them food and clothing when they were down on their luck. She would often offer her criminal partners (and there were many of them) an additional payment, in advance, to acquire a certain type of merchandise she was looking for. Her fencing business began to thrive, so much so that the legitimate dry-goods business became merely a front for her growing criminal enterprise. Soon Mandelbaum needed a warehouse to store her stolen loot before reselling it to interested parties who were more than willing to keep their mouths shut about the incredible deal they had received. Soon she needed several warehouses to accommodate her illegal operations.

In order to keep her business up and running, she found herself having to pay off everyone from Boss Tweed right on down to the cop on the beat. It didn't matter. Business was booming and Mandelbaum was making a fortune. She didn't mind spreading her ill-gotten gains around—as long as her criminal escapades were allowed to go on unhampered by either the police or politicians. And this is exactly what happened. She quickly became the undisputed receiver of stolen goods in all of New York City and remained so for the next thirty years. A smart and enterprising businesswoman, Mandelbaum saw that the future of her criminal transactions lay with diversifying her interests, and so she began to surround herself with some of the top criminals in the city who remained at her beck and call, including strong-arm thug John "Red" Leary, safecracker Johnny Dobbs, and confidence man Tom "Shang" Draper. With them and an assortment of other ruffians and hoodlums, she began to actively plot and finance larger criminal operations, including bank heists. The bank-robbing business turned out to be not quite as successful as her fencing operations, primarily because many of the gangs she hired to pull off the bank jobs were not the most sophisticated of criminals. They relied on brute force and explosives, techniques that often ended in disaster with hardly any profits to show for it.

She financed one bank robbery to the tune of $5,000, only to have the gang she'd hired destroy the bank safe by using too much dynamite and nearly killing two of her operatives. The end result of the caper was a mere $1,600 in cash—everything that wasn't burned up in the vault explosion. Marm knew she'd have to improve her talent pool before attempting another bank heist.

—⚏—

Life in the neighborhoods along the East River was already unsavory and dangerous, but the New York City slums along the waterfront featured a far more treacherous ingredient—gangs. Thugs and hoodlums of all types inhabited the slums, seeking refuge in the dark alleys and damp cellars. They lurked in hallways and darkened doorways, preying on strangers who had legitimate business in the tenement district, along with the tenement dwellers themselves, and even each other. Gang wars were frequent, and deadly.

The homeless street children who roamed the area, sleeping in alleys and on the streets, gravitated toward petty crimes like pickpocketing and shoplifting. They soon graduated to more serious crimes—including murder—as they grew older and were inducted into gang life. Young girls at the age of fourteen began working as prostitutes in whorehouses, dance halls, and seedy dives.

New Yorkers and tourists alike were warned against venturing into these sections of the city at night. Even the police assigned to these sordid areas patrolled the streets in pairs. All types of crime grew like bacteria amid the poverty and squalor of block upon block of shameful tenements, decrepit flophouses, warehouses, old factories, seedy saloons, gambling dens, and houses of prostitution.

One of the most notorious areas was the Gashouse District, from Fourteenth down to Twenty-seventh Street, where huge gas tanks loomed over the landscape, blotting out the skyline. Rows of these giant, ugly tanks rose up in the neighborhood, first built in 1842. The tanks leaked gas day and night, filling the air with noxious-smelling fumes. The gashouse gangs, made up of dangerous, uneducated, out-of-work young men, terrorized the community and often plundered other unsuspecting neighborhoods.

If they were looking for trouble they would find it soon enough in Mulberry Bend, a one-block stretch that ran through Little Italy. The alleys between the rows of filthy tenements were barely wide enough for a person to walk through and nearly knee-deep in garbage. Many of these torturous paths led to dives and cellars where an assortment of criminals lurked. The crisscrossing, interconnecting alleyways, with names like "The Rat Trap" or "Bandit's Roost," were safe havens from the law. Day and night, rape, mayhem, and murder exploded in the Mulberry Bend alleys. The *New York Tribune* called it "New York's Black Hole of Calcutta."

Hell's Kitchen on the West Side was another spawning ground for gangs. It was filled with saloons, whorehouses, gambling dens, slaughterhouses, and dance halls crammed in among the brick tenements, grimy houses, old warehouses, and freight yards along the Hudson River. It ran from Twenty-third Street to Forty-second Street, down Seventh Avenue to the Hudson River. A section of Twenty-eighth Street was known as "The Tub of Blood" because of the explosive violence and murder that frequently erupted there. It became known as the most lurid slum in America. The Hell's Kitchen gangs were mostly Irish thugs, often armed with brass knuckles. They were considered the toughest of the gangs that roamed through New York City slums.

John "Red" Leary, a notorious member of Marm Mandelbaum's inner circle, came from Hell's Kitchen. Leary was once implicated in an armed robbery of a Hudson River freight train. The gangs shook down merchants and businessmen throughout the neighborhood and inflicted retribution in the form of severe and oftentimes crippling beatings to anyone not willing to pay them tribute on a regular basis. Hell's Kitchen was under the control of the Gophers, a gang of thieves known for robbing freight cars and boats carrying cargo along the Hudson River. The gang was led by "Mallet" Murphy, a diabolical gangster whose calling card was a life-threatening wallop with his heavy mallet.

The worst of all the slums was the villainous Five Points, a den of almost unspeakable gore and horror. It was the home to the city's most vicious criminals, prostitutes, and confidence men. There were no legitimate businesses in Five Points except for a very few grocery, dry-goods, and clothing shops. The nearly falling-down tenements and sheds housed hundreds of poor immigrants who were at the mercy of the gangs, many of which worked for absentee landlords, collecting rents. Anyone who couldn't pay the high rents they were charged were physically tossed out of their filthy, vermin-laden tenement dwelling, often beaten severely and left in the road as a warning to anyone else who could not come up with their weekly rent payment. Day or night, Five Points was the scene of an uncontrolled abundance of crime. No one, not even the police, dared to venture into this den of thieves and murderers.

Tom "Shang" Draper, another of Mandelbaum's intimates, was from Five Points. Draper was known for perfecting the "badger" game at his saloon at 466 Sixth Avenue. Draper employed poor young girls into enticing drunken men to come with them to a nearby hotel on Prince Street, promising sex. Once at the hotel, as the man was in the middle of disrobing in one of the dingy hotel rooms and the young girl was stripping off her clothes, one of Draper's thugs would break into the room, assault the drunken, startled man, and steal all his money and valuable possessions. The girl would flee with Draper's thug.

This routine was repeated over and over again, lining Shang Draper's pockets with thousands of dollars in ill-gotten gains. The girls earned a paltry sum, and many were forced into outright prostitution. Draper was always on the lookout for beautiful young girls to use for his scheme. Draper worked closely with Mandelbaum, using her both as a fence for stolen property and as a financial resource for his other criminal endeavors, including bank robberies. Mandelbaum financed and managed many of Draper's bank jobs, none of which had been very successful. The wages of sin hadn't been paying well . . . but all that was about to change.

—⚍—

The Mandelbaums may have lived in meager surroundings on the upper floor of the Clinton Street address, but Marm's guests experienced only luxury in the lavishly furnished back portion of the building, where she did all of her entertaining. As she had accumulated wealth and stature in the criminal community, she gained a certain notoriety in the legitimate world. She became adept at living in both worlds, learning how to deftly balance between the legitimate world and the underbelly of the criminal one.

Although Mandelbaum was the leading criminal fence in New York City, she was, by her own account, still a lady. She had exquisite taste and manners and was an avid admirer of intelligence and sophistication. She wouldn't tolerate foul language around her, especially at her dinner parties. She expected everyone, especially the rough trade she surrounded herself with, to be on their best behavior when they were in her company. Those that couldn't abide by these rules were seldom allowed to do business with her. She was constantly trying to improve the lagging social graces of her criminal friends, imploring them to read and aspire to proper etiquette and good manners.

Her parties were considered the highlight of the city's social season, where thieves and thugs would mix freely with businessmen and politicians.

Many of these legitimate guests ironically had homes and businesses that had probably been robbed by the very crook sitting next to them at the lavish banquet table Mandelbaum always set. Still, no one who was anyone in New York City could resist an invitation to one of her parties. George Leslie was no exception.

Leslie arrived at his first dinner party at Marm's wearing his best attire: a Highland frock coat, an elegant Wyatt striped shirt with a string tie, wool tailcoat pants, and a Farrington vest, with its high-cut, notched collar—the kind so many businessmen in New York City were wearing at the time. He wore a black Victorian top hat and white formal gloves and carried a cane, a hardwood staff topped with a shiny brass three-knob crown.

Leslie had the carriage drop him off at the front door of Mandelbaum's store on Clinton Street. He held a package under his arm. The store was dark. He strode to the door and knocked loudly, but there was no answer. He was sure he had the right date and the right address. He knocked again and finally heard someone coming.

Mandelbaum's teenage son Julius, fair-haired and slim, opened the door and let him in. Behind Julius stood Herman Stroude, Mandelbaum's part-time clerk and full-time bodyguard. Muscular and tall, he towered over Leslie, who was himself at least six feet tall. Stroude was bald, wore a gold earring in his ear, and had a bushy black mustache. Julius reluctantly made eye contact with Leslie as he explained that he'd been invited to the party by Jim Fisk. He gave Julius one of his cards. Stroude took the card and went upstairs to verify Leslie's story with Jubilee Jim, who was already enjoying the gala event with Josie Mansfield. When Stroude returned a few minutes later he whispered something to Julius.

Julius led the dandified Leslie through the darkened store to a long corridor, up several flights of stairs, and into a huge, brilliantly lit dining room, filled with a bustling, noisy crowd. Guests were laughing, chatting, and eating while a piano player off in the corner played a rousing version of "Little Brown Jug." It was one of the most popular songs in 1869, played in respectable saloons and dance halls throughout the city, as well as being a musical staple in the city's so-called "free and easies," the more disreputable drinking establishments that provided music as well as prostitutes. These large riotous taverns proliferated throughout the New York City slums. "Little Brown Jug" was written by Joseph Eastburn

Winner, the brother of another popular composer during the same period, Septimus Winner. Septimus's songs "Listen to the Mockingbird" and "Oh, Where Has My Little Dog Gone" were both popular dance hall and tavern favorites.

Mandelbaum's dining room was spacious, elegant, and comfortable, with plush carpets of red and gold and an assortment of formal dining tables and chairs, as well as upholstered couches and high-back leather chairs. The room featured a coffered ceiling and hand-carved woodwork, including an ornate fireplace and bookcases. Huge pocket doors separated the two parlor sections. The windows were covered with luminously embroidered silk drapes along with carved wooden shutters that concealed guests from prying eyes. The ceilings rose nearly twelve feet high, where the cut-glass chandeliers hung at a lower level, in keeping with the practice during the Gilded Age, when lighting needed to be closer to arm's reach for quick replacement.

More than sixty guests dined at the many tastefully set, Chippendale-style mahogany tables with matching chairs, each of which had a shaped crest with acanthus carving on it. Mandelbaum, who was too huge to fit comfortably into one of the chairs, was seated on an embroidered, cushioned bench. All the tables were covered with ornate linen tablecloths and decorated with gold candelabras. The walls were covered with paintings, some framed, some not. The elaborate decor of the dining room was abundant with Victorian elegance and whimsy, all of it stolen from some of the best homes and offices throughout the city and country. Mandelbaum had exquisite taste in stolen property.

Guests dined on lamb and sliced ham that was provided at the party by "Piano" Charlie Bullard. Bullard was a former butcher who now focused on his talent for safecracking. However, when called upon, he still provided the best cuts of meat for Marm's parties. Bullard was also a trained pianist, able to perform the most intricate piano concertos. He was known throughout the underworld for having the most sensitive fingers in the safecracking business. No bank safe tumbler was safe from Bullard's nimble fingertips. Bullard often entertained Marm's dinner guests, playing anything from Beethoven to the most popular songs of the day on the white, baby grand piano that adorned Marm's lavish dining room. It was Bullard who was playing the rollicking version of "Little Brown Jug" as Leslie entered the room.

As Leslie stepped out of the dark hallway into the crowded, gaily lit, and festive dining room, George Leslie knew he had arrived—in more ways than one.

Leslie recognized John Roebling, the Brooklyn Bridge engineer, who was seated at one of the long dining tables by himself. Roebling again invited Leslie down to the East River ferry landing to view the proposed site of the Brooklyn Bridge. Work on what would become the greatest feat in American engineering history would begin soon.

It was easy to locate flamboyant Jubilee Jim in the crowd, as he was carrying on in his usual animated, jovial manner. Fisk was wearing his cobalt blue, specially made Ninth Regiment uniform. His ample chest was covered with any number of silver and bronze medals, and he had gold epaulets on both shoulders. He sported a Napoleonic hat with crimson feathers on the top. Fisk had recently been elected colonel in the city's Ninth Regiment militia. His election was a month before at the Ninth Regiment Armory on West Twenty-sixth Street, only a few blocks away from Erie Castle. Of the twenty officers present, all but two had voted for him (and those two were summarily dismissed from service).

Before the election, Fisk had told the group of officers, "You know I'm no military man. I've never trained a day in my life; never shot off a gun or a pistol; and don't even know the A B C's of war yet. Fact is, I doubt whether I could shoulder arms or file left, or make a reconnaissance in force, or do any of them things, to save my boots . . ." It wasn't Fisk's military prowess the officers wanted; it was his prestige and his money. After being elected, Fisk bought the whole regiment new uniforms and arms and hired a one-hundred-piece marching band.

News of Fisk's election was met by thunderous applause and cheers from the regular soldiers. A *New York Herald* reporter covering the event referred to the newly elected Colonel Jim Fisk of the Ninth Regiment as "the Mushroom Mars" (referring to the Roman God of War, Mars, and Fisk's portly appearance) and "Colonel Napoleon Fisk." It didn't bother Fisk. Nothing ever did. A reporter for the *Herald* wrote: "The great God of war mounted the dais and the trembling centurions were summoned before him. In a deep bass voice he then issued a pronunciamento, and to the obsequious satraps declared that there was a tide in the affairs of the militia which taken at the flood leads me on to glory."

In order to bolster the sagging enrollment of the regiment, Fisk immediately offered a $500 prize to the company that enrolled the most new soldiers by July of that year. He also quickly put together a list of employees of the Erie Railroad and the Grand Opera House whose jobs would be in jeopardy if they did not enlist in the Ninth Regiment. With his new title, added to that of admiral, a rank he had ceremoniously bestowed on himself as owner of the Fall River Steamship Line, there was a great deal of speculation over whether Fisk should be called "Colonel-Admiral Fisk" or "Admiral-Colonel." After outsmarting Wall Street financier Daniel Drew into selling him the Fall River steamship fleet, Fisk had declared, "If Vanderbilt's a Commodore, I can be an Admiral!" Fisk had bought himself a showy naval uniform, much like his new Ninth Regiment getup, and had a matching one made for Mansfield so she could wear it whenever the two of them traveled together aboard one of his many magnificent steamships.

Fisk had outfitted the steamships with plush carpeting and new furniture and fixtures, and he'd even hired a crew of ship's stewards to serenade the passengers. On each of his two most luxurious steamships, the *Bristol* and the *Providence*—both huge steamers able to carry close to eight hundred passengers—he arranged to have on board more than 250 yellow, singing canaries in huge gilded cages.

Many New York newspapers regarded his election as colonel of the Ninth Regiment as a joke by Fisk on polite society. Fisk was the first person to ever simultaneously hold the titles of colonel and admiral, an accomplishment he relished.

Seated next to Fisk was his mistress, the exquisitely dressed and beautifully seductive Josie Mansfield. She concealed everything but her dark, oval eyes behind a Chinese fan. Leslie couldn't take his eyes off her; hardly anyone could. It was difficult for him to hide the knowledge of the intimacy they had recently enjoyed in Fisk's absence, but he did the best he could under the circumstances. Mansfield had an advantage: She was able to hide her excitement at seeing Leslie behind her fan. Besides, she'd had plenty of practice. Leslie wasn't her first paramour; with Jubilee Jim away in Washington, setting in motion his and Jay Gould's scheme to corner the gold market, Mansfield was free to cheat on Fisk whenever it pleased her—and it pleased her to do so often. Mansfield was left to her own devices, and she had many . . . and even more vices. Men were at the top of that list. Not only had Mansfield enjoyed a dalliance with Leslie, but she was also carrying on a secret affair with the handsome but mentally unbalanced Ned Stokes.

Mansfield's roving eye was not content with the affections of her two male lovers. She also began a clandestine relationship with a woman, Victoria Claflin Woodhull. A former cigar girl from San Francisco, Woodhull moved to New York where she appeared in a string of bad theater productions. But acting, or at least acting on the stage, was not Woodhull's real vocation. Instead, the tall, leggy blonde became the titular head of a band of New York City intellectuals, bohemians, and free love advocates, among them Josie Mansfield. Their relationship was kept out of the public eye through a series of elaborate schemes involving Woodhull using her questionable thespian talents in any number of musical productions at the Twenty-third Street Grand Opera House. "The Cleopatra of Twenty-third Street" carried on her illicit affairs with Leslie, Stokes, and Woodhull, depending upon what mood she happened to be in, at her beautiful brownstone within sight of Fisk's Erie offices at the theater.

Woodhull later became a leader in the American women's suffrage movement and a notorious advocate for women's rights and free love. In 1870, she became the first woman stockbroker on Wall Street, opening her firm, Woodhull, Claflin & Company, with financial backing from wealthy robber baron Cornelius Vanderbilt. Some argued that Vanderbilt's financial assistance to Woodhull was payback to Fisk for his underhanded dealings in wrenching control of the Erie Railroad from him. Vanderbilt cherished the knowledge that besides going head to head with Fisk in the financial arena, Woodhull was also going toe to toe with Fisk's mistress, Josie Mansfield.

In 1872, despite women not having the right to vote, Woodhull became the first woman in America to run for president. Then-incumbent Ulysses S. Grant was easily elected to a second term in office, despite all the scandals that had plagued his administration.

That evening at Marm's party, Leslie paid his respects to Fisk, thanking him profusely for inviting him. He kissed Mansfield's outstretched hand, once again never losing eye contact with the beautiful woman. Fisk told Leslie that Marm was anxious to meet him, advising him to introduce himself to her, posthaste. Despite his desire to stay and enjoy Mansfield's company, he did what Fisk suggested and made his way over to Marm's table straightaway.

—m—

Mandelbaum was busy holding court in a far corner of the busy dining room. When Leslie introduced himself, Mandelbaum's otherwise downward-curved mouth turned into a smile. Marm asked Shang Draper to move down so that Leslie could sit next to her, a place of honor by anyone's account. The request annoyed Draper, who had become, or so he imagined, second in command to Mandelbaum. He didn't like the idea of having anyone take his place next to Marm, either physically or figuratively. Nonetheless, Draper grudgingly moved over and Leslie sat down next to Mandelbaum.

Leslie immediately thanked Mandelbaum for the invitation to the dinner party, and especially for helping to retrieve his stolen wallet. Leslie had learned from Sheriff O'Brien, to whom Leslie had paid a handsome reward, that he owed his gratitude to Marm. It was only through her efforts that the wallet had been returned, almost intact—sans the two hundred dollars, of course. Leslie had only been concerned with the return of his little joker, which was now sitting safely in the Fifth Avenue Hotel's safe, along with many of his other precious possessions.

Mandelbaum took an immediate liking to George Leslie. Perhaps it was his good looks, or his manners. Perhaps it was because Marm always prided herself on being a good judge of character, and she sensed that the handsome, well-mannered gentleman from Cincinnati had a larcenous heart. In fact, being a good judge of character, she knew he did.

5

THE GREAT ESCAPE

They left behind them a large lot of burglars' implements, comprising jimmies, mauls, powder, [and] fuses, and though the safe bears the marks of hard usage, all the securities, amounting to some $100,000, were held safe by its faithfulness.

—JAMES C. TOWNSEND, PRESIDENT,
GLEN COVE MUTUAL INSURANCE COMPANY (1868)

Once Leslie was seated comfortably next to Marm, she clapped her hands and a young boy maneuvered through the noisy crowd, carrying a tray of wineglasses. Leslie recognized the boy immediately. It was the young pickpocket from the train station. Along with his many other attributes, Leslie was also gifted with a near-photographic memory. He could look at something or someone for the briefest time and recall the person or place in the minutest detail.

The pickpocket—who was called Johnny Irving—had a shock of blond hair and wide blue eyes. He wasn't dressed in the rags he'd been wearing earlier at the train station; instead, he now sported a white shirt, black vest, and bowtie. Leslie politely took a glass of wine and handed it graciously to Marm. He then took one for himself, all the while keeping his eyes fixed on Irving, who grew more uncomfortable by the minute.

Leslie asked after the boy's younger sister. Irving pretended not to understand. Marm intervened, asking if Leslie knew the boy. Leslie explained how he had run into the boy and his sister at the train station. Marm told him that she made every attempt to care for the poor orphaned street children by finding them work. She boasted of running a small school for them on Grand Street. Leslie had heard all about the "school" she ran.

Leslie was bright enough to realize that it was Irving who had stolen his wallet that day at the train station, and that he worked for Marm as one of her many criminals in training. It was the only way he could have gotten his wallet back nearly intact. Irving had stolen it and dutifully returned it to his teacher and benefactor, Marm Mandelbaum. It made perfect sense. Still, Leslie had to wonder, of all the possibly hundreds of wallets stolen by Mandelbaum's cadre of young pickpockets, why had his been so readily returned to him? Sheriff O'Brien had only been the go-between. It was Marm who'd had the wallet and Marm who returned it to him. It was a puzzle to Leslie.

With Irving still standing in front of them, Leslie quickly brought up the issue of the stolen wallet. He again thanked Mandelbaum for returning it to him. Marm took no credit for finding the wallet, explaining that it had been all Sheriff O'Brien's doing. She explained that the wallet had simply and miraculously come into her possession when someone, she could not remember who, had brought it into her store claiming that they had found it. It was pure coincidence as far as she was concerned. God, she told him, worked in mysterious ways. So did Marm Mandelbaum, Leslie suspected.

It was just too bad that he'd lost his one hundred dollars, Marm said. Leslie winked at Irving, who looked as though he was about to drop his tray and bolt at any second. Both Leslie and little Johnny Irving knew that his wallet had contained *two* hundred dollars. For one brief moment the knowledge of that fact struck a tenuous bond between Leslie and Irving.

Marm waved Irving off. Before he could make his getaway, Leslie reached into his pocket and handed him a silver dollar, commending the boy for his fine service. Irving looked at Marm before taking Leslie's tip. She nodded approvingly and Johnny Irving snatched the silver dollar and tucked it safely away, no doubt relieved that Leslie hadn't revealed his deception to Mandelbaum.

Irving's secret was safe with Leslie. Based on what the police offi-cer had told him, Leslie knew that Mandelbaum's little pickpockets only received a small percentage of what they stole for her. There was, of course, no honor among thieves. Irving must have returned only half of what was in Leslie's wallet. The rest he must have kept for himself and his sister. *Enterprising boy*, Leslie thought.

After Irving left, Leslie explained that he didn't care so much about the money; it was the contents of the wallet that mattered most to him. Some of it was irreplaceable, he said. Marm understood completely. Of all the people in the world who might have appreciated what it was George Leslie was trying to perfect—the Holy Grail for bank robbers—Marm Mandelbaum was at the top of the list. Leslie wasn't the first to try to create a device that could be used to surreptitiously uncover the combination to any bank safe. And now that Marm knew he had a safe-cracking instrument tucked away in his wallet, she was anxious to find out why. This handsome young man from Cincinnati didn't look or act like any of her other employees. For the first part of the evening, Man-delbaum would not let Leslie leave her side, much to the chagrin of her other criminal guests, always eager to bask in her ample limelight and good favor.

—⚹—

It was difficult for Leslie not to notice the young, dark-skinned girl in the gold earrings and red bandana across the room. She was surrounded by a bevy of men, young and old alike, all vying for her attention. The beautiful "Black Lena" Kleinschmidt was, among other nefarious things, a gifted pickpocket and blackmailer. She was a product of Mandelbaum's infamous school for thieves. She had been given the dubious nickname of "Black Lena" not so much for her skin color but for the cold black heart that beat in her ample breast. Lena had a streak of independence, and on occasion she had used her invitations to Mandelbaum's parties to line up potential victims and replenish her coffers. Mandelbaum invited her rebel-lious student because, with her toffee-colored skin, long black hair, Asian eyes, full red lips, and powder-blue eyes, Black Lena was a favorite among the men who came to the dinner parties. Lena knew how to use her beauty and her body to get what she wanted.

Mandelbaum always made it perfectly clear to everyone in her employ that guests at her dinner parties were not to be sized up as easy marks. If her guests felt they were only being victimized at Mandelbaum's parties, they wouldn't come, and she relished the modicum of respectability her parties provided her with. Knowing Black Lena's modus operandi, Mandelbaum excused herself from Leslie's company and made her way through the crowd to where Lena was entertaining a throng of male guests. Taking her aside, Mandelbaum reminded the beautiful young woman about her rule— Hands off! She also warned Lena to put any thought of approaching the handsome Mr. Leslie out of her mind. Mandelbaum wasn't about to share the attention of her young gentleman with anyone, and especially not with Black Lena.

—⚉—

The gentlemen at the dinner, having finished their dessert, were now smoking the cigars that were being passed around on silver trays by a host of Marm's little part-time waiters and full-time pickpockets, such as Johnny Irving. With Mandelbaum away from the table, Leslie was left sitting beside Shang Draper, who gave him the cold shoulder. Feeling uncomfortable with Draper's silent treatment, Leslie decided to wander through the crowd alone. Handsome and debonair, Leslie easily introduced himself to various guests. He was always under the watchful eye of Marm Mandelbaum, but she wasn't the only one keeping an eye on him. Josie Mansfield was also keeping watch, as was Shang Draper. And despite her vow to Marm that she had no interest in the handsome stranger, Black Lena was also observing Leslie.

Mansfield was seated between Fisk and Ned Stokes. Fisk was in rapt conversation with the man seated next to him, while Stokes incessantly fawned over Mansfield, hanging on her every word. But Mansfield only had eyes for George Leslie. She managed to catch Leslie's attention with a dramatic flutter of her Chinese fan, and Leslie quickly made his way across the crowded room to where she was sitting.

Ned Stokes was oblivious to anyone except Mansfield, and did not bother to acknowledge Leslie when he extended his hand to him. Leslie, in his usual gentlemanly way, bowed and kissed Mansfield's extended hand. She slipped something into his other hand as he bowed. Stokes suddenly jumped to his feet, wild-eyed and raving. He angrily reprimanded Leslie for what he perceived as unwanted advances on Miss Mansfield, scolding him for interrupting their conversation. Someone put a huge hand on Stokes's shoulder and in a firm, authoritative way, spun him around. Red Leary was nicknamed as such not only because of his fiery red hair and beard but also because of his violent temper. Leary always served as the bouncer at Mandelbaum's shindigs, not that any of her legitimate guests would be thrown out, even though the wine, women, and song could have a destructive effect on some of them.

Leary held onto Stokes firmly. Standing over six feet tall, Leary had broad shoulders and muscular forearms from years of working on the docks, his chosen career before turning to a life of crime. His shoulders and barrel chest were stuffed into an ill-fitting suit, and a small derby was perched on the top of his flaming red hair. As he held Stokes nearly up off the floor with one arm, Leary looked like an avenging angel, plucking a sinner up and out of the firmament.

In the face of the burly former dock worker, Stokes quickly saw the error of his ways. He apologized to Leslie and sat back down quietly next to Josie Mansfield. It was not the first time Stokes had lost his head when it came to someone expressing interest in Mansfield.

Fisk paid no attention to the mild ruckus and continued an animated conversation with Samuel Tilden. Doffing his brightly feathered cap, Fisk introduced Leslie to Tilden. Leslie slipped the note Mansfield had given him into his vest pocket before shaking Tilden's hand.

Samuel Tilden was an eminently successful lawyer, with many railroad companies as clients. Tilden also had political aspirations. Although he was no friend of the criminal culture, his political ambitions required him to stay in contact with *all* the many elements of New York City's society, including the likes of Mandelbaum and her crowd. Besides, Tilden had bigger fish to fry than mere petty criminals. Tilden had set his sights on New York's biggest criminal, Boss Tweed, and his notorious Tweed Ring. Tilden was serving as the state Democratic chairman and was reluctantly spearheading a reform movement in the city that included getting rid of Tweed. Leslie listened raptly to Tilden's plans to reform the city and rid it of the likes of Boss Tweed.

Tilden had studied law at Yale University and served as legal counsel for New York City. He was elected to the New York Assembly in 1846 as a Democrat. Three years earlier, in 1866, he had become the New York Democratic Party chairman. A compulsive hypochondriac, Tilden often interrupted his conversation by periodically touching his nose with his handkerchief and placing his hand on his brow to check his temperature. Several times he stopped and asked if he looked in some way flushed or out of sorts. When someone coughed nearby, he would hurriedly cover his mouth and nose with the silk scarf he had draped around his neck.

Tilden had come under fire from some New York City newspapers for tolerating the corrupt shenanigans of the political chief of the city, William "Boss" Tweed. It was impossible to do anything in New York City, from holding political office to running a school for pickpockets as Marm Mandelbaum did, without the support of Boss Tweed and his three loyal companions, Peter Sweeney, Richard Connolly, and Oakey Hall. They ruled New York City as if it were their private domain.

—⁓—

The 52 Chambers Street courthouse project was at the heart of Tweed's financial empire. Begun in 1861, the building was supposed to have cost the city $350,000. By 1869, it had cost the city nearly $11 million, with much of the difference lining the pockets of Boss Tweed and his Tammany Hall Ring. From his headquarters, located on East Fourteenth Street, Tweed orchestrated bribes and kickbacks that he demanded in exchange for city contracts. The county courthouse project was mockingly referred to as Tweed's "Little Alaska," since the building ended up costing twice as much as the purchase of Alaska did in 1867.

The litany of graft and corruption at the site ultimately became Tweed's downfall. Records later revealed that one carpenter at the courthouse project was paid nearly $400,000 for one month's work. Interestingly, the building was practically devoid of woodwork. A furniture contractor received nearly $200,000 for delivering three tables and several dozen chairs. Another of Tweed's friends on the courthouse payroll, plasterer Andrew J. Garvey, reportedly was paid more than $100,000 for two days' work. To add insult to injury, when public clamor arose as to why the project had taken so long and cost so much, a lengthy report was published detailing the vague incidentals. The report was printed at a cost of approximately $8,000 by a company owned by Tweed.

Cartoonist Thomas Nast of *Harper's Weekly* depicted Samuel Tilden as a "sham reformer" whose intent was not to dismantle corrupt city government but instead, to create his own political machine and take over from Tweed. Tilden had been reluctant at first to pursue Tweed, but as political and public pressure grew, he decided to make political hay out of reforming city government and getting rid of Boss Tweed.

—ᴡ—

Red Leary tapped Leslie on the shoulder. He pointed to Marm who was standing on the other side of the room, waiting for him. Leslie bid Tilden, Fisk, and the beautiful Mansfield good-bye. Stokes now sat sullenly beside Mansfield. Leslie saw no reason to engage him further. He headed across the room to where Marm was waiting to take him downstairs to the storefront, the only place they could talk privately. Leslie graciously took the arm of his hostess as she led him out of the brightly lit room into the dark corridor and down the stairs.

Although Marm was taken by the gentlemanly Leslie, she was nobody's fool. She needed to test him to be sure he wasn't an agent for the police or the Pinkerton detectives. Mandelbaum had enough money to bribe police and politicians in order to stay one step ahead of the law, but the uncompromising Pinkerton detectives were different. They were incorruptible, which made them dangerous to Mandelbaum and her criminal empire.

The Pinkerton Detective Agency was started in 1852 by Allan Pinkerton, a deputy sheriff in Chicago. It quickly grew to become the vanguard of criminal detection, known for its high moral standards and relentless pursuit of criminals. It was reportedly the prototype for the Federal Bureau of Investigation. During the Civil War, Allan Pinkerton was the head of the Union secret service, responsible for spying on the Confederacy. The agency was also given the job of guarding President Abraham Lincoln. Their slogan was "We Never Sleep," and the sign that hung over their offices in Chicago depicted a huge, black-and-white, wide-open eye. This logo led to the term "private eye."

In later years, the Pinkerton Detective Agency became known as an instrument of big business, acknowledged more for squashing union riots and strikes than for pursuing criminals. Notably, in 1875, the Pinkertons infiltrated and crushed the Molly Maguires, a secret coal miners' organization in Schuylkill County, Pennsylvania. They also broke up the strike of the iron and steel workers' union at Andrew Carnegie's Homestead plant in Pittsburgh. But before their image was forever tarnished by their link to big business and efforts to suppress the burgeoning labor movement in America, the Pinkerton Detective Agency, under the leadership of Allan Pinkerton and later, his two sons, Robert and William, was engaged in the pursuit of known criminal gangs and most conspicuously, Marm Mandelbaum. They were a dangerous force to be reckoned with, and Mandelbaum was not about to take any chances. She had to be sure that George Leslie was not a Pinkerton agent sent to infiltrate her operation.

Alone downstairs in the dingy storefront, far from the gaiety upstairs and from prying eyes, Mandelbaum confronted Leslie. She wanted to know what he was doing with something like the little joker in his wallet. Although she didn't know Leslie's name for his invention, she certainly knew what the contraption was supposed to be used for. She had seen similar devices before, dozens of times, and she had seen them all fail to produce the desired result—miraculously opening up a bank safe. She laid her cards on the table: She knew what he had in his wallet; what she wanted to know now was why someone of Leslie's upbringing, education, and social standing would have such a device.

Leslie gave it to her straight. He wanted to rob banks, and his little joker would help him do it. He explained to her how it worked and how it would revolutionize bank robbing. Mandelbaum had heard it all before. Leslie explained he'd tested it on his own safe and it worked like a charm. Mandelbaum still wasn't convinced. There was a big difference between using the device on a safe he had in his room, with all the time in the world to fiddle with it, and actually using it in a real bank robbery where you potentially had someone breathing down your neck. Leslie agreed. He told her that was why he wanted her to give him a chance to prove it to her.

Mandelbaum feigned surprise. Whatever made him think she knew anything about robbing banks? She stared at him suspiciously, complaining that the rich food and wine had upset her stomach. Leslie played along, boasting that if she was looking for somebody to rob a bank, he was the man to do it. He provided a litany of his qualifications, explaining that he had been gifted with a photographic memory. That, along with his understanding of architectural design, allowed him to practically memorize the layout of any building after seeing it only briefly.

She agreed that this was an amazing ability, to be able to size up any room or building so quickly, a gift that must be helpful in his career as an architect. Helpful in perhaps other careers as well, Leslie told her—including robbing banks.

Mandelbaum wanted to know why he wanted to rob a bank. It was dangerous, and if he was caught he could spend years in prison. Leslie assured her that he would never get caught, and that his device would take all the danger out of robbing a bank. There would be no need for laborious safecracking, no need for dynamite or any other explosives, and no need for guns or weapons of any kind. He said he had it down to a science.

He still hadn't answered her question about his motive for robbing a bank. He already appeared to be fairly wealthy. He didn't need the money, did he? It was easy enough to answer. People like Jubilee Jim Fisk robbed everyone—banks, trains, other Wall Street brokers, even the government. And Boss Tweed and his political machine—well, they robbed the city blind. The Carnegies, Belmonts, and Vanderbilts, they all robbed from each other and called it good business. And they all put their money in banks for safekeeping. He just wanted to eliminate the middleman, Leslie explained. If all the robber barons put their money in banks, he would just rob the bank. It made perfect sense to him.

It was beginning to make perfect sense to Mandelbaum as well. Still, no matter how taken she was with this handsome young gentleman, she was a shrewd businesswoman, and an even shrewder criminal. No matter how much she liked him, his loyalty had to be tested—and it would be, soon enough.

—⁓—

THE GREAT ATTEMPTED BANK ROBBERY AT THE NEW YORK EXCHANGE BANK

Herring's Safe Foils the Burglars and Saves $500,000

New York, March 27, 1867, Messrs. Herring & Co., No. 251 Broadway:

GENTLEMEN: You have already been well informed through the columns of the daily newspapers of the desperate attempt made upon our money vault and the Fire and Burglar-proof Safe made by you for our bank a few years ago. Although our vault was very strongly built and provided with heavy doors and the best of locks, the attempt upon the vault was successful.

The rogues succeeded in undermining the vault by digging a tunnel some seventy feet long under the adjoining building, and terminating at the base of the vault itself. Here they commenced their operations upon a large scale, and, after removing the front part of the heavy stone foundation, which was strongly laid in cement, they reached the large flag-stone which formed the floor of the vault. This stone was broken by means of a jack-screw of great power, and the interior of the vault thus reached.

Your safe now became the great point of attack; and bravely did it resist every effort, holding secure its entire trust (property amounting to $500,000) against all the tools and ingenuity of the burglars.

The first great aim seemed to be to drill into the safe; but, although some thirty holes were made in the outer casing, the hardened iron forming the centre lining turned the point of every tool. Disappointed here, they now attempted to dissect the safe, and endeavored to force the strong framework apart. After removing one bar, and partially cutting off another, they gave this up; and all further operations proved unavailing. Our confidence in your safe has been reassured; and we would further add, for the benefit of the public, and to your credit, that, had they even succeeded in getting through the outer casing or shell of the safe, which they did not do, three more thicknesses of metal still remained; and each of these, in our opinion, would have given them more trouble than the single one by which they were so completely foiled.

When the great resources of these burglars were considered, the opportunity to work from Saturday night to Monday morning, the great number of the best of tools in their possession, and the skill and ingenuity displayed, we have reason to feel proud of your safe.

We wish you to send the large safe purchased by us at your store to our new banking-house in Greenwich St., and as soon as we get moved you shall have the old one as a trophy.

—S. Van Duzer, President of the New York Exchange Bank
(*The New York Sun,* 1867)

—⁂—

Leslie spent much of the remainder of the evening seated in the chair of honor next to Mandelbaum, an act that prompted some speculation and a great deal of envy, especially from Marm's criminal cohorts at the party. Across from Leslie was Max Shinburn, a German-born criminal whose expertise was burglary and safecracking. He was also one of Mandelbaum's favorites because of his gentlemanly demeanor. Shinburn liked to be referred to as "The Baron." He had spent some of his ill-gotten gains buying a title of royalty in Monaco. He and Leslie hit it off famously.

During dinner the guests drank an array of fine sparkling wines from Victorian etched wineglasses, but after the meal they were treated to a variety of mixed drinks prepared by New York City's most famous mixologist, Jerry Thomas. Thomas was the principal bartender at the Metropolitan Hotel, on the corner of Broadway and Prince Street. He was known as the city's premiere bartender, popular among all the best "club men" and widely known for his famous mixed drink inventions, including the "Martinez," a drink wrongly described as the original martini. Thomas's Martinez was made with sweetened gin, red vermouth, maraschino liqueur, and bitters.

Seeing the attention Marm paid to the stranger infuriated Shang Draper, who didn't take lightly to some tinhorn from Cincinnati cutting in on his turf. Draper worked closely with Mandelbaum, using her as both a fence for stolen property as well as a financial resource for bank robberies. He didn't know who Leslie was or what role he might play in the ongoing business of New York City crime, especially as far as his association with Marm was concerned, but he wasn't about to let anyone come between him and his dealings with Marm, especially not the handsome, sophisticated George Leslie. Draper, who had grown up in the horrific Five Points, had a suspicious mind, and worse, an abiding hatred of the upper class.

Another underworld thug who was not pleased with Leslie's encroachment of Mandelbaum was Johnny "The Mick" Walsh, the leader of the notorious Walsh Gang in the Bowery section of the city. Walsh's violent gangland tactics, including shakedowns of businesspeople and immigrants for protection money, dominated the Bowery. Walsh was no friend of Shang Draper's; he was looking to expand his criminal operations throughout the city, and Draper stood firmly in his way. The two gang leaders had been engaged in a long-running feud, and their gangs had fought turf wars in a series of bloody knife fights and gun battles, with neither gang besting the other. A successful albeit shaky peace had been brokered by Mandelbaum, who saw the feud as bad for business. The truce between Draper and Walsh would be shattered many years later during a bloody shootout at Shang Draper's saloon in 1883, with Draper finally getting the best of "The Mick."

Leslie left the dinner party with private invitations extended to him from three people: Mandelbaum, who wanted to discuss his little joker in more detail; Josie Mansfield, who gave him the dates that Fisk would be in Washington; and exotic beauty Black Lena Kleinschmidt, who, despite Mandelbaum's orders, had found a way to arrange a secret rendezvous with Leslie.

All in all, it had been a very productive evening for George Leslie.

—◊◊◊—

It was the bad luck of "Piano" Charlie Bullard that became good luck for George Leslie. It was Bullard, the former meat cutter turned safecracker extraordinaire, who ultimately secured a place of honor for George Leslie at Marm Mandelbaum's crooked table. Although Mandelbaum was impressed with Leslie's fine manners, good looks, architectural mind, and the construction of his little device, it was Leslie's help in springing Bullard from jail that convinced Mandelbaum to give Leslie a chance to try his hand at his first heist, the robbery of the Ocean National Bank in the summer of 1869. Not only was it Leslie's first bank robbery, but it was the most lucrative bank heist in New York City history (that is, until Leslie pulled off the Manhattan bank job nine years later).

Although Mandelbaum was readily taken by the gentlemanly George Leslie that first night at the dinner party, she was nobody's fool. Mandelbaum demanded loyalty from everyone she worked with, and Leslie was no exception. Although she instinctively felt that she had found a kindred spirit in him, she still needed to test his loyalty, and she did it by asking him to help plan a jailbreak.

Bullard had been apprehended by Pinkerton detectives for stealing close to $100,000 worth of merchandise from the Hudson River Railway Express. Mandelbaum, who'd had Leslie on her mind ever since their first meeting, summoned him to a meeting along with "Baron" Max Shinburn and several other of her closest associates. Mandelbaum wasn't able to get Bullard out of jail using the usual "legal" means, so she decided to break him out. Together, she and Leslie planned Bullard's escape.

Leslie was sent to visit Bullard in jail, where he memorized the layout of the building. The gang, led by Shinburn and another notorious robber, Adam Worth, rented a vacant office in a building across the street from the jail and hung out a sign advertising appraisals. The front windows were boarded up to keep out prying eyes. In the basement of the building, with the help of several of Mandelbaum's strong-armed cohorts, a tunnel was dug under the street and beneath the wall of the jail, directly into Bullard's cell. Leslie's blueprints of the street and jail, plans he had drawn up after just one visit, pinpointed the exact location of Bullard's cell. With the tunnel dug, and after two willing guards were sufficiently bribed to look the other way, Bullard was freed. No one was hurt and not a shot was fired. The plan had worked to perfection. Within the week, Piano Charlie Bullard was back entertaining guests at Mandelbaum's parties and George Leslie had gained entry into Mandelbaum's inner circle. Following Bullard's successful and intricately planned jailbreak, Mandelbaum suggested that Leslie try his hand at something more potentially rewarding—robbing the Ocean National Bank.

—ᴍ—

Mandelbaum organized a gang for the bank job and put Leslie in charge. Shang Draper didn't like the idea of a "tenderfoot" being in charge of anything, particularly not a bank robbery. And he especially didn't like taking orders from Leslie. Mandelbaum remained adamant about Leslie being in charge. If Draper wanted in on the Ocean National Bank job, he would have to follow Leslie's orders. Begrudgingly, he did, even to the point of wearing one of the fake beards and wigs Leslie made everyone in the gang wear, including Abe Coakley, Jimmy Hope, Johnny Dobbs, Red Leary, and "Banjo" Pete Emerson. Leslie borrowed the disguises from the dressing room at the Grand Opera House, where he was a frequent visitor and close to Josie Mansfield's home, where they carried on their amorous relationship out of sight of her benefactor, Jubilee Jim. The dressing room at the Opera House was a treasure trove of costumes and disguises that

Leslie readily availed himself of. Disguises were just one of the many innovations Leslie used on the Ocean National Bank robbery. The most important, however, was the use of his little joker, which worked like a charm.

During this period, Leslie sought not only the affections of Josie Mansfield but those of Black Lena as well. Along with his almost weekly visits with Mansfield, Leslie made frequent trips to Hackensack, New Jersey, for liaisons with the dark-skinned beauty. Their relationship would prove to be short-lived, however—especially after Mandelbaum found out about it.

It was difficult to keep any secrets from Mandelbaum. She had informers everywhere. Black Lena had decided to emulate the successful Mandelbaum by setting herself up in a fashionable home in Hackensack. The home was purchased with the loot she had accumulated from her pickpocketing and blackmailing schemes. She introduced herself to polite New Jersey society as the widow of a wealthy mining contractor. Lena's house was made up to look just like Mandelbaum's palatial salon in the rear of the building on Rivington Street.

Similarly, Black Lena gave elaborate dinner parties in hopes of endearing herself to New Jersey high society for the express purpose of finding an array of new victims for her criminal pursuits. Although in some circles imitation might have been considered the sincerest form of flattery, Black Lena's attempts to mimic Mandelbaum's success ultimately led to her downfall. It was not simply the fact that Lena imitated Mandelbaum's successful salon in Hackensack; two other transgressions, considered unforgivable by Mandelbaum, led to her demise.

First, Black Lena was not satisfied with merely imitating Marm; she actually boasted of outdoing her, to the point where she asked Johnny "The Mick" Walsh, leader of the Bowery Walsh Gang and an archrival of Mandelbaum's, to join her. Walsh had designs of not only taking over all the criminal activity in the Bowery, but also of running everything in New York City, including the profitable fencing business controlled lock, stock, and barrel by Mandelbaum.

When word spread that Black Lena was joining forces with Johnny Walsh to take over Mandelbaum's lucrative criminal empire, Mandelbaum set the wheels in motion to get rid of Lena. If teaming up with Walsh wasn't enough to make Mandelbaum decide to put an end to her, Black

Lena's amorous liaison with George Leslie was the straw that broke the camel's back. Mandelbaum didn't blame Leslie; after all, he was a handsome, debonair young man, attractive to many women. Mandelbaum herself was attracted to him, but not for romantic purposes. Hers was more of a business proposition, and Black Lena's involvement only complicated matters.

Mandelbaum employed Johnny Irving's pickpocketing skills to undo Black Lena, asking Irving to steal an emerald ring from one of Black Lena's high society guests. Mandelbaum then had the ring sent to Lena in the guise of a gift from George Leslie. Leslie was known to spend lavishly on his paramours, so the beautiful emerald ring came as no surprise to Lena. She displayed the ring prominently at her next dinner party, claiming it came from a secret admirer, little suspecting what was in store for her. The woman who had actually owned the ring was at the party. When she recognized the emerald ring on Lena's finger, she immediately informed her husband, a New Jersey district court judge, who called in Pinkerton agents to investigate. Black Lena's criminal career, along with her relationship with George Leslie, came to an abrupt end when Pinkerton agents and police raided her Hackensack home and discovered rooms filled with stolen property. Lena was hauled off to jail and received the stiffest sentence any district court judge could hand down. That was the end of Black Lena's attempt to dethrone Mandelbaum, and the end of her relationship with George Leslie.

The incident did not endear either Marm or Johnny Irving to Walsh, who vowed to get revenge. He had invested a great deal in his partnership with Black Lena, and now his plans for the takeover of the criminal underworld in New York had been dashed. For years following the Black Lena incident, Walsh engaged in a long and bitter feud with both Johnny Irving and Marm Mandelbaum.

With Black Lena out of the way, Mandelbaum felt Leslie could now concentrate his full attention on what was most important: the robbery of the Ocean National Bank.

6

THE OCEAN NATIONAL BANK ROBBERY

I never met a thief in my life, provided he could benefit by peaching on his confederates, from whom [I] could not find out anything I was desirous to know. There is no such thing as honor among thieves.

–THOMAS BYRNES, NEW YORK CITY POLICE DETECTIVE (1869)

The old adage "One man's floor is another man's ceiling" wasn't lost on George Leslie as he prepared to undertake his first bank heist. It was more important for Leslie to know whose ceiling was another's floor as he planned his intricate robbery of the Ocean National Bank. The robbery was one part planning and another part hocus-pocus, but it was all sheer criminal genius.

—∿—

George Leslie pulled off his first bank heist in June 1869, a few short months after his introduction to Marm Mandelbaum. Mandelbaum supplied Leslie with a handpicked gang of her best and most trusted associates, including Johnny Dobbs, Billy Porter, Jimmy Hope, Gilbert Yost, Red Leary, and Shang Draper. Leslie's gang robbed the Ocean National Bank located at the corner of Greenwich and Fulton streets, getting away with close to $800,000, an unprecedented amount of cash. The take in the Ocean Bank robbery would have been even higher if Leslie hadn't decided that they would only take what they could carry, and only those items— cash, checks, and jewelry—that were untraceable. He saw no point in stealing bank certificates that could only be cashed at the bank itself, or gold that would weigh them down. Leslie was particular about what he wanted to steal and how he wanted to steal it, which branded him among other criminals he was working with as a prima donna. Prima donna or not, this was his first heist, but would by no means be his last.

It was the largest take of any bank job in the city's history up and until then, and it was pulled off without firing a shot or blowing open the bank safe. Leslie's little joker did all the work. Although Mandelbaum financed the operation at a cost of $3,000, it was Leslie who masterminded the caper. Leslie had clearly demonstrated his amazing knack for planning and pulling off successful, not to mention highly rewarding, bank robberies. It was the beginning of a great career in crime for George Leslie, and an opportunity afforded him solely by Marm Mandelbaum, a fact that Leslie never forgot. Throughout his reign as "the King of Bank Robbers," the title that was later given to him by friends in the criminal world, as well as New York City police officials and newspaper reporters. Leslie paid tribute to Mandelbaum either through a direct percentage from every bank job he pulled or by laundering stolen securities and other valuables through her, whether she'd financed the caper or not. This relationship would last throughout his short life.

Shang Draper had not been so keen on Leslie, seeing him as a challenger to his own lofty position within the crime world, and especially with Marm. He would later come to see Leslie as a threat to someone even more important to him—his wife, Babe Irving.

Planning for the Ocean National Bank heist took three months, much to the chagrin of Draper and the others, who wanted to simply break into the bank vault and blow up the safe. This wasn't what Leslie had in mind and, over almost everyone's objections, Marm put the novice bank robber Leslie in charge of the whole operation. Leslie promised her the biggest payday in criminal history, and he wasn't far off the mark. It would take another nine years before Leslie tried to make good on his promise by pulling off the greatest heist in American history, the robbery of nearly $3 million from the Manhattan Savings Institution on October 27, 1878.

Leslie put Mandelbaum's financial backing to good use, providing his gang with the best burglary tools available, bribing several officials, drawing up a full set of plans for the bank's layout, and actually constructing a room identical to the one inside the Ocean National Bank in one of the many empty warehouses Mandelbaum owned. In the end he needed to borrow another $1,000 in cash from Mandelbaum to rent office space. Although it sounded strange to her, Mandelbaum complied. She had complete trust in Leslie, even though he was a novice in the criminal world. She knew true criminal talent when she saw it, and George Leslie had the quickest criminal mind she had ever witnessed. Besides, she knew that Leslie was good for any amount of money she put up to finance the bank job.

No one had ever gone to the extent Leslie did in planning a bank robbery. At the vacant warehouse, Leslie rehearsed with the gang how the entire operation would work—like clockwork, with each member of the gang performing a specific function at a specific time. He had all the gang study the blueprints and drilled into them the step-by-step process they would take during the robbery. Leslie timed each of the steps so that everything would be done within split seconds. Timing was everything as far as Leslie was concerned. Leslie also reenacted the bank heist over and over, throwing in various possibilities and forecasting alternative measures. He even had the gang reenact the robbery in the dark in case something happened to the lighting inside the bank.

Draper and the others weren't accustomed to Leslie's style of lengthy, meticulous planning. They were more adept at blowing things up and taking what they could grab. Leslie wanted a more sophisticated operation, one that he could export to other gangs in the city and across the country— for an advisor's fee, of course. The Ocean National Bank job would be not only his trial run but also his initiation into the New York City crime world. Leslie passed his test with flying colors, not to mention the nearly $800,000 payday in stolen cash, securities, and precious jewelry.

To pull off the bank job, Leslie deposited a large sum of his own money into the Ocean National Bank. This gave him ample opportunity in the months leading up to the heist to visit the institution in the guise of a new depositor. He withdrew his money prior to the robbery. Leslie's many visits to the bank yielded invaluable information, not to mention an in with the bank president. The grounds of the bank were scrutinized until every square inch of the building was known to Leslie. He memorized and then committed to paper the entire layout of the bank, which was located on the first floor of a five-story brownstone. With his knowledge of architecture and his photographic memory, Leslie was able to draw up blueprints of the bank's interior and the outside surroundings that would have put even the most knowledgeable architect to shame. The plans were used to build the replica of the bank where he and the gang rehearsed.

Dining with the bank president and others associated with the bank and its operations, Leslie, who was readily accepted into upper-crust society, was able to learn the name of the company that had built the bank's safe. Leslie did this under the pretense of verifying that the safe where he was depositing his money was indeed one of the best around. He said that as an architect, he would know a good safe from a bad one, and wanted to see for himself what kind of product the safe maker was known for. He was able to ingratiate himself with the Yale locksmith responsible for the bank's safe. The locksmith boasted that the lock was impenetrable. It had been tested time and time again, and no one had been able to pick the lock. The safe had even been exhibited in Paris where a bevy of international locksmiths had all tried their hands at picking the lock but had failed.

Leslie wasn't about to leave anything to chance. With the information he had obtained from the locksmith, Leslie was able to make the necessary adjustments to the little joker—specifically, to accommodate the size and shape of the dial on the Ocean National Bank safe. Yale lock or not, nothing was safe from the little joker.

Once inserted inside the safe's dial, the joker would duplicate where the tumblers stopped after it was opened and secured several times. Of course, there was the matter of breaking into the bank so that he could remove the dial on the safe, place the joker inside, and then replace the dial so no one was the wiser. That meant he and the gang had to break into the bank twice: once to insert the joker, and once again to remove it, determine the safe combination, and then actually open the safe. With the safe combination known, it would just be a matter of having a skilled safecracker like Johnny Dobbs, one of the best in the business, try any of the various combinations that showed up on the joker to open the safe. This all seemed too elaborate for most of the gang, but that didn't matter; Mandelbaum had designated Leslie as the boss of the operation, and they all fell into line—most of them, anyway.

Draper remained skeptical of Leslie's plan and his motives. He had already secretly ordered Red Leary, the strongman and muscle behind the gang, to be ready to "take care of" Leslie if he did anything stupid. Draper was sure that the dandified Leslie, with no known experience in robbing banks, would fail miserably. If indeed Leslie was a spy, sent by the Pinkertons to infiltrate Mandelbaum's operation, then Draper, with Red Leary's help, would make sure Leslie never lived to tell about it.

Leary told Draper he was ready to take care of Leslie if and when the bank job went south on them. In fact, Leary had no such intentions. Leary knew which side his bread was buttered on, and it was Marm Mandelbaum who was doing the spreading. If she said Leslie was in charge, then Leslie was in charge. Leary was working for Marm, not Draper, and took orders only from her. And her orders were to do whatever George Leslie wanted him to do—even if he told him to kill Draper. Leary was a company man, and the company was Marm Mandelbaum as far as he was concerned.

The most difficult part of the whole operation was trying to introduce one of the gang into the confidence of the bank. The problem was twofold: First, it had to be someone that the bank trusted to hire in some humble capacity. Leslie needed someone on the inside who could let them into the bank after hours to place the joker inside the dial of the safe and then let him in again to retrieve it. The inside man had to be someone Leslie trusted implicitly, because that person would hold Leslie's career—if not his life—in his hands. It also had to be someone the bank would never suspect. Breaking into the bank once was hard enough. Doing it two times was, in most people's estimation, impossible.

But Leslie knew just the man for the job—a boy, actually: Johnny Irving, the young pickpocket. Leslie knew that he had established an unspoken bond with Irving ever since he chose not to reveal to Mandelbaum that Irving had stolen from her. Using his newfound connections at the bank, Leslie was able to persuade the bank president to hire Johnny Irving, who with his blond hair and sad blue eyes looked his angelic best, to sweep up the bank after hours. It was perfect. Leslie now had his trustworthy inside man.

—ɯ—

Besides having an inside man in Johnny Irving, Leslie also needed a backup plan and a way to get his burglary tools inside the bank without anyone noticing. A trip down to the Hartz Magic Repository on Broadway took care of one part of the problem. The second part would be far trickier.

Disguising Jimmy Hope with a fake mustache and curly black wig, he had Hope rent office space in the basement of the bank. The bank only occupied the first floor of the building. The entire basement was rented by William Kell. Posing as an insurance agent, Hope was able to rent a small office that opened out onto Fulton Street. Using forged documents, Hope showed Kell his credentials signed by the New York Insurance Department. Claiming to be Lewis Cole, president of the fictitious insurance company, Hope was able to rent the small office for $1,000, paid in advance. (Leslie chose the name Cole because of his admiration for outlaw Cole Younger, who rode with his hero, Jesse James.) Shortly afterward he had a desk, chair, and a huge cabinet moved into the office.

Having carefully surveyed the structure of the bank, Leslie knew that the small office in the basement that Jimmy Hope had successfully secured sat directly below the bank vault. *One man's ceiling, another man's floor.*

When the time came to enter the bank the second time around, during the weekend, Johnny Irving wouldn't be working at the bank so he wouldn't be able to let them sneak inside. Leslie decided he would simply drill a hole in the ceiling of the rented office, which would give them direct access to the bank vault and the safe. Of course, there was the question of all the saws and tools they would need, but Leslie had already thought of that. Everything they needed was stored in the huge cabinet that Hope had delivered to the rented office—pure genius on Leslie's part.

—⁓—

Over the course of a weekend in June 1869, George Leslie, Johnny Dobbs, and Red Leary were able to slip into the Ocean National Bank—twice. Billy Porter, the wheelman for the heist, was parked up the street in a getaway carriage. Gilbert Yost, Jimmy Hope, and Shang Draper all served as lookouts. Leslie made all of them wear theatrical disguises procured from the Opera House, different disguises each time. On the night of the second break-in of the bank, Leslie asked Draper to dress as a woman and keep watch in front of the bank. No one would ever suspect that a well-dressed woman, sporting a parasol and a hat, would be a lookout for a bank robbery. Draper balked at the idea, so Leslie went to Mandelbaum. Of all the members of the gang, Draper had the slightest build. He had small, round shoulders and small, delicate hands, and he was clean-shaven. It would not take very much to disguise him as a woman, Leslie thought. He knew Red Leary wouldn't do, not with his brawny build and flaming red beard.

The night of the robbery, Shang Draper, dressed in a powder-blue gown and wearing a long blond wig and carrying a parasol, stood watch in front of the Ocean National Bank while Leslie, Dobbs, and Leary broke in. The humiliation of it only fueled Draper's animosity toward Leslie.

On the night of the first break-in, Johnny Irving, working late sweeping up around the bank, let the three men in the back door. Using his renowned dexterity and nimble fingers, Johnny Dobbs removed the dial from the safe, following the instructions Leslie had given him. After becoming friends with the safe maker, Leslie had bought a smaller version of the same safe and had it delivered to the warehouse where he had built the replica of the bank. Using what he had learned, Leslie and Dobbs both had ample time to practice removing the safe dial without harming it. The three long months of planning that Leslie had put into the bank heist was paying off.

Dobbs removed the dial on the safe and inserted the little joker inside. Then he replaced the dial so that it appeared as though nothing was out of the ordinary. When bank officials opened the bank vault the next day, Leslie's joker would take care of the rest, recording the combination stops on the lock whenever someone opened the safe during normal business hours.

Leslie knew that there would be more money kept in the bank over the weekend than during the week, so they waited two days until Saturday night. Then they broke in again. This time they drilled a hole in the ceiling of the Lewis Cole & Co. office in the basement of the bank and gained access to the vault through the hole that came up directly opposite the vault. Leslie, Dobbs, and Leary climbed up through the hole to enter the bank for the second time.

Dobbs once again expertly took off the safe dial, removed the joker, and placed the dial back on the safe. Using the series of notches etched into the flat tin plate that had been inserted into the bank dial, Dobbs was able to record the tumbler stops. There were only so many different combinations, and Dobbs began the meticulous process of trying them out. It was only a matter of time before Dobbs established the right combination, and the door to the safe opened easily.

They were in.

—⟡—

Johnny Dobbs was one of the most successful safecrackers in New York City. Although there were plenty of deserving candidates to choose from, he was the best. His real name was Michael Kerrigan, and he had earned his reputation as one of New York City's finest criminals by working his way up the criminal ladder, starting as a fence for stolen merchandise and later graduating to bank robbery, safecracking, and ultimately murder. He was in on George Leslie's 1878 world-record bank robbery of the Manhattan Savings Institution, handpicked by Leslie. After the Manhattan bank robbery, Dobbs bought a small saloon where he tried his hand at going straight. Ironically, it was located almost across the street from the New York police headquarters on Mulberry Street. It was reported that when asked why he'd chosen a saloon so close to police headquarters, he replied, "The nearer to church, the closer to God." His attempt at leading a legitimate life didn't last long, and soon he was back plying his trade in the underworld. Johnny Dobbs enjoyed a near twenty-year criminal career. In 1898 Dobbs was found lying in a gutter, beaten to death. His body was taken Bellevue Hospital. He died penniless. He was just fifty years old.

—⟡—

Leslie and his gang made off with close to $800,000 in cash, securities, and jewelry in the Ocean National Bank robbery, the largest bank heist in the city's history. They took only what they could carry and only what Leslie told them to steal—no secured certificates and no bags of heavy gold. Not a shot had been fired. Not a single person injured. Not a stick of dynamite used. Not one bit of property wrecked.

Nothing like it had ever been pulled off in the annals of New York City crime. Even the city newspapers gave credit to the culprits: "A masterful bank job pulled off by one very special bank robber," the *New York Herald* proclaimed after authorities were notified of the robbery the following Monday morning. Boss Tweed was reported to have commented, "I couldn't have done better myself."

Leslie had thought of everything, including the fact that if the bank job was performed on the weekend, then bank officials and authorities would not discover it until the following Monday morning, giving Leslie and his gang plenty of time to unload the stolen cash with Marm and make their individual getaways.

Newly appointed police detective Captain Thomas Byrnes was put in charge of the robbery investigation. Despite his expert criminal detection skills, Byrnes's investigation went nowhere fast. Neither Byrnes nor any of the other detectives assigned to the case were able to uncover a single lead in the case. The only puzzlement about the robbery was why the robbers had left behind close to $2 million in cash and securities lying on the vault floor.

Although Byrnes, a top-notch investigator who would go on to become the chief inspector for the city and an incorruptible force in law enforcement, had no leads in the Ocean National Bank robbery, his instincts told him that he was dealing with a whole new breed of bank robber—someone whose intellect was far superior than the usual run-of-the-mill criminal. The only incident noted by Byrnes during his short-lived investigation was the complete withdrawal of funds from the Ocean National Bank by one George L. Leslie. Byrnes was concerned with even the tiniest detail. Through his various sources, Byrnes learned that Leslie was an architect by vocation and a well-to-do gentleman of solid upbringing and education. He wasn't, in Byrnes's estimation, the criminal type. When he learned that Leslie was a frequent guest of Marm Mandelbaum's many dinner parties, Byrnes reportedly remarked, "This can't lead to anything good." How very right he was.

—∭—

HEAVY BANK ROBBERY

The Safes of the Ocean Bank of New York City
Opened and Robbed of Their Contents

HOW AN ENTRANCE WAS EFFECTED

The Probable Loss-Rumors, etc.

Between the hours of six o'clock Saturday evening and eight o'clock this morning, the Ocean National Bank of New York City, situated on the corner of Fulton and Greenwich streets, was robbed to a heavy amount.

The bank building is a brownstone, five stories, and belongs to the Bank. The upper stories are rented for offices, the first floor is occupied as a place of business for the bank, and the basement is rented to Mr. Wm. D. Kell, who is engaged in some business which does not require the use of the entire basement.

As remarked, the first floor of the building is occupied by the Bank, the large portion is used for the transaction of business with the public. In the rear two small rooms take off ten or fifteen feet. One is the Bank parlor, or President's room, and the other is the safe-room, the room where all the safes are kept and where the valuables are placed at such times, when the employees cannot watch them, for safekeeping. The Bank parlor has two windows looking out upon Fulton Street; the safe-room has none.

Three weeks ago there appeared in the office of Mr. Wm. D. Kell a gentleman of prepossessing exterior, intensely respectable and very business-like in appearance and address. He said his name was Cole—Lewis R. Cole—and he represented the firm of Lewis R. Cole & Co., and that the firm was just organized to enter into the insurance agency business, that the firm was already recognized as agents of the Chicago Insurance Company in New York, and he exhibited credentials from Superintendent Barnes, of the Insurance Department of this State. He was desirous of renting one of the offices in the basement, the door of which opened on Fulton Street, which he saw was for rent. He understood that Mr. Wm. D. Kell had control of it, and that he was anxious to obtain possession of it. There was some obstacle in the way, which he got over by offering one thousand dollars. So he gained possession, and the first point was gained.

In a day or two, a bureau, or closet, or cabinet, or whatever it may be called, was moved into the office. What it was we shall see presently. Then they gave out that something had occurred and that they could not open their office for business for a month yet. That was the second point gained.

This morning when the bank was opened by the porter, a hole was found in the floor in the corner of the bank parlor. It should have been stated that this office hired by the parties representing themselves to be Lewis R. Cole & Co. is directly under the parlor. As a matter of course, the discovery of this hole in the floor created a decided sensation in the breast of the worthy porter. What did he do? Immediately he rushed to the safe-room and his worst fears were confirmed. The bank had been robbed. By this time other employees of the Bank had made their appearance, and word was immediately sent to the Station-house in Liberty Street. Two or three officers soon made their appearance. The safe-room was inspected. The large safe which contained all of Saturday's deposits was opened. The locks were inspected. The outer door was locked with one of Yale's combination locks. This had not been pried open, or busted, or exploded. It was intact, yet open. The natural inference is that it was picked. A thing never heard of before. The owners of the lock have guaranteed time and time again that it could not be picked. At the Paris Exposition in 1867 a lock of the same pattern was submitted to the best lock workmen of France, England and America, and they worked for days, endeavoring to pick it, and finally all gave up in despair. Yet this lock was open, without the aid of bars, powder, or the knowledge of the combination, at least so it is supposed. The inner locks were pried open and exploded.

LOSSES

In the due course of time the officers came to the bank and commenced an examination of affairs. They found that the gold had not been touched, because they had undoubtedly made such a nice haul of valuables, easily carried, that they would endanger their safety endeavoring to transport a quantity of gold. The drawers were emptied, and many of the boxes which had been placed in the safekeeping of the bank by depositors were emptied of everything of value. It is impossible at this early period to obtain information of the exact loss of the depositors, but it is thought by the officers of the Bank that it reaches $30,000. The Assistant Cashier stated to our reporter that the Bank could not have lost over $25,000. This is discredited by those who were about the Bank, and the impression seems to be that the loss is over a million. However, the authorities of the Bank assert that the robbers left gold certificates to the amount of $120,000, exchanges for the clearinghouse this morning to the amount of $90,000, and a bag of gold containing $30,000, while in the innermost safe was $300,000 in legal tender and national bank notes, which they could not have seen at all.

It seems strange after making all the careful arrangements and preparations that they did, that they should have left so much behind them when they might so easily have carried it off.

So the total loss is figured at $70,000—$20,000 in bills, $20,000 in checks payable to the Bank and bills receivable, and $30,000 lost by the depositors from their boxes.

The police say that the tools discovered in the Bank were the finest that have ever been used by burglars in New York. The cabinet moved in the room was of the panel order, or the kind which Hartz used to use in his entertainments. It is entered, shut the door, and on opening it again no one is seen, yet no one has passed out. Shut it again and then open it, and the occupant is seen. This was undoubtedly intended as a place of retreat, in case the burglars were discovered at work.

The bank was in a fearful state of confusion. Notes and securities were thrown in every direction, and the floor was littered up with paper. Around the bank gathered a large and anxious crowd who were bent on discovering all they could, but a stalwart policeman stood at the door and prevented all but those having business with the bank from entering. The wildest rumors were afloat, among others that the bank had lost $27,000,000 and would have to suspend operations, but the assistant cashier positively asserted that the bank would continue to do business as it had done before.

Detectives Hay and Thompson have the matter in charge and will work it up.

—*The New York Times* (October, 1876)

Joseph Hartz was a magician who performed both in England and America under the stage name of Professor Hartz. He performed his magic act professionally at the Adelaide Gallery in London in 1859. Besides performing, he and his brother established the first magic store, called the Hartz Magic Repository on Broadway in New York City, where he sold, among other illusionist devices, his famous "Disappearing Cabinet."

—⟋⟍—

There wasn't a single clue left behind for the police to follow. The heist had been a complete success. None of the members of the gang were remotely implicated in the crime, and they were able to go about their daily routines without being questioned by the police. Leslie too went about his business, attending Marm's dinner parties and shows at the Grand Opera House, and secretly meeting with Josie Mansfield whenever Jubilee Jim was out of town.

John Roebling had invited Leslie to visit the proposed Brooklyn Bridge site along the East River ferry landing several times. And although Leslie had graciously agreed, between his visits to Josie Mansfield in Fisk's absence, his trips out to Hackensack to be with Black Lena, his devotion to Marm Mandelbaum, and the planning for the robbery, he was never able to take Roebling up on his offer. Now that the robbery was behind him, Leslie decided to visit the site; in addition, John Roebling was one of the few legitimate friends he had.

Although the news about the Ocean National Bank robbery had made headlines in all the newspapers for weeks, coverage was soon relegated to the inside pages as interest in the robbery waned and no suspects were identified. Other tragic news would soon replace the headlines about the robbery—news that would hit Leslie close to home.

—⟋⟍—

The Brooklyn Bridge was to span the East River from Park Row in Manhattan to Sands and Washington Streets in Brooklyn. The New York State Legislature had considered a bill to build a bridge over the East River in 1857. At the time, the population of Brooklyn was approximately 266,000. By the time work began on the bridge in early 1869, Brooklyn's population had grown to almost 400,000, an increase of nearly 50 percent, making it the fastest-growing city in the country. In 1866, the bill calling for the construction of the Brooklyn Bridge was approved, and Roebling was appointed chief engineer at a salary of $8,000 a year.

Roebling proposed building a 1,600-foot suspension bridge at a projected cost of $7 million. It was Roebling's dream that the Brooklyn Bridge would not only be the safest bridge in the world, but a colossal work of art as well. Once built, it would be 50 percent longer than any other suspension bridge in America; it would be the first bridge to use pneumatic caissons and it would be the first steel-cable suspension bridge. Pneumatic caissons used compressed air pumped into the caissons to keep them dry in order for laborers to complete work on the famous bridge. Roebling proposed that steel wire rather than the usual iron be used in the construction of the bridge. The proposed bridge would be anchored across the lower East River by two neo-Gothic towers supported by an intricate network of steel-wire cables.

In his report to the New York State Legislature, Roebling said,

The contemplated work, when constructed in accordance with my design, will not only be the greatest bridge in existence, but it will be the great engineering work of the Continent and of the age. Its most conspicuous feature—the great towers—will serve as landmarks to the adjoining cities, and they will be entitled to be ranked as national monuments. As a great work of art, and a successful specimen of advanced bridge engineering, the structure will forever testify to the energy, enterprise, and wealth of that community which shall secure its erection.

The Fulton Ferry landing in Brooklyn was buzzing with activity, but not the kind anyone ever expected. On June 28, 1869, while surveying the landing, trying to determine exactly where the Brooklyn tower for the bridge would be erected, John Roebling caught his foot between a piling and the rack of an incoming ferry. Absorbed in his calculations, Roebling completely forgot about the incoming boat. He was standing on a cluster of piles at the end of the Fulton Street ferry slip when the boat slid into the dock. The force of the ferry's fender rack hitting the pilings caused Roebling to lose his footing and slip. His foot was caught against the piling and crushed by the force of the incoming vessel. Workers at the site freed Roebling and tried to attend to him while someone rode off to get an ambulance.

Roebling would have none of it, and instead had the men help him to his own carriage, asking that they drive him to his son's house, not far away. Several carriages, wagons, and a police ambulance arrived at the scene, but despite being in excruciating pain, Roebling was helped to his own carriage and driven to his son's house on Hicks Street in Brooklyn. Once he'd arrived there, a physician was called. Following an examination of the injury, it was recommended that the toes on the crushed foot be amputated.

Roebling was an uncooperative patient following the operation. He all but dismissed the physician his son had called to care for him and assumed the treatment of the injury himself. He was determined to manage his own recovery without relying on a doctor, even after an infection developed. Roebling continued to refuse a doctor's care and directed care by his family and attendants himself. Lockjaw set in. Within a week of his injury, Roebling began to lose his mental faculties, and shortly thereafter, his ability to speak. Still, he continued to direct those caring for him by writing notes to them. A strong-willed man, no one, not even his own son, could convince him to give up the folly of treating himself.

Two weeks after the accident, on July 22, 1869, John Roebling died from tetanus, never living to see the completion of his beloved Brooklyn Bridge. He was sixty-three years old.

OBITUARY

John A. Roebling, the Engineer

MR. JOHN A. ROEBLING died, at the residence of his son in Hicks Street, Brooklyn, yesterday morning at 6 o'clock. While MR. ROEBLING was engaged in making some measurements connected with the East River Bridge, on the 28th of June, a boat at Fulton Ferry caught and severely bruised one of his feet. The immediate result of this accident was the amputation of his toes. A serious illness followed, which led finally to his death. It is also said that MR. ROEBLING's determination to conduct his own case, instead of wholly and unreservedly relying upon the advice of his physicians, had much to do with the result which so many of his friends now mourn. Up to 3 o'clock yesterday morning he continued to direct his attendants in writing, but soon after that time he showed signs of mental weakness, and he was observed to sink rapidly. In these last wandering moments his mind dwelt upon the East River Bridge plans. His last days were very much embittered to him by the loss of his power of speech, lockjaw having silenced him about four days ago. About an hour previous to his death he failed to recognize his friends, and was soon attacked by three spasms which operated upon his heart and lungs. The remains of the much lamented engineer will be removed to Trenton, N.J, and the funeral will take place on Sunday . . .

The last and crowning triumph of engineering anticipated by MR. ROEBLING was the projected bridge over the East River, an enterprise of the most gigantic proportions, and which, if finished, will be an enduring monument to his name and fame.

—*The New York Times* obituary (July 23, 1869)

Roebling last words were "It will be a beautiful bridge." His son and partner, Washington A. Roebling, took over as the chief engineer for the construction of the Brooklyn Bridge, which was begun in January 1870. The Brooklyn Bridge was completed in 1883.

—₥—

George Leslie was able to get off scot-free from his first bank job, due in no small part to his meticulous planning—what would become his trademark throughout his nine-year criminal career.

Nearly all of the $800,000 taken in the Ocean National Bank robbery was turned over to Marm Mandelbaum to launder through her various and sundry channels. Not a penny of it was spent by any of the gang. Mandelbaum gave Leslie and his gang the usual 10 percent cut of which Leslie took 50 percent with the remainder divided up among the rest of the gang. They all received their cuts from the robbery only after Mandelbaum had successfully laundered the stolen cash and securities and the robbery had drifted out of the newspaper headlines.

7

Black Friday

I was born to be bad.

—JUBILEE JIM FISK (1869)

There were more ways to steal a man's money than just by robbing a bank, and the citizens of New York City (and the rest of the country, for that matter) discovered that fact soon enough. Newspaper headlines quickly turned from stories about the extraordinary and masterful robbery of the Ocean National Bank to the national economic frenzy surrounding Black Friday, September 24, 1869.

For months, Jubilee Jim Fisk and his partner, Jay Gould, had been secretly trying to corner the market on gold. Their elaborate scheme included the brother-in-law of President Grant, Abel Rathbone Corbin, as well as a highly decorated war hero, General Daniel Butterfield, who was appointed as assistant treasurer of the United States at Corbin's urging. Since his election in 1868, Grant had committed his administration to a gold-backed currency, and he was adamant that the Civil War bond debt would be repaid with gold.

During the war, the government had issued an enormous amount of money that was only backed by credit. When the war ended and Grant was elected, most American citizens were led to believe that the government would buy back the "greenbacks" using gold. Grant endorsed a plan to use gold to buy back dollars from Americans at a discount rate and replace them with a gold-backed currency.

Grant's Treasury secretary, George Boutwell, began selling the Treasury's gold for "greenbacks." His financial policy kept the the price of gold low and the national money supply at a balanced level; in addition, it enabled Grant's administration to reduce the national debt by $50 million. Fisk and Gould quickly realized that by getting insider information from corrupt administration officials, they could buy massive amounts of gold at a low price and then, when gold was withheld from the market, sell it at an incredibly high price.

Using the president's brother-in-law as a go-between, Fisk and Gould arranged to meet Grant at several social gatherings in Washington, as well as New York City. At their meetings, Fisk, Gould, and Corbin tried to persuade Grant that Boutwell's financial policy was lowering the price of gold and hurting Wall Street investors. Grant neither agreed nor disagreed with their arguments but did listen to the three men.

Next, they were able to get advance notice from General Daniel Butterfield, their well-placed inside man, regarding if and when the government was going to sell more gold. As assistant secretary of the Treasury, Butterfield was responsible for handling the government's gold sales. Butterfield was paid $10,000 for his troubles, an amount he later claimed was a loan when appearing before a congressional committee investigating the gold scheme. At the time, Butterfield's annual salary was a mere $8,000.

Fisk and Gould's bribery didn't stop with Corbin or Butterfield. They twice offered to invest $500,000 in gold for Grant's personal secretary, Horace Porter. Porter refused their entreaties. Gould also brazenly offered Grant's wife, Julia, half interest in a quarter-of-a-million dollars' worth of securities. She too declined.

Boutwell was onto the scheme. After discussions with some of New York City's leading banking and financial concerns, Boutwell alerted Grant to what was going on. Grant ordered his brother-in-law Corbin to put an end to the gold scheme. He then ordered Boutwell to issue a government sale of $4 million of gold. When the government gold hit the marketplace on September 24, 1869, the price of gold plummeted and widespread panic erupted. By September 24, the price of gold had reached nearly $162 an ounce. When the government sale of gold was issued, the price fell to $133 within a matter of minutes. Financial speculators scrambled to sell off their holdings in gold, but it was too late; many of them, including Abel Corbin, were financially ruined. Fisk and Gould escaped any significant financial harm by selling off their holdings early, thanks to the insider information provided to them by Butterfield.

Fisk and Gould had bought all of the available gold on the market during the month of September, with the hope of driving up the price of gold and then selling it all for huge profits. In order for their plan to succeed, Fisk and Gould needed the cooperation of the high-level people in Grant's administration. They had to halt the sale of government gold. They also had to convince investors that Grant himself agreed with the idea. They were able to accomplish that, and then some, making themselves a tidy profit estimated at nearly $11 million. Many other investors went bankrupt and were ruined by the financial panic.

Black Friday shook President Grant's presidency to the core and caused a near collapse of the country's economy. The near two-week buying frenzy on the gold market all but halted the nation's foreign trade, since it relied solely on gold as the exchange medium. Stock prices fell approximately 25 percent, while the country's agricultural export business, which also relied heavily on the gold standard, fell nearly 50 percent. Several brokerage firms went bankrupt, leading to the ruin of many investors, some of whom committed suicide. The economic health of the country was destabilized for months afterward.

Ironically, Corbin's financial shenanigans and ultimate ruin came about because of an incident of bad punctuation on behalf of a Western Union telegraph operator. Confronted by Grant about the scheme, Corbin sent the president a lengthy letter explaining his association to Fisk and Gould, as well as another plea to Grant to hold off on the sale of government gold. Corbin then alerted Gould about Grant's intent to sell government gold back into the market, and he too sent Grant a letter. He followed up the letter by telegraphing Grant, asking if he had received his letter. Grant responded to Gould by telegraph, "Letter delivered all right." The message was mistranslated by the telegraph operator to read: "Letter received. All right." Gould misconstrued Grant's mistranslated message as meaning he was *not* going to sell government gold. Gould relayed the information to Corbin, who thought the matter was dead and continued to buy up gold at an amazing rate. When Grant did introduce the government gold into the market, it was too late for Corbin. He was financially ruined.

Despite the near financial collapse that Fisk and Gould had caused the country, not to mention the bribery and influence-peddling charges against them, they were once again able to escape prosecution, thanks to the legal maneuverings of their high-priced legal counsel and the corrupt Tammany Hall judges. There was a subsequent congressional investigation, but two star witnesses were not permitted to testify: Virginia Corbin, the wife of Abel Corbin (who was also President Grant's sister), and the president's wife, First Lady Julia Grant. Daniel Butterfield was forced to resign his position from the Treasury.

Following the debacle, Fisk was forced into hiding to escape a mob of angry and ruined investors. He hid out at his luxurious offices at the Grand Opera House on Twenty-third Street. From there he resumed his dalliance with his mistress, Josie Mansfield.

—⚖—

General Daniel Butterfield's name might have gone down in infamy for the role he'd played as a corrupt government official were it not for his illustrious military career during the Civil War. More to the point, it was not for his role in the infamous Black Friday scandal that Butterfield is most remembered, but rather, for his contribution to the musical repertoire of the military. Butterfield was a New York businessman, employed at times by the American Express Company, established by his father. During the war he was wounded twice and became a recipient of a Medal of Honor. In July 1862, while encamped with the Army of the Potomac, Butterfield summoned Private Oliver Wilcox Norton, his bugler, to his tent. He whistled to Norton a new tune that he wanted substituted in his brigade for the regulation "Taps" (extinguish lights). Later that evening Norton played Butterfield's new version of "Taps" for the first time. The tune was soon adopted as the new regulation "Taps" and used by armies in both the North and South. It is the melody used by the military to this day.

—⚖—

THE BLACK FRIDAY GOLD OPERATIONS—

The Suit against Gould and Fisk for About $2,500,000

A motion was made at the United States Circuit Court before Judge WOODRIFF, yesterday, for an adjournment of the suit of JAMES BROWNE and HERMAN A. KONGER against JAY GOULD, FISK, Jr., and others until the April term, for the purpose of giving the defense an opportunity to send commission to Berlin, Prussia, in order to obtain the testimony of EUGENE ZOUDY, formerly of the firm of ZOUDY & SPRUNGER, of this City. The suit arises out of the celebrated "Black Friday" gold transaction, and is brought to recover from FISK, GOULD, et al., the amounts lost on account of the non-fulfillment by the latter of the contracts which they alleged to have made. The amount involved is said to be about $2,500,000. ZOUDY'S evidence is represented to be important to the defense. The case was adjourned until today, in order to allow the counsel for the defense time to prepare an argument in support of the motion for an order to show cause why an order for the commission should not be granted. D. D. Field appeared as counsel for the defendants.

—*The New York Times* (December, 1870)

After masterminding the Ocean National Bank robbery, George Leslie became Marm Mandelbaum's closest confidant. He was dubbed by Mandelbaum and others within the underworld as "the King of Bank Robbers," an unsavory title that he would rightly earn over the next nine years. The title was later picked up by New York City newspaper reporters as well as city police. From 1869 until 1878 Leslie was credited by the New York City police department as having had a hand in over one hundred robberies throughout the city. This did not include bank heists he was involved with all across the country, including a bungled bank robbery in San Francisco in 1874.

Following Leslie's death, when his role as a criminal mastermind was finally revealed, New York City police chief George Walling called

Leslie's gang "one of the strongest bands of burglars and thieves that ever existed." According to Walling, "[T]he operations of the Leslie gang . . . in nine years, in this city alone, amounted to around half a million dollars. Throughout the United States, plundering could not have been less than seven million dollars, comprising 80 percent of all the bank robberies perpetrated from the late 1860s to the date of Leslie's death."

Leslie and his handpicked gang pulled off a succession of lucrative bank heists, including the robbery of the South Kensington National Bank in Pennsylvania, the Third National Bank of Baltimore, the Wellsboro Bank in Chicago, and the Saratoga County Bank in New York, all of them financed by Mandelbaum. His reported take from his entire string of capers amounted to approximately $10 million, proving without question that he was the best in his field. Not only did Leslie rob banks with his own gang, but he also established himself as a senior advisor to other bank robbers, often collecting $20,000 in advance for each heist he planned. He was considered by most in the underworld as a criminal mastermind, and his unblemished record of success up and until then, served him well. Leslie continued his symbiotic relationship with Mandelbaum, who considered him her best and most productive protégé, and his reputation spread well beyond the boundaries of New York City. From the East Coast to the West, his talents were always in demand.

Despite the long string of successful bank heists, Leslie adroitly managed to avoid detection, even though his name did surface occasionally among both police officers and Pinkerton detectives. Still, no one was ever able to directly link Leslie to any of the bank robberies. Some of Leslie's unsavory cohorts would boast of Leslie's uncanny criminal mind and word of this slowly filtered to police operatives. Outwardly Leslie maintained the appearance of a respectable society gentleman. He became a patron of the arts and a lover of good literature. His enormous collection of books filled room after room of his apartment. His clothing was made by the most fashionable tailors in New York City. By all accounts he was a handsome, sociable, intelligent man of means, slipping seamlessly through the many layers of New York City high society. No one would have suspected that this was the same man responsible for 80 percent of the great bank robberies in the country during the early part of America's Gilded Age, unprecedented in the annals of American crime.

—m—

ROBBERS AT WORK

The Boylston National Bank, Boston, Robbed of about $500,000—How the Robbers Entered —Two Foot Thick Wall Pierced

BOSTON, Nov. 22—The Boylston National Bank, corner of Washington and Boylston streets, was entered between Saturday and this morning and a clean sweep made of all the valuables on deposit in the outer vault, mostly belonging to private individuals. These valuables were largely in United States bonds, and were contained in twenty-five or thirty tin boxes belonging to as many different individuals . . . it is believed by the cashier that from $400,000 to $500,000 have been stolen . . .

—The New York Times (November, 1869)

ANOTHER BANK ROBBERY

The Auburn City Bank Robbed of $31,000

AUBURN, N.Y., April 26—The Auburn City National Bank was robbed today, between the hours of 12 and 1 o'clock, of $31,000 in greenbacks . . .

—The New York Times (April, 1870)

BOLD BANK ROBBERY AT SCRANTON, PENN.

$30,000 in Currency Stolen

SCRANTON, Penn., Aug. 1—The banking house of JOHN HANDLEY & CO. was robbed of $30,000 in currency at 10 o'clock this morning by parties entering the vault from the rear of the bank . . . The plan was boldly and adroitly accomplished. There is no clue to the robbers . . .

—The New York Times (August, 1870)

NEW JERSEY

The Bank Robbery at Trenton—A Daring Operation
TRENTON, Sunday, Jan. 21—The robbery of the old Trenton Bank on Sunday evening has occasioned great excitement here. The affair was well planned, but miscarried owing to the merest chance. Seven persons in all appear to have been concerned in the burglary. Some days ago they rented a building two doors from the banking house under the pretense that they intended setting up a millinery establishment . . . So far as is known up to this time, the bonds carried off amount to about $25,000 . . . As yet no trace of the robbers has been found . . .

—The New York Times (January, 1872)

HEAVY BANK ROBBERY

**The Third National Bank of Baltimore Robbed of More Than
$234,000—List of the Stocks, Bonds and Other Valuables**
BALTIMORE, Aug. 19—The provincial City of Baltimore has had an unusual sensation today in the shape of a wholesale bank robbery, the amount being stolen being variously estimated at from $200,000 to $250,000 in money, stocks and securities. The bank victimized is the Third National, situated on South Street, No. 32. . . . These scamps proved to be experienced bank robbers . . . [I]t was discovered that the vault had been entered from the next house, occupied by Stabler & Co., and three out of the four safes within the vault were found broken open and the contents abstracted. Upon examining the house adjoining, a large hole was found through a four foot wall . . .

—The New York Times (August, 1872)

GIGANTIC BANK ROBBERY

**Over Half a Million in Bonds and Money Stolen
—The Cashier and His Family Gagged**

WATERFORD, N.Y., Oct. 14—The Saratoga County National Bank of this village was robbed of $500,000 in stocks and bonds, and $9,500 in money, between the hours of 1 and 4 o'clock this morning. The robbers were nine in number. It is not known how they secured entrance . . .

—The New York Times (October, 1872)

Editorial

RECENT BANK ROBBERIES

Where, then, is safety to be found, and what is the price of security? Well might some of the luckless sufferers in recent bank robberies, parodying the poor man whose hard fate they are in some degree experiencing, ask this question. When a bank is robbed people are, of course, interested in hearing all about the burglary, but are not ordinarily, unless personally concerned, racked with any distressing sympathy for the sufferers. A bank is, in this country at least, generally a corporation . . .

A great authority, a long time since, laid it down that bowels of compassion were not a part of a corporation's constitution, and that being so, people naturally do not think it necessary to display for it feelings for which the entity itself has no credit . . . because in this nineteenth century, with abundance of wealth and mechanical resources, we cannot for the life of us contrive a perfectly secure receptacle for the object upon which we are credited abroad with bestowing a love more intense and absorbing than that which we have aught beside—the almighty dollar? . . .

. . . We can't keep it; there is no perfectly safe place to put it.

. . . Not a single building for money or security exists in this country in which the public has that sort of confidence which our kinsmen across the sea have . . . if we had in New York a perfectly-isolated building, guarded each night by a different detachment . . . we are disposed to believe that it would be a receptacle which would, under right surveillance, prove absolutely secure.

—*The New York Times* (October, 1872)

—ᴍ—

Leslie made it a point to continue his relationships with New York's "fashionable four hundred," ingratiating himself with many of the finest of New York City's social set. In 1872, Ward McAllister, the self-appointed leader of New York City's glittering high society, chose a group of men from prominent New York families who were intended to lead society as its patriarchs. Dubbed the "Four Hundred Club" by McAllister, this organization was made up of businessmen such as Alexander Turney Stewart, known as the "Merchant Prince," a pioneer in retail and wholesale business and manufacturing; railroad magnate Cornelius Vanderbilt; John D. Rockefeller, who formed the Standard Oil Company in 1870, the first industrial enterprise to exercise a virtual monopoly on the growing oil industry; financier and banker John Pierpont Morgan; self-made multimillionaire miner and rancher, William Randolph Hearst; newspaper magnate Joseph Pulitzer; and Caroline Webster Schermerhorn Astor, the prominent American socialite and wife of real estate heir, William Backhouse Astor Jr., among others. They had all made their fortunes from honest (and sometimes dishonest) enterprises, and were all eager to display their vast wealth. Although not listed among them, George Leslie made sure to curry favor with this elite group.

If he was adamant about maintaining his presence among New York City's high society, he was equally unyielding when it came to refusing to openly associate with any of the criminal class—except for Marm Mandelbaum, who remained his chief benefactor. Leslie grew contemptuous of most criminals, even members of his own specially selected gang. He regarded most of them as too stupid to make crime pay, and pay well. Because of his incredible success rate, Leslie was able to have the pick of the cleverest criminals in New York City's underworld, and he soon settled on a gang that he felt comfortable with, including Red Leary, Gilbert Yost, Shang Draper, Billy Porter, and Johnny Irving. Leslie was not particularly enamored of Draper, but in order to preserve the peace at Mandelbaum's request, Leslie kept him as part of his outfit.

Not many bank robbers had the patience, intelligence, or aptitude to rob a bank the way Leslie did. Using his little joker, he was able to pull off bank heists without leaving a clue, and without all of the previously necessary paraphernalia of drills and dynamite. Other members of the criminal underworld were in awe of his cool demeanor and self-assured poise. Even Shang Draper, who was disdainful of Leslie because of his notoriety, and more so, because of his reputation as a ladies' man, gave the devil his due. When it came to robbing banks, George Leslie was indeed the king.

What started to concern Draper the most was not so much Leslie's standing in the criminal community, but his apparent attraction to "Babe" Irving. Draper himself had already become infatuated with the young sister of Johnny Irving, who was, at just fourteen, already a beautiful young woman.

Leslie's liaisons with Josie Mansfield had been thwarted because of Jim Fisk's return to New York City. In order to hide from angry crowds pursuing him over the Black Friday debacle, Fisk was in self-imposed exile at the Opera House, sneaking out only to visit Mansfield at her brownstone on Twenty-third Street. With Mansfield and Fisk back together, at least for the time being, and Black Lena in jail, Leslie had turned his amorous attentions toward Babe Irving. As was his custom with all the women he romanced, Leslie showered Babe with expensive gifts—diamond rings, pearls, gold bracelets—all of which Draper forced her to return, or simply sold. Draper had developed deep feelings for the innocent-looking blue-eyed blonde, and perhaps out of spite toward Leslie, Draper intended to marry her.

Leslie's roving eye was not limited to Babe Irving. He was also captivated by another young woman, Kate Leary, the fiery red-headed wife of another of his partners in crime, Red Leary. It was a dangerous liaison. Red Leary had a short fuse and a mean temper. He reportedly had killed at least sixteen men in his years as a New York City criminal, and he posed an immediate and dangerous threat to Leslie if he ever found out about the affair with his wife, Kate.

The rumors and innuendo surrounding Leslie's reported womanizing was a cause of concern for Marm Mandelbaum. Mandelbaum saw trouble brewing on the horizon—not only for her protégé, Leslie, but also for her entire criminal operation. If Leslie continued his clandestine relationships with Babe Irving and Kate Leary, or, for that matter, with Josie Mansfield, it would be bad for business. Mandelbaum took a cut from every bank job Leslie was involved with, and was, at least for the time being, the sole fence for stolen goods, securities, and cash for much of New York City's underworld. But she was facing competition—much like competition was invading the legitimate business world.

John D. "Traveling Mike" Grady had organized the new Grady Gang, which was in direct competition with Mandelbaum for control of New York City's fencing operations. Operating out of a Broadway saloon, Grady began regularly fencing $10,000 a week in stolen goods. Although this was a mere pittance compared to the quantity of stolen goods and money laundered by Mandelbaum, Grady was aggressive, employing the likes of Johnny "The Mick" Walsh, leader of the Bowery's Walsh Gang, as an enforcer and for protection against any moves that Mandelbaum might contemplate making against his growing organization. Walsh already had it in for Mandelbaum and her crowd because of the Black Lena affair.

The one thing that Mandelbaum didn't need was to lose George Leslie—her own goose that laid the golden eggs—because of his uncontrollable libido. Although Marm had orchestrated the end of Leslie's relationship with Black Lena, there was nothing she could do about Josie Mansfield—at least, not yet.

Knowing she was skating on thin ice if she tried any of her devious maneuvers regarding either Babe Irving or Kate Leary, she decided on another tack. She needed to get Leslie out of the city, as far away as possible, in order to let his relationships with the two dangerous young women cool down. Mandelbaum arranged for Leslie to plan a robbery in San Francisco for Ace Marvin, a noted West Coast criminal. She explained that getting out of the city would be good for Leslie, since his string of successful (and as yet unsolved) bank robberies had aroused some intense scrutiny by the police and Pinkerton agents.

Leslie agreed to the plan.

—⚒—

Red Leary was the muscle in Leslie's gang, even though Leslie's robberies were cerebral affairs and fortunately hadn't yet required any of Leary's strong-arm talents. Leslie's heists were all about sophisticated planning rather than brute force. Still, having Leary on board guaranteed Leslie some modicum of backup should something go wrong with the police, or even with his own gang. Leary was a well-known Brooklyn criminal famous for his bravado and sagacity who had spent nearly half of his early life in prison. His face adorned New York City police detective Thomas Byrnes's criminal "rogues' gallery"—photos of known criminals used for identification purposes. A photo of Leary's wife, Kate, was also part of Byrnes's gallery.

For the sake of appearances, Leary ran a run-down boardinghouse in a section of Coney Island considered well beyond most civilized development, called The Red Light. The place became a harboring place for criminals and a safe deposit for stolen merchandise. Leary often buried stolen loot in the sand dunes behind his saloon, or took it out to sea concealed in a water-tight chest and anchored the items deep in the water.

Once, after police were tipped off about the whereabouts of some stolen bolts of silk, New York City police raided The Red Light but found nothing inside the place. Later, after digging in the surrounding sand dunes, they unearthed more than $30,000 worth of silk wrapped in oilcloths and buried in the sand. Both Kate and Red were arrested, but thanks to various political connections and the expertise of Mandelbaum's legal counsel, Howe and Hummel, they were not prosecuted. Both Kate and Red always managed to have a few friends at court and usually managed to escape punishment.

The barroom at Leary's Coney Island fleabag hangout was often visited by Brooklyn politicians and sporting men. Leary himself was a renowned sportsman and gambler, and took pride in the fact that men of wealth and reputation were his patrons. Known bank robbers, many with national reputations, bank sneaks, and other "first-class" criminals invariably dropped in at Red's place, as well. However, petty thieves were not welcomed at the place and faced a hard clubbing by Red if they dared to show up.

Leary was over six feet tall with bright red hair and mustache, broad shoulders, and the powerful frame and the muscles of an athlete. He was afflicted with ingrown eyelashes that often made him half blind, and his large red eyebrows gave Leary a foreboding presence. Although he was reticent and circumspect among those he didn't know, his friends found him to be easygoing, a joker, generous to a fault, and an absolutely loyal and fearless companion. It was these qualities that Leslie admired about Leary. He knew that no matter what, Red Leary wouldn't crack under any circumstances; Leslie was sure that neither the police nor the Pinkertons would ever get anything out of him if he were ever apprehended in a bank heist.

Leary lived with his wife, Kate, a woman whose hair was as red as his. She was youthful and pretty and had a winning smile. Men found her fascinating, and George Leslie was among her many admirers. Although she professed her undying love and fidelity to Red, she was always found in the company of various men when her husband wasn't around. The police knew Kate as one of the cleverest shoplifters in the city, even at her tender age of seventeen. Kate was so clever that although the police were constantly tailing her, recording her activities, they were never able to catch her in the act. She reportedly was the instigator for many of Red's daring burglaries.

When her husband was arrested for his involvement in a Northampton, Massachusetts, bank robbery, she located his jail cell, rented an apartment next door to the jail, and, with the help of accomplices, dug a tunnel through the walls into the jail and rescued Red. She was someone to be reckoned with, both as a criminal and as a woman of seductive powers.

—⚹—

Billy Porter and Johnny Irving, two other trusted members of Leslie's gang, lived together in a handsome Gothic-style house on Patchen Avenue in Brooklyn. The house was some distance from the road and surrounded by a large shaded yard. Opposite the house was the little Church of St. Stephens. Billy Porter, like Leslie, disliked any form of violence. He never harmed or threatened anyone with any weapon, knife or gun. A gentleman through and through, Porter had dark features, a thick mustache, and heavy eyelids. Like Leslie, he was a man of brains, not brawn. Porter steered clear of the limelight and kept a low profile at his Patchen Avenue home. He wore expensive derbies and silk bowties, and his one addiction was expensive cigars. He was seldom seen without one jutting from his mouth.

Porter may have looked like a well-to-do gentleman, but he had carried out every form of criminal pursuit, including check forging, swindling, larceny, safecracking, and bank robbery. His real forte was forgery. It was Porter who had forged the insurance documents that were used to rent the office space in the basement of the Ocean National Bank. Also very much like Leslie, Porter had a taste for the finer things in life, and filled his Patchen Avenue home with expensive furniture, oil paintings, bric-a-brac, antiques, and rare books. He even had a tennis court built in back.

Johnny Irving had graduated from being a pickpocket to becoming a full-fledged—and the most trusted—member of Leslie's gang. He lived at Billy Porter's Patchen Avenue address with his sister, Babe. With her blond curly hair, red valentine lips, and porcelain skin, she was quickly becoming one of the most desirable young women in the underworld, yet remained very modest and genteel. Babe dressed inauspiciously but always with great elegance, and wore only the finest jewelry—stolen, of course— that criminals like George Leslie and Shang Draper lavished upon her.

Draper did what he had promised and married Babe. The two moved into a house a few blocks away from the Patchen Avenue home of Porter and Irving. Along with money, jewelry, and expensive clothes, Draper also provided his young bride with her preferred drug of choice, laudanum, which often left her grasping at sanity, incapable of free will. She was soon addicted not only to the drug but to her sole supplier, her husband.

Shortly after Babe married Shang Draper, Johnny Irving took a wife of his own. Jane Cookson was a small, frail woman who had no idea what her husband's occupation was and didn't care, as long as he continued to bestow clothes, money, and jewelry upon her, which he did. But Irving also became addicted to both drugs and alcohol, and soon his inebriation became chronic. He and his new wife drifted apart. Irving would disappear into a fog of alcohol and drugs for days on end, spending his time and money in cheap brothels.

Discovering she was pregnant and hoping that a family might straighten him out, Jane made vain attempts to keep Johnny sober, but nothing helped. Finally, after much soul-searching, she left him. Irving spent his time at the Patchen Avenue address with a series of prostitutes. Although his behavior was a worry to Leslie, Irving still managed to sober up long enough to take part in any of Leslie's bank heists whenever he was called on.

The last member of Leslie's gang, Gilbert Yost, had worked his way up the criminal ranks, beginning by forming his own gang of pickpockets and later organizing jewel robberies and heists. Early in his criminal career, Yost was caught stealing a cash box from a mail wagon and was sentenced to six years' imprisonment at Sing Sing, the 800-cell prison originally built in 1825. It was erected by a quarry on Mount Pleasant, near the Hudson River town of Sing Sing. Sing Sing's name comes from the Indian phrase, *sin sinck,* meaning "stone on stone." Yost managed to escape the prison within a year and returned to the streets of New York to resume his criminal career. To conceal his face from police officers, Yost grew a mustache and a set of artful muttonchop whiskers, making him look more debonair and affluent.

Yost was the best safecracker in the business, and he focused all of his attention on this art. He didn't squander his money on drinks or food or women. Yost saved most of his money, kept a low profile, and avoided violent confrontation. He was a perfect fit for Leslie's gang.

—⟋⟍—

If George Leslie looked for gang members who were like him in certain ways, the notorious duo of financial buccaneers, Jubilee Jim Fisk and Jay Gould, couldn't have been more different. Fisk, flamboyant, jovial, and charming, was offset by the dour, shy Gould. What they had in common was their ruthless, dogged pursuit of wealth, at any price, as evidenced by their manipulation of gold during the Black Friday fiasco.

Unlike the rotund Fisk, Gould was slim and slight. Fisk's fiery red-blond hair was counterbalanced by Gould's jet-black hair and full beard. Fisk's merry, watery blue eyes were the exact opposite of Gould's deep-set and darkly intense ones. And Fisk's penchant for showy diamond jewelry and flashy clothes was again equalized by Gould's drab, dark-gray banker's suits. Despite their being opposite in both appearance and demeanor, together they constituted the two most cold-blooded financial minds on Wall Street.

Gould's childhood, to a certain extent like Fisk's, was one of seemingly endless poverty and deprivation, something he never forgot and the engine that drove his undying quest for great wealth. He made his first real money as the inventor of a mousetrap. His next foray into business ended in disaster, however, when he joined a wealthy Pennsylvania merchant named Charles Leupp in the tannery business. Gould used much of the profits from their joint venture in speculation, and suffered some severe losses. When his partner discovered the losses, he became so despondent over the possibility of being ruined that he shot and killed himself.

Soon afterward Gould married Helen Day Miller, the daughter of a wealthy grocer, and with his father-in-law's financial backing began investing in an assortment of poorly managed railroads. Buying the railroads cheaply, he worked tirelessly at giving the trains the appearance of profitability and then sold them off to the highest bidder at a huge profit. He, like Fisk, stayed out of the Civil War and instead spent the war years working as a speculator and amassing a small fortune.

At thirty-three years old, Gould was one year younger than Jim Fisk when they caused Black Friday. In 1868, he was elected president of the Erie Railroad Company, and with Jim Fisk and Daniel Drew wrestled control from Cornelius Vanderbilt. A shrewd and ruthless steamship and railroad tycoon, Vanderbilt's total wealth is estimated at $143 billion at today's value, qualifying him as the second-richest man in American history behind Standard Oil Company founder, and the country's first billionaire, John D. Rockefeller. Vanderbilt was the owner of the New York Central Railroad and was attempting a hostile takeover at the time. Gould, Fisk, and Drew outmaneuvered Vanderbilt and became controlling shareholders in the Erie Railroad Company, causing Vanderbilt to suffer heavy financial losses.

In 1870, Gould and Fisk betrayed Drew by manipulating the stock price of the Erie Railroad Company. Drew sustained a loss of some $1.5 million and Fisk and Gould assumed control of the railroad. One of the first orders of business conducted by the two was to name William "Boss" Tweed to the Erie board of directors. In turn, Tweed arranged favorable legislation for them at the state level. It was, therefore, not unusual for Gould to put up $1 million in bail for Tweed in 1871 when the Boss was arrested on charges of corruption. Another small irony was that Gould ultimately gained control over the Western Union Telegraph Company, the company that nearly brought him to ruin during the Black Friday debacle when one of its employees wrongly transcribed a telegraph message from President Grant.

—ɯ—

Daniel Drew was a fierce Wall Street speculator with a multitude of nick-names, including "The Deacon," because of his deep association with the Methodist Church where he sang psalms every Sunday, and "The Great Bear," because of his operating techniques. It was a risky proposition to go up against him in any business dealing, as Vanderbilt and others discovered. However, Gould and Fisk did get the best of him in the Erie Railroad Company transaction. Drew founded the brokerage firm of Drew, Robinson & Company in 1844 and is credited with championing "watered stock," a Wall Street term used for shares whose price has been manipulated upward. Supposedly the phrase came from Drew's longtime association with the cattle business, where he reportedly increased the weight of his cattle by having them drink a lot of water before he sold them at market.

Shifty and cunning, Drew lost most of his money in the country's financial Panic of 1873 and filed for bankruptcy in 1876. He died virtually penniless in 1879, after living off the kindness of his son.

—ɯ—

The San Francisco bank robbery that Leslie had agreed to help plan for West Coast criminal Ace Marvin did not turn out as well as planned. Leslie's plan called for Marvin and his gang to rob the bank over the weekend, much like the Ocean National Bank had been robbed, so that the theft would not be discovered until the following Monday. He also thought that there would be more money being held in the vault over the weekend than during the week.

Ace Marvin was not a bank robber by trade, but instead was a jack-of-all-trades criminal. Marvin hoped that the bank heist would set him up nicely for a time. Marvin had recruited a "pete" man—a dynamite expert—who, encouraged by Marvin, had brought along enough explosives to blow up half of San Francisco. Marvin also hadn't done any of the prerequisites that Leslie had ordered him to do. He hadn't planted an inside man in the bank, and he hadn't bribed any of the local police for the purposes of looking the other way. Leslie saw these two things as essential to any bank heist. Marvin also hadn't planned out an escape route. Leslie demanded a getaway plan, so Marvin finally enlisted a carriage driver and had him hide with his carriage in the alley behind the bank, so they could escape from anyone pursuing them.

Leslie worked for weeks on his intricate plan for Ace Marvin, which, per his usual routine, included breaking into the bank twice—once to hide the little joker in the safe knob, and a second time to retrieve it and decipher the combination. Marvin didn't think it could be done—and breaking into the bank twice made no sense to him. Getting inside once would be enough . . . but twice? Marvin thought Leslie had lost his mind. But Leslie persisted.

Two days before the weekend of the heist, Leslie, Marvin, and his gang of six men—including a lookout, the carriage driver, his overzealous "pete" man, and a locksmith—forced the lock on the side door of the bank. There were no alarms, and the night watchman had left early. Leslie had the locksmith replace the broken lock on the door so that no one would suspect a forced entry. Leslie's eye for detail mesmerized Ace Marvin and the others.

Marvin's safecracker delicately pried the dial off the bank vault using a specially designed file. Leslie had him cover the area immediately surrounding the lock dial with cheesecloth so his filings wouldn't leave any scratches. When he was finally able to pry the dial off, Leslie carefully inserted his thin wire-and-steel contraption inside the dial, arranging it carefully. Leslie let the safecracker replace the dial knob so that no one would suspect a thing. Even though Leslie explained to Ace Marvin exactly how his joker would crack the combination to the safe, Marvin remained skeptical. If everything went as planned, they would break back into the bank over the weekend, open the safe, and clean the place out. No one would be the wiser—until they discovered the theft on Monday morning. It was a perfect plan.

But Marvin grew nervous waiting. He was sure someone would notice the dial being tampered with, or the lock on the side door being forced open and fixed. Leslie had all he could do to convince Marvin to leave the bank that night, to at least give his joker a chance to do its job. Marvin agreed to wait—for one day. There was no talking him out of it. Leslie sensed disaster on the horizon and he didn't want any part of it. Rather than go along with Marvin the next night, Leslie packed his bags, checked out of the San Francisco hotel he had been staying in, and boarded a train back to New York City.

The next day Leslie read in the newspaper about a $100,000 bank robbery in San Francisco. *Peanuts*, he thought. If he had been allowed to do his job properly, Leslie would have counted the money in the vault before making his haul. If he had found the pickings that slim (and by Leslie's standards, $100,000 *was* slim), he would have left the money in the vault, closed things up nice and neat, and left. He would have broken in several more times if he had to, and he would have struck only when he found the vault filled with sufficient cash and securities.

Leslie had to be content with his advance payment of $20,000 for the botched San Francisco bank job.

8

THE PATH OF THE WICKED

Let no guilty man escape if it can be avoided.

—PRESIDENT ULYSSES S. GRANT (1872)

U lysses S. Grant was reelected for a second term in 1872, despite the scandals that had plagued his presidential administration. It was also the year that saw the downfall of the infamous Boss Tweed and his corrupt Tweed Ring, and the murder of Jubilee Jim Fisk.

A year before, fire had raged through the city of Chicago, destroying the city's North Side. Thousands of wooden buildings burned to the ground and left behind a smoldering pile of rubble. Thousands were forced to flee their homes. By the time the fire was under control, an estimated three hundred people had lost their lives, 18,000 buildings had been lost, and the damage was estimated at nearly $200,000,000. Much of the stolen merchandise and belongings looted from homes and businesses during the Great Chicago Fire ended up in the hands of Marm Mandelbaum.

—⚏—

Republicans nominated Grant for a second term in June 1872, despite the scandals that had plagued his first term, including the infamous Black

Friday fiasco that nearly brought the country to a standstill. The Democrats nominated New York City publisher and outspoken antislavery advocate, Horace Greeley. During the campaign, *The Sun* (New York) broke a story on the Credit Mobilier scandal, which involved the Easton, Massachusetts, congressman and wealthy shovel manufacturer, Oakes Ames. In the scandal, the Union Pacific Railway formed the Credit Mobilier of America, a dummy construction company, which was then awarded all the construction contracts for completing the last 600 miles of the transcontinental railroad. Union Pacific stockholders and the federal government were then bilked out of approximately $20 million. When Grant called for a complete investigation, Ames was able to halt it by bribing several influential congressional officials. No individuals associated with the gigantic fraud were ever prosecuted, and despite the *Sun*'s exposé, Grant won the election in a landslide, tallying 3.5 million votes to Greeley's 2.8 million.

—ᴍ—

If the New York City newspapers were unable to bring about an end to Grant's scandalous administration, they were far more successful in bringing about the demise of William "Boss" Tweed and his infamous Tweed Ring. A government reform movement was growing in New York City, and officials were determined to expose and overthrow Boss Tweed. The effort was led by George Jones, publisher of *The New York Times*, and Samuel J. Tilden, New York City's attorney general. *Harper's Weekly* cartoonist Thomas Nast played no small part in Tweed's downfall by creating wicked caricatures of him in the magazine. The Tweed Ring was brought down in 1871, when *The New York Times* published an exposé on the graft and corruption of Tweed and his cohorts.

In July 1871, two low-level city officials with a grudge against Tweed provided *The New York Times* with reams of documentation that detailed the corruption. The newspaper's articles about Tweed, coupled with Nast's political cartoons, created a national outcry, and Tweed and many of his cronies were soon facing criminal charges and political oblivion. Questioned about the charges of corruption by a reporter, Tweed responded, "What are you going to do about it?"

Thomas Nast created scathing cartoons depicting Tweed as thief, a convict, or an enormous glutton. Tweed tried to bribe Nast, *Harper's*

Weekly, and even the publisher of *The New York Times* to leave him alone, but they rejected his advances. Tweed reportedly exclaimed, "Stop them damned pictures. I don't care so much what the papers say about me. My constituents can't read. But, damn it, they can see pictures!"

Pressure was put on Harper Brothers, the company that produced the magazine, and when they refused to fire Nast, the company lost the contract to provide New York schools with books. Nast himself was offered a $500,000 bribe to end his campaign—a hundred times more than his salary of $5,000—but Nast still refused to back down.

In July of 1871, *The New York Times* published the contents of the New York County ledger books, which revealed that the county was being charged $7,500 for thermometers and a staggering $41,190 each for brooms. Tweed's friends were commissioned to do the construction work. Carpenter George Miller was paid $360,747 for a month's labor, and James Ingersoll received $5,691,144 for furniture and carpets.

In late 1871, Samuel Tilden was named to lead a contingency of the city's most prominent businessmen, dubbed the Committee of Seventy, to prosecute Tweed and his cronies. Tilden was able to trace money directly from city contractors to Tweed's private bank account. Ultimately a grand jury handed down 120 indictments against Tweed. In December of 1871, Tweed was arrested and held on $1,000,000 bail. It was Jay Gould who rescued his longtime crony and business associate, putting up the one million dollars to bail Tweed out of jail.

A year later, the overconfident Tweed was finally brought to trial, which resulted in a hung jury. Tilden believed that Tweed had bribed the jurors, so when he retried the case in 1873, he assigned one police officer to guard each member of the jury, another police officer to watch the first one, and a private detective to watch over all three. Tweed was found guilty at the end of the second trial and given a twelve-year prison sentence, which was reduced by a higher court. He served just one year. When he was released in 1875, he was rearrested on civil charges, sued by New York State for $6,000,000, and held in debtors' prison until he could post $3,000,000 as bail. On December 4, 1875, Tweed escaped from prison and fled to Spain.

—m—

Mary Henrietta Coath was just fifteen years old when she met George Leslie. She was a beautiful girl with long black hair and huge dark eyes. Her lips were like those Leslie had seen in Renaissance paintings—small, red, and pouting. Leslie had taken up a brief residency in a Philadelphia boardinghouse owned by Molly's mother while helping to plan another one of his bank heists.

Mrs. Coath was alone; her husband, a tailor, had left her when it was rumored that Molly was not his child. At the time Leslie first laid eyes on the beautiful dark-haired girl, she was being wooed by another boarder, Thomas Parnell. "Pretty Tom" Parnell was a burglar, although not a very successful one. Molly was enamored of the dashing Tom, and equally charmed by the attention paid to her by the handsome Leslie. While at the Coath boardinghouse, Leslie masqueraded as an Internal Revenue agent, going by the name of George L. Howard. Young Molly Coath had no idea about Leslie's secret life as "the King of Bank Robbers."

Getting Pretty Tom out of the way was going to take some doing, so Leslie decided to rely on Marm to help him. Mandelbaum was more than happy to assist. Recent developments in New York had given rise to concern over Leslie's marital status and love life, especially as it related to Josie Mansfield. By the time Leslie had returned from his work with Ace Marvin in San Francisco, the whole Mansfield affair had blown wide open in the newspaper—not her relationship with Leslie, but with Mansfield's benefactor, Jubilee Jim Fisk. The last thing Mandelbaum wanted was for Leslie to be dragged into the whole sordid Mansfield-versus-Fisk affair.

Mandelbaum suggested that it might be time for Leslie to settle down, even if only for the sake of appearances. Leslie was smart enough to realize that given his relationship with Josie Mansfield, he could possibly be named in the newspaper as one of her lovers. Neither Mandelbaum nor Leslie needed publicity at this time, given that Leslie's string of successful bank heists had been unprecedented. They both realized that publicity of any kind might shine a spotlight on their whole nefarious operation. Hearing of Leslie's interest in Molly Coath—he wanted to marry her—Mandelbaum was more than happy to oblige her protégé in his endeavor to capture the young girl's heart.

Using her many contacts, Marm arranged for Pretty Tom to burgle a jewelry store in Norristown, Pennsylvania. Pretty Tom, who had been in and out of jail and was considered on the bottom rung of the criminal lowlife ladder, readily accepted the chance to work for the infamous Marm Mandelbaum. Mandelbaum gave Pretty Tom explicit instructions on how to go about the burglary. He broke into the jewelry by smashing a window in the rear of the store at night, just as Mandelbaum told him to, and slipped inside. The sound of the window breaking alerted neighbors, who summoned police. The owner of the jewelry store lived only a block away; when he was contacted by police, he raced right over to the store and opened the doors. They found Pretty Tom in the act of filling a burlap bag with jewelry and watches. He was promptly arrested and dispatched to jail.

With Pretty Tom out of the way, Leslie was able to woo young Molly Coath without competition. He stayed in Philadelphia longer than he had expected, and two months after their first meeting, Leslie married Molly Coath in a brief ceremony held at the boardinghouse and conducted by a justice of the peace. His name on the marriage certificate was listed as George Leslie Howard, the assumed name he'd chosen to conceal his identity from authorities in New York City.

At Mandelbaum's urging Leslie brought his new bride back to New York City where they settled into a luxurious third-floor apartment on Fulton Street. There Leslie maintained a triple identity. To his new wife, he was George L. Howard, an Internal Revenue agent. To most of New York society, he remained George Leslie, the gentleman from Cincinnati, book lover and patron of the arts. And to his underworld cohorts he remained the King of Bank Robbers.

—m—

Boss Tweed wasn't the only notorious New York City figure who was experiencing trouble. Fisk was slowly watching his financial empire as well as his love life unravel right before his eyes—and everyone else's, as well. Not only was Fisk being sued in court by his ex-lover, Josie Mansfield, and her new lover, Ned Stokes, but his partnership with Jay Gould was also dissolving. His legal and financial troubles became fodder for the many New York City newspapers. Fisk had always thrived on public attention, but now he was getting far more of it than he'd bargained for.

Because of all the bad publicity, Fisk's friend and business partner, Jay Gould, knew that Fisk would have to resign from the Erie Railroad board of directors. In December, a few days before the court was to begin hearing the case of *Mansfield vs. Fisk*, Gould decided it was time for Fisk to go. Too much was at stake for Gould and the financial empire he had created. Josie Mansfield was suing Fisk for $50,000, an amount she claimed had been invested on her behalf by Fisk. The sensational case had the potential to blow the lid off not only Fisk's sordid affair with his mistress, but also to expose the plethora of criminal activities perpetrated by Fisk, Gould, and Boss Tweed at the Erie Railroad. According to *The New York Times*, the case would provide a "complete and damaging exposure of the crimes of said Fisk, Jay Gould . . . and their division of the Erie Railroad spoils with the Tammany Ring."

Gould decided to get rid of Fisk and reform the Erie Railroad board of directors, under the respectable financial leadership of men such as August Belmont and John Jacob Astor. Gould's plan did not include his own personal loss of control over the railroad, but it would at least give the scandal-ridden company the appearance of respectability—something that wouldn't be possible as long as Fisk remained on the board. Gould finally confronted Fisk with his inevitable conclusion: "The time has come when we must set our house in order. [T]he only thing that can prevent utter annihilation for the whole of us is your resignation . . ."

Reluctantly, Fisk complied.

—⁂—

Not only was Fisk being sued by his former mistress Mansfield, but he was also being sued by Ned Stokes for $200,000, as a settlement in a previous case involving his business dealings with Fisk in the Brooklyn oil refinery.

At the heart of both cases were Fisk's private love letters to Mansfield, which Mansfield and Stokes had been using to blackmail Fisk. Mansfield's affair with George Leslie had cooled as Leslie began making more and more trips afield at the clever urging of Marm Mandelbaum. Mandelbaum saw Mansfield as a potential danger to the business relationship she had with Leslie, and since she was unable to get rid of Mansfield the way she had Black Lena, she did the next best thing: She sent Leslie off on bank heists all over the country, the furthest being the bank robbery in San Francisco with Ace Marvin.

With Leslie out of the picture, Mansfield had turned her attention to Ned Stokes, who had become a fixture at her Twenty-third Street brownstone, especially after she'd thrown Fisk out. Together, Mansfield and Stokes blackmailed Fisk, threatening to release the incriminating love letters to the newspapers unless Fisk paid up. Heartbroken at the betrayal by Mansfield, and fearful of the bad publicity that would ensue if the letters were published, Fisk paid them off in amounts between $5,000 and $50,000. It was not enough for either of them.

Stokes, because of his chronic gambling debts, wanted more. Armed with the compromising love letters, Stokes demanded more money, threatening to expose Fisk's underhanded dealings at Erie along with news of his scandalous affair with Mansfield (even though the latter was already common knowledge throughout New York circles). For Fisk, perhaps the most damaging information contained within the letters was the revelation that Mansfield had cheated on him with the young and handsome Stokes. Fisk would be held up to the highest of public ridicule if the letters were ever published. It was one thing to have his inner dealings within the railroad company revealed to the world—he felt that he could weather that storm. It was still another for all the world to know that he had been cuckolded.

Although Mansfield and Stokes had made copies of the love letters, the originals were being held by mutual agreement by a third party. Stokes filed suit in court to have the original letters returned. Although the newspapers were chomping at the bit to publish the letters, Fisk knew that once they were published, neither Mansfield nor Stokes would hold the upper hand. Their threat to him would be over. Bitter over the alliance his former adored mistress had made with the younger, handsome Stokes, and angered that they could never seemingly have enough, Fisk counterattacked. First he contacted his wife, Lucy, and confessed all of his many transgressions with Mansfield, asking for her forgiveness. Lucy Fisk, who had lived throughout most of their marriage in the lap of luxury in Boston, far away from her husband's many illicit relationships, was traveling in Europe at the time. She reluctantly forgave him.

Next, Fisk countersued both Mansfield and Stokes. His lawyers dug deep into Mansfield's past, turning up evidence that blackmail was and always had been part of her modus operandi, something Fisk had little knowledge of himself. News of Mansfield's tryst with D.W. Perley, a

California lawyer, was dug up. Perley had been blackmailed by Mansfield's stepfather after Perley was caught in a compromising position with the fourteen-year-old beauty. According to the story, which was verified in court by Mansfield's first husband, Frank Lawlor, a theater manager living in Albany, New York, Mansfield's mother ran a boardinghouse on Sutter Street in San Francisco where Perley had stayed. Perley had become infatuated with the young but seductive Josie. Old enough to be her grandfather, Perley had showered her with attention and expensive gifts. According to Perley, he was lured one night to Mansfield's bedroom with the promise of carnal delight. The melodramatic affair was broken up when Josie's stepfather burst into the room, finding the two in various degrees of undress. Playing the irate parent, Mansfield's stepfather demanded money in order to keep the whole affair quiet and out of the newspapers. It was the beginning of Mansfield's career of trading on her beauty and sex for money, and blackmail. The revelations in court more than satiated the curious public's prurient interests.

Despite the scandalous revelations about Mansfield's tawdry past, Fisk gained no sympathy—at least not from the journalists covering the case. Paraphrasing the noble comments made by congressman Henry Lee about President George Washington, *The New York Times* wrote of Fisk, "Perhaps of him it may one day be said that he was first in war, first in peace and first in the pockets of his countrymen."

In the course of the trial, the love letters were circulated among various trial lawyers for both sides, along with the presiding judge, Daniel Ingraham. Ned Stokes claimed that the letters contained incriminating evidence about Fisk's underhanded dealings at both the Brooklyn Refinery where he and Fisk were engaged as partners and the Erie Railroad.

Judge Ingraham read the letters and disagreed with Stokes. He denied any claim Stokes might have had, which infuriated the already-unstable Stokes. Still, the two cases dragged on. Fisk relished the fact that he had finally gained the upper hand after several years of being blackmailed by the two of them.

Unfortunately, it was not just Mansfield and Stokes who were suing Fisk. He was also being sued by more than a dozen people for his alleged swindle during the Black Friday gold fiasco. There were others who had filed suit against Fisk, including a case that involved his ownership of the Fall River steamship line. There were so many cases, in fact, that not even Fisk knew the exact number. According to Fisk, ". . . some gold suits are pending; I don't know how many suits there are against me, nor the amounts claimed against me."

Although the love letters contained no incriminating evidence against Fisk or Gould or their criminal dealings with the Erie Railroad, and even though many of his friends and associates, Gould included, pressured him to publish the love letters of his own volition in order to dispel the many rumors circulating about them, Fisk refused. His vanity and his pride had been wounded by Mansfield, and he was not about to allow publication of the love letters regardless of what they might contain because he was afraid they would contribute to his public humiliation. Furthermore, in his own curious way, Fisk loved his wife, Lucy, and did not wish to have her face the ridicule that would be brought about by his thoughtless deeds. It was too much for him to bear.

Again, instead of putting the whole matter to rest, Fisk filed off a flurry of new lawsuits against Mansfield and Stokes. An injunction against the publication of the love letters was handed down by the courts. Fisk next filed an affidavit in court signed by one of Mansfield's most trusted servants (whose salary was paid by Fisk), stating that Mansfield and Stokes had conspired to blackmail Fisk. Both Stokes and Mansfield countersued for libel. On November 25, 1871, the cases—both blackmail and libel—were heard at the Yorkville Police Court by Judge B. H. Bixby. The courthouse was packed and the newspapers had a field day. It was easy to mock Fisk, the once-invincible Wall Street buccaneer turned cuckold, but both Mansfield and Stokes faced their own share of the reporters' attention.

The *New York Herald* described Mansfield in the courtroom as ". . . the beauty and gorgeous heroine of Jersey City and the owner of the palace in Twenty-third Street . . . Mrs. Mansfield looked so lovely that she created quite a flutter . . ." *The Herald* continued, noting that she was "well known from Maine to Oregon from her connections with Marc Antony Fisk and Octavius Caesar Stokes," alluding to Mansfield's moniker as the Cleopatra of Twenty-third Street.

The Herald also described Stokes: "The exquisite Stokes was all glorious . . . An elegant diamond ring glowed on his little finger . . . and a cane was swung carelessly to and fro between his manly legs. Stokes looked so handsome that Mrs. Mansfield found it quite impossible to take her eyes off his face . . ."

The ridicule was reserved for Fisk, who arrived at the courthouse wearing his gold braided admiral's uniform, the one he'd had specially made, and an exact copy of which he'd had made for Mansfield. "His moustache bristled ferociously . . . a big diamond pin shone out of his fat chest like the danger light at the Sandy Hook bar," *The Herald* reported. Fisk took it all in stride. He had weathered worse storms, and he was confident he would weather this one as well. Besides, thing were looking up—at least legally. The case was continued. Mansfield's libel suit against Fisk had been heard, and now Fisk would have a chance for rebuttal. Stokes's countersuit for libel was going nowhere. His own attorneys had advised him to abandon the suit against Fisk. Fisk felt himself bouncing back as he always had. Even the Black Friday scandal hadn't hindered him.

On January 6, 1872, the case reconvened. While Fisk was busy in one courtroom defending himself against Mansfield's libel charge, the grand jury was meeting separately. By the time the case adjourned at one o'clock that afternoon, the grand jury had handed down an indictment against Stokes and Mansfield on Fisk's charges of blackmail. Word of the indictment spread quickly.

Following the day's adjournment, most of the lawyers and witnesses, including Ned Stokes, headed for Delmonico's for lunch. The rumor of the indictment for blackmail reached the ears of Ned Stokes, who was busy eating oysters and drinking beer. Although he had been conferring with his own legal counsel, Stokes, saying nothing to anyone, abruptly left the restaurant and took a carriage to Mansfield's house.

Fisk had returned to his offices at the Grand Opera House where he freshened up. He had made arrangements to meet with Mrs. Morse and her two daughters, who were resting after their long trip from Boston. The Morses were longtime friends of Lucy's, and Fisk always entertained them when they visited New York City, taking them to the best restaurants and serving as their host. Fisk, still wearing his ornate uniform, put on his silk cape and admiral's hat and headed by carriage to the Grand Central Hotel on Broadway where the Morses were staying.

At approximately four o'clock that afternoon, Fisk, worn out from the laborious days at court, tired and bewildered by the way things had turned out for him, lumbered slowly up the staircase at the Grand Central Hotel on Broadway and Fourth Street. There was someone standing in the shadows at the top of the landing. Fisk could barely make out who it was. Finally, he discerned that it was John Redmond, one of the hotel porters. Redmond knew Fisk and had been told to meet him and show him to the Morses' room.

Redmond informed Fisk that Mrs. Morse and one of her daughters had gone out, but the other daughter was still in her room. Fisk told Redmond to let her know he was here and that he'd be waiting for her in the second-floor sitting room. Fisk, already out of breath from climbing up the first flight of stairs, began his second climb up another set of stairs to the waiting room. Redmond followed a few steps behind him.

Again, standing at the landing at the top of the stairs, Fisk saw someone waiting. It was Ned Stokes. He was wearing a double-breasted gray coat and a silk top hat, and holding a cane in one hand. In the other hand was a small revolver and he was aiming it at Fisk.

"I've got you now," Stokes calmly proclaimed. He fired the revolver twice in rapid succession, hitting Fisk in the arm and the stomach.

"For God's sake, will anybody save me!" Fisk yelled. Blood was spurting out of his arm and the wound in his belly. Fisk staggered but clung to the handrail as Stokes ran off. He was apprehended shortly thereafter by the police.

Fisk managed to walk down the stairs. The gunshots had attracted a crowd. Several hotel employees helped Fisk back up the stairs where they took him into a vacant room.

When the hotel doctor finally reached Fisk, he discovered the wounded man standing on his feet. Blood was running down his arm and the front of his vest was soaked. The doctor managed to get Fisk to lie down on the sofa. He gave Fisk some brandy and bandaged the wound in his arm. It was the wound in his stomach that worried the doctor. He tore open Fisk's shirt and washed and then probed the wound in his belly, looking for the bullet. It had penetrated deep into Fisk's bowels.

The hotel sent messages across the city, and soon eight doctors, including Boss Tweed's personal physician, arrived. Newspaper reporters, friends, and curiosity seekers all jammed into the Grand Central Hotel, trying to get into the room to see the wounded Fisk.

Jay Gould arrived, as well as Boss Tweed, who was still out on bail. More than a dozen friends and associates were let into the room to see him. The doctors conferred. They gave Fisk chloroform to knock him out and probed his stomach wound for the lead slug. It couldn't be retrieved. Fisk lay on the bed, dying, just as he lived, the center of attention.

News of Fisk's shooting spread throughout the city like wildfire. Within hours newspapers began publishing extra editions announcing the deed. Thousands of people converged on the Grand Central Hotel. Hundreds of police were called out to keep order. Total mayhem broke out throughout the city.

JAMES FISK MURDERED

He is Deliberately Shot Down in the Grand Central Hotel.
Edward S. Stokes the Author of the Desperate Deed.
Fisk Twice Wounded and Reported as Dying.
His Ante-Mortem Statement Taken by the Coroner.
The Murderer Promptly Arrested On the Spot.
Exciting Scenes in and About the Hotel.

The startling intelligence that EDWARD S. STOKES had shot and mortally wounded JAMES FISK, Jr., flew like lightning through the City yesterday afternoon about 4 o'clock . . . For some time past the respectable dwellers in our City have been shocked and disgusted with the unavoidable publicity of their licentious amours; unavoidable, because they have been discussed in the Police and Law Courts. No sympathy with plaintiff or defendant was possible . . . The natural consequences of a vicious life has happened. A man lies dying—murdered; and his enemy—his murderer—is now discussing with himself the folly of his crime in a prison cell. And what of the wretched woman who has caused all this trouble? . . . The plaintiff and EDWARD S. STOKES were both present in the Court-room from 10 o'clock in the morning until 2 o'clock in the afternoon. Both were upon the witness stand, and subjected to examination by the opposing counsel. By a strange coincidence, it happened that STOKES was interrogated as to whether he had threatened FISK in any way. He seemed somewhat embarrassed by the question but finally said that he had never threatened him otherwise than with legal proceedings. During all the time he was in the Court-room STOKES was entirely self-possessed, with this one exception, and did not in any way betray the deadly purpose which he executed two hours after leaving the Court-room with MRS. MANSFIELD. . . .

At the Grand Central Hotel, late into the night, the halls and corridors were alive with excitement. Policemen were stationed in the hall leading to the room where the wounded man had been carried, and also on the staircases to prevent the crowd from rushing up the stairs to satisfy their curiosity. The news spread rapidly through the streets and soon became the topic of conversation in barrooms and other places of public resort. Many who heard it thought at first that it was a joke and could scarcely be made to believe it . . . MR. FISK'S friends, hearing of his shooting, hurried to the hotel on foot and in carriages, and soon a large number of Erie Railroad employees and others interested in MR. FISK'S fortunes were present. The feeling among these was of strong indignation. Said one, pouring out a volley of oaths, "Let's us go to the Station-house, and take STOKES and hang him."

—*The New York Times* (January 7, 1872)

After shooting Fisk, Ned Stokes had dashed across the second-floor lobby, stopped briefly at a nearby sofa to stash his revolver, and then headed down a staircase to the first-floor lobby of the hotel. He was followed at a safe distance by one of the hotel bellhops who had witnessed the shooting. H. L. Powers, the manager of the Grand Central Hotel, was alerted. Powers rounded up several employees and onlookers and they pursued Stokes, who ran inside the hotel barbershop. Inside the barbershop Powers and his employees and several patrons subdued Stokes, who gave up without a fight. The police were summoned and Stokes was arrested. The gun he had used to shoot Fisk wasn't in his possession. Police later found the small Colt revolver stuffed into the sofa in the second-floor lobby where he had hidden it. Stokes was taken to the room where Fisk was being treated by doctors. With Stokes in tow, surrounded by several police officers and a posse of citizens, the police asked Fisk if he recognized Stokes as the man who had shot him. "Yes, that's the man who shot me. That's Stokes," Fisk said.

Stokes was led away by police to the Tombs, the city prison, otherwise officially known as the Hall of Justice and House of Detention in Lower Manhattan. On the way Stokes nonchalantly asked the officers if he could stop off for a drink. The police officers refused his request.

Later, locked in a cell, Stokes asked the police to bring him several cigars that were in his top coat, and they complied. Stokes began smoking one cigar after another, filling the small cell with a cloud of tobacco smoke.

"What do you think—is the man seriously injured?" Stokes asked one of his jailers.

Two hundred and fifty police had to be sent to the Tombs to protect Stokes from an angry lynch mob.

—ɷ—

A newspaper reporter reached Josie Mansfield at her home within an hour after the shooting and informed her of what had happened. "Stokes must have been insane," she said, her face going pale. "I am in no way connected with this sad affair. I have only my reputation to maintain," she told the stunned reporter. A contingent of police officers was sent to Mansfield's home to protect her from an angry mob, and from a series of anonymous death threats.

—ɷ—

The room at the hotel where Fisk was being cared for was a hubbub of activity, throughout the day and into the night, filled with nearly a dozen physicians all trying to treat and comfort Fisk, as well as friends and business associates and newspaper reporters running in and out. Boss Tweed stayed by Fisk's side throughout much of the ordeal, as did his nearly lifelong business partner, Jay Gould.

Fisk asked for his wife, Lucy. She had already been sent for. By the time she arrived from Boston the next morning, her husband had slipped into a coma. Although theirs had been an unconventional marriage—her living in luxury in her familiar surroundings in Boston for most of their eighteen years of marriage, and Fisk living his flamboyant lifestyle in New York City—he had remained in his own way dutiful to her, much more like a son to a mother than a husband to a wife. But even after all she discovered about his many transgressions and the abundance of humiliation he had heaped upon their marriage, she forgave him and stayed at his bedside for hours, holding his hand and wiping his brow.

Jubilee Jim Fisk, the circus barker who became the flamboyant terror of Wall Street, died shortly before eleven o'clock on the morning of January 7, 1872, with his wife and friends at his side. When he was pronounced dead, Lucy Fisk kissed him on the forehead and whispered, "My dear boy. He was such a good boy."

Jim Fisk was only thirty-seven years old when he died. His estate at the time of his death was estimated to be a mere $3 million. Most of it, $2 million, was bequeathed to his wife. The rest of his fortune, at least by best estimates, was squandered on his mistress, Josie Mansfield, his own vast luxuries, legal fees, and charity to the poor.

—ɷ—

Jim Fisk, or He Never Went Back on the Poor
Let me speak of a man who's now dead in his grave,
A good man as ever was born.
Jim Fisk he was called and his money he gave
To the outcast, the poor and forlorn.

We all know he loved both women and wine,
But his heart it was right, I am sure.
Though he lived like a "prince" in a palace so fine,
Yet he never went back on the poor.

If a man was in trouble, Fisk helped him along
To drive the "grim wolf" from the door.
He strove to do right, though he may have done wrong,
But he never went back on the poor.

Jim Fisk was a man who wore "his heart on his sleeve,"
No matter what people would say,
And he did all his deeds (both the good and the bad)
In the broad open light of the day.

—BALLAD GENERALLY BELIEVED TO HAVE BEEN WRITTEN
BY WILLIAM J. SCANLAN (1872)

—⚓︎—

Jubilee Jim Fisk's funeral was a massive affair, featuring appearances by a 200-piece band and his own state militia unit. His body lay in state at the Opera House. More than 20,000 people filed into the Opera House to pay their respects, and more than 100,000 mourners lined the streets of New York. The Ninth Regiment gave Fisk a military funeral unequaled in its regalia. Afterward, his body was returned to his native Brattleboro, Vermont, for burial.

Thomas Nast published a cartoon in *Harper's Weekly* showing Boss Tweed, Jay Gould, and other Erie Railroad robber barons mourning over the grave of Jim Fisk. The caption under it read DEAD MEN TELL NO TALES.

George Leslie attended the funeral. Although not a personal friend of Fisk's, he felt a certain kinship with him. Leslie told Mandelbaum that Fisk's only mistake had been to trust his girlfriend too much. Mandelbaum agreed; it was a fatal mistake, and one all men should avoid at all costs. Leslie absolutely concurred.

—⚓︎—

Editorial

THE LESSON OF THE DEATH AND LIFE OF FISK

. . . The murder in itself, stripped of all its cowardly and sensational incidents, strikingly illustrates a few very homely and ancient principles. Honesty, after all, is the best policy, and it is at the lowest, the best and safest "to enter not into the path of the wicked, and go not in the way of evil men. . . ." The house of the woman "who forgeteth the covenant of her God does incline unto death"; "her house is the way to hell, going down to the chambers of death . . ." It was inexorably inevitable that his life would come to an abrupt and bloody period. His business was organized theft, robbery, and corruption. His pleasures were systematized incontinence, profligacy, and shamelessness. His tactics were principally remarkable because they discarded the obligations of all human and Divine law . . . The best service the world and nation in all his thirty-seven years, was to die at the climax of his course of violence and debauchery, in a way which rendered that course not a fascination, but a warning to his surviving fellow men . . . Thousands thought on Saturday that smartness and utter unscrupulousness were passports to fame; that to steal a railroad, maintain a dozen strumpets, buy whole Legislatures and defy justice by purchasing judges, were efforts which the position of him who made them rendered worthy of emulation . . . The murderer's motive is the measure of his claim to consideration. That motive was vulgar, deliberate malice, and revenge not for outrages inflicted on Stokes innocent, but on him as a willing, eager, and outwitted coadjutor and confederate in every interest they had . . . The influence he exerted can hardly be exaggerated. He was a standing incentive to millions of young men to copy his career—till that career so terribly terminated . . .

—*Brooklyn Daily Eagle* (January 8, 1872)

In June 1872, Ned Stokes went on trial for murder. The district attorney demanded the death sentence, and much of the public agreed. Josie Mansfield appeared as a witness for his defense. The dazzlingly stunning Cleopatra of Twenty-third Street was called a harlot by the district attorney.

Stokes claimed he had shot Fisk in self-defense. He claimed that Fisk had been brandishing a gun when they met on the staircase of the Grand Central Hotel, but that he had managed to fire first in order to save himself. Mansfield testified that Fisk owned nearly a dozen pistols and had repeatedly threatened to kill Stokes. No gun had been found on Fisk, and other witnesses testified that Fisk owned no guns at all.

Stokes also claimed that he had been driven temporarily insane by Fisk's persecution of him in the courts, and that Fisk had not died because of the bullet wound but because of the incompetence of the physicians attending to him. Stokes also claimed the doctors had killed him by giving Fisk a lethal dose of morphine.

The jury disagreed with the prosecution in the first trial and a mistrial was declared. At his second trial, Stokes was found guilty and sentenced to death. He won an appeal, and at the end of a third trial in 1873, Stokes was convicted of manslaughter and sentenced to six years in prison. He served fours years in relative comfort at Sing Sing before being released in 1877. He was shunned by New York society for the rest of his life, and was no longer welcomed at his previous favorite haunts, including Delmonico's. He became the proprietor of the Hoffman House and several other restaurants and hotels. For the rest of his life he was haunted by the specter of Fisk's ghost, along with severe paranoia, fearing that friends of Fisk's would seek revenge. According to a report in *The New York Times*, "He feared assassination . . . He always ate with his back close against the wall . . ." It was reported that he also slept with the light on for the rest of his natural life.

—ᴟᴟ—

DID STOKES PUT THE PISTOL IN THE SOFA?

The trial of Edward S. Stokes for the murder of James Fisk, Jr., is drawing very rapidly to a close. All the evidence, unless there should be something very extraordinary, has been put in. Mr. Tremaine has commended his summing up for the prisoner . . . He claimed that the crime of murder required four different elements: That the wound was premeditatedly inflicted by the prisoner; that the deceased died of it and nothing else; that the prisoner had no justification or excuse; and that he was sane. All these four elements, he claimed, had not been proved . . . Mr. Fisk's death, at the time it occurred, resulted not from the wound which was not to a certainty fatal, but from the malpractice of Drs. Tripler and Fisher . . . Henry the parlor man says he did not go near that door, and in this the prisoner agrees with them. He wished that they could see that sofa, to see how improbable it was that this pistol should have been put where it was found . . .

—*Brooklyn Daily Eagle* (July 13, 1872)

—ᴟᴟ—

Josie Mansfield sued Lucy Fisk, Jim Fisk's widow, for $25,000 she claimed Fisk owed her from previous investments. She lost the suit and shortly thereafter moved to Paris, where she was reportedly accompanied by Annie Hindle, an actress whose specialty was male impersonations. Mansfield's reputation preceded her to Paris, England, and other parts of Europe, where she was known as "The Courtesan Josie." Newspapers and magazines kept her legacy alive with sensationalist headlines, such as JOSIE MANSFIELD, THE SIREN . . . HOW A BEAUTIFUL WOMAN CAPTIVATED AND RUINED HER VICTIMS. She ultimately married a wealthy lawyer and lived in luxury for the rest of her life.

Of all the many ironies associated with the Fisk, Mansfield, and Stokes scandal, the least known centers on an engraved image of Josie Mansfield. The $1,000 Silver Certificate issued in 1891 is known as the Courtesan Note because the engraving on it is of the Gilded Age's most famous courtesan, Josie Mansfield. The image was printed on the certificate by the Bureau of Engraving and Printing for use on the currency. It depicts Mansfield leaning on a shield with sword in hand; a star-studded necklace adorns her neck and she is wearing a tiara of stars and leaves. *The New York Times* uncovered that the engraved portrait of the woman on the certificate was taken from a photograph of Mansfield. She had always been very fond of money and now she is forever bound to it by way of the $1,000 Silver Certificate.

—∭—

THE MANSFIELD-FISK SUIT

In the suit of Josephine Mansfield against Lucy D. Fisk, the Executrix of the estate of the late James Fisk, Jr. in which a verdict for $25,000 was recently rendered in favor of the plaintiff, a motion was made yesterday, before Judge Donohue, in Supreme Court, Chambers, for an order granting defendant a new trial. The motion was made on the grounds of newly discovered evidence, it being claimed on behalf of the defendant, that a Mr. Shearman and a Mr. Cole are prepared to give testimony to the effect that the proceeds for the bonds sold by

Fisk, which forms the subject of the suit, was paid by him for "Josie's" Twenty-third Street house, with her knowledge and consent . . .

—*The New York Times* (March, 1875)

—⁓—

While part owner of the Hoffman House hotel, located at Broadway and Twenty-fifth Street, Ned Stokes bought French painter William-Adolphe Bouguereau's famous painting, *Nymphs and Satyr*. The celebrated painting of the beautiful naked nymphs at play with the amused satyr hung for many years over the bar in the hotel. The painting was displayed with great splendor under a red velvet canopy and lit by a chandelier. It shocked the public but drew massive crowds to the hotel bar just to view it. Stokes sold the painting when he sold his interest in the Hoffman House. In 1930 the painting was discovered in storage at the hotel. It is now on display at the Clark Art Institute in Williamstown, Massachusetts.

—⁓—

While the turmoil of the times swirled around him in 1872, Leslie and his young, beautiful wife, Molly, gained the goodwill and esteem of their neighbors on Fulton Street. A gold plate with the number 478 in inlaid silver marked their Fulton Street home, a three-story frame house surrounded by a beautifully manicured lawn. Years before the site had been bought and the house built as a summer residence for a retired city merchant. In the center of a square block the house was buried in thick borders of shrubbery and flower beds. The picturesque home was rumored at be worth approximately $100,000 when Leslie and his wife moved into it. They occupied both the first and second floors of the house.

Outside the door leading upstairs to their apartment, Leslie hung out a business sign that read GEORGE L. HOWARD, TAX REVENUE DETECTIVE. Leslie had chosen one of the most desirable locations in the city to carry out his criminal activities. The elegant home was a perfect front for Leslie, and the exorbitant mortgage of $100 a month, an astronomical amount at the time, was no challenge to Leslie. From the Fulton Street address, Leslie could easily carry on his underworld business and at the same time maintain an image of prosperity and acceptance. He and Molly were perfectly content.

Sam Devere and his wife eventually moved into the third-floor apartment of the house. Devere was a noted comedic songwriter and actor. He often visited with the couple downstairs and entertained Leslie and Molly by playing the banjo or piano for them. Molly was a striking brunette, young but self-assured with refined manners, always dressed impeccably in expensive handmade dresses and shawls. She was a perfect match for Leslie's debonair manners and appearance.

Theirs was a palatial home, furnished with expensive (most of them stolen) household goods—rugs, couches, rich wood tables, thick ornate curtains and drapes, chairs, mirrors, and embroidered love seats. Molly kept, with the help of a maid, a clean home often filled with vases of flowers. Leslie had an extensive library and there were musical instruments throughout the lavish apartment including a baby grand piano. Between the two floors of the Fulton Street house, they had ten rooms. Each was more lavishly furnished than the next—mostly with plunder that Leslie had acquired from Mandelbaum's warehouses filled with stolen merchandise. Some of it, like the baby grand piano, he had bought outright, using money he had taken as payment from one of the many bank robberies he was credited with.

Rich imported carpets covered the floors and much of the furniture, tables, and chairs were made of expensive wood such as rosewood or black walnut. The seats on the chairs throughout the place were red velvet or satin or often embroidered with colonial hunting scenes. There was a baby grand piano in the center of the main room where a hallway lined with gilded paintings was located. The hallway lead to an exquisite dining room filled with walnut furniture and glass cabinets filled with expensive china and cut glasses. Leslie kept an abundant well-stocked liquor cabinet although he seldom ever drank.

Outside on the ample lawn facing the street, Leslie had erected a croquet grounds surrounded by lawn furniture and comfortable hammocks and swings, which gave the place the air of style, ease, and comfort. Leslie even had several outhouses built in the back of the home, hidden from view by shrubbery and flower beds. On summer days and evenings Leslie, Molly, and the Deveres would play croquet. They were happy and fun-loving couples, seemingly pleased to be in each other's company. Although Molly and Anne Devere made few or no acquaintances in the neighborhood, they always appeared friendly and polite. Molly was often outside gardening, cutting flowers or weeding. Sometimes she spent whole afternoons relaxing and reading on one of the hammocks. George and Molly were looked upon as model neighbors and citizens. George Leslie gave them no reason to think otherwise. He never invited any of his underworld cohorts to his home, not even Marm Mandelbaum, so that his association with other criminals in the city could not be readily tracked.

Although Leslie was lavish in his expenditures he was always prompt in his payments, and was looked upon as a special customer in the eyes of the business owners he frequented. No one ever asked about his business since Leslie made it clear from the beginning that as an income tax detective, most of his work was classified. He could not speak a word of it to anyone.

These were idyllic times for George Leslie and his new wife. They spent time at their luxurious home on Fulton Street. They often went on strolls through Madison Square Park on East Twenty-sixth Street. They entertained themselves with visits to P. T. Barnum's famous American Museum, on the corner of Ann Street and Broadway. It was one of the most famous places of amusement in the world, filled with oddities such as the Feejee Mermaid and the original bearded lady. Life was good for George Leslie, and he had plans to make it even better with the greatest bank robbery in history. He had already set his plans in motion to rob what most people considered an impenetrable financial fortress: the Manhattan Savings Institution. It would take almost five years before he was able to pull off the robbery, but Leslie was in no rush. Life was good, and could only get better—or so he thought.

9

THE NORTHAMPTON BANK ROBBERY

To be a citizen of New York is to be a disgrace.

–GEORGE TEMPLETON STRONG, NEW YORK CITY DIARIST (1870)

The Northampton Bank robbery went wrong from the start. It began when Leslie did not go on the heist. If he had been there, perhaps the robbery would not have gone so terribly off course. Since the beginning of his bank-robbing career in 1869, Leslie had enjoyed an unprecedented string of successful heists. He had never been caught, and all of his robberies—at least the ones he had been directly involved with—had gone off without a hitch. They had all made considerable money, lining both his pockets and those of his gang, not to mention fattening the bank account of Marm Mandelbaum.

Leslie had been living a life of luxury, happy and settled into his new role as husband and respected member of the community. He had not become sloppy in his endeavors as some might have done, given the ease of each success, but he had generally begun to parcel out his heists to other gangs and to collect an advisor's fee instead of a cut from the profits. It allowed him more time to plan his greatest robbery.

He had turned the Northampton Bank heist over to what he had considered to be a band of seasoned criminals, headed by Robert C. Scott and

James Dunlap, two Illinois penitentiary ex-convicts, and Billy Connors, a well-known New York City criminal. Leslie had never worked with any of the three men before. Scott had been the one to seek out Leslie's expertise in planning the Northampton robbery, and Leslie had agreed to the plan.

On January 26, 1876, Scott, Dunlap, and Connors, along with a gang made up of Red Leary, Billy Porter, Johnny Irving, Shang Draper, and Gilbert Yost—men that Leslie trusted and had worked with before—made their way to Massachusetts with Leslie's intricate plan for the robbery in hand. Even though Leslie had planned everything down to the last detail, they still managed to bungle the heist. Going under the code name "The Rufus Gang," they were able to successfully rob the bank of a record amount of more than $1.6 million in cash and bonds, one of the largest heists on record in the country, breaking even Leslie's Ocean National Bank job record. Unfortunately, much of the loot was in nonnegotiable bonds, which made the heist useless. Worse, the massively bungled job led to the almost immediate apprehension of Scott and Dunlap, placing Leslie's role as mastermind for the caper in jeopardy, a situation Leslie could not afford. Up until this point, law enforcement authorities had remained baffled by the string of unprecedented bank heists and had few leads in the case.

Leslie never forgave himself for not taking part in the robbery himself, which he determined might have circumvented the costly disaster. He promised himself he wouldn't let it happen again. He would organize and lead the next bank heist he planned, making sure that whatever gang he put together would follow every one of his instructions down to the very last detail. But even his participation in the next bank heist—robbing the bank in Dexter, Maine, in 1877—was not enough to forestall the far worse consequences in store for him there. Like Fisk and Boss Tweed before him, Leslie's luck would soon run out.

—⚏—

The Panic of 1873 was created when the country's preeminent investment firm, Jay Cooke and Company, failed. Jay Cooke was a prominent American banker and the principal financier of the Union Army during the course of the Civil War. During the war, Cooke was able to secure more than $3 billion for the Union effort. Afterward, Cooke helped finance the building of the transcontinental railroad. His company failed when it overextended itself, causing Cooke to lose almost his entire fortune, and leading to the economic Panic of 1873, which touched off a series of economic events that crippled the country. The New York Stock Exchange was forced to close its doors for nearly two weeks; banks failed and factories closed; most of the major railroad companies went under; and thousands of workers lost their jobs, leading to countless foreclosures on businesses and homes. It was even more devastating than Black Friday.

The tax rate in the city had grown from a little over $4 per citizen at the start of the Civil War to more than $25 per person by 1870, and the city's incurred debt nearly tripled, from $36 million to more than $97 million during the same ten-year period, pushing the city to near bankruptcy. But not even this latest economic disaster could deter the lavish spending habits of New York City's robber barons. Their appetite for amusement remained insatiable as they continued their unrestrained spending on themselves. As the city crumbled, they adorned the copious robes of Nero and fiddled away their fortunes on wine, women, food, and any other decadent habit that suited their fancy. The city's elite ignored the fact that the streets were overrun with filth and garbage. The sewer system, in constant disrepair, pumped death and disease through the grimy tenement districts.

New York City government had been under the control of the notoriously corrupt William "Boss" Tweed until his arrest and conviction. But during his tenure, Tweed had let public buildings and streets fall into disrepair. His oversight of the city produced graft and outright thievery of the greatest proportions. At the height of his corrupt political powers, Tweed and his henchmen controlled everything in the city and the state; there was nothing that Tweed didn't have a hand in. He was the leader of Tammany Hall, the president of the county board of supervisors, the street commissioner, and a state senator. He had his handpicked mayor in Abraham Oakey Hall, a dandified eccentric with the nickname "Elegant Oakey," as well as his specially chosen governor in John T. Hoffman, a former New York City mayor. He had stacked the state courts with his own appointees, including George G. Barnard as the presiding justice and Albert Cardozo on the State Supreme Court, and John H. McCann as a justice sitting on the Superior Court. Tweed also had Peter Barr Sweeney as city chamberlain controlling the state judiciary and Richard B. Connolly serving as city controller, with oversight of the city's purse strings.

Through this amalgamation of corrupt officials, the Tweed Ring controlled all branches of the city and state government, doling out patronage and city contracts to more than 10,000 colleagues as they saw fit. Tweed controlled the police department through bribes, and kept the various newspapers in his pocket by spending the city's advertising budget where and when he saw fit. Bribes, graft, and kickbacks were their calling cards, and corruption was rampant. Tweed and his cronies stole a reported $1 million a month from the city treasury while the city fell into ruin.

Tweed was one of the largest property owners in the city, lived in a Fifth Avenue mansion, and owned a sumptuous country home. His stables were cleaner and more hospitable than any tenement in the city. His horses ate better than most of the poor men, women, and children living in the city's vast and growing slums.

No matter how much money George Leslie stole during his nine-year reign as the King of Bank Robbers, it never came close to the amount of money Boss Tweed and the Tweed Ring stole from the City of New York during Tweed's nearly twenty-one-year iron-fisted control over the city government. Although the exact amount of money embezzled by Tweed and his cronies has never been determined, it has been estimated in the vicinity of $30 million in cash outright. Bribes, graft, rigged construction bids, plunder, and the sale of privileges are estimated to have cost the City of New York close to $200 million during Tweed's unchallenged sovereignty as political boss.

If Tweed's unbridled greed, corruption, and spending were grotesquely remarkable, it was no more extraordinary than the flagrant disregard for the human condition symbolized by the abundant and extravagant spending of the city's well-to-do.

—⚏—

Between Delmonico's exclusive restaurant and Morrissey's, a lavish gambling parlor located at 5 West Twenty-fourth Street, practically next door to the opulent Fifth Avenue Hotel, New York City's robber barons found ample opportunities to shamelessly squander their vast fortunes. Gambling at places like Morrissey's grew more and more outrageous. Banking tycoon August Belmont reportedly lost nearly $60,000 in just one night, spending the rest of the evening dining on two finely cooked ducks—making the ducks, at a sinful $30,000 each, probably the most expensive meal ever eaten during the Gilded Age.

Belmont and his closest friends, Leonard Jerome and William Travers, often tried to outdo each other when it came to who could throw the most lavish dinner parties. Using Delmonico's as their usual base of operations, the trio would hold parties for their friends and families where women dinner guests would find expensive gold bracelets hidden within their dinner napkins and men would smoke cigars rolled in $100 bills. Delmonico's was more than pleased to present epicurean delights known as "Silver, Gold and Diamond Dinners" for these men and others, for whom money was no object. Reportedly a single pair of opera glasses, its frames surrounded with diamonds and sapphires, was purchased for the wife of one patron of the arts for $75,000. Leonard Jerome's magnificent home came with an $80,000 stable and included hardwood walnut paneling, plush carpeting, a ballroom, a theater that could accommodate more than 500 guests, and luxurious domestic quarters for Jerome's wife and children.

—⁊⁊—

Like most of Leslie past plans, the Northampton Bank robbery involved an inside man. Over the course of his reign, Leslie had relied on bribing an inside bank official, crooked police officer, or even placing one of his own men inside the bank by prevailing on his many associates in the banking industry to hire some down-on-his-luck man or boy for some menial job inside the bank. This time was no different, except for the fact that it wasn't Leslie who secured the inside man. Instead, Scott, Dunlap, and Connors found their own in the form of a crooked salesman from the Herring Safe Company, William D. Edson.

During a preliminary meeting in a saloon on Prince Street, near Broadway, Edson agreed that for $50,000, he would help the gang with the robbery of the Northampton National Bank. It was known through a variety of sources that the Northampton bank kept large cash reserves in its vaults. The locks on the bank vault had been installed by the Herring Safe Company in 1874 by none other than William Edson.

Leslie made several trips to Northampton to survey the bank, doing what he did so well, making mental notes of the bank's layout, along with relevant details about the town, including possible escape routes. After several months of intricate planning, Leslie turned his plans over to Scott, Dunlap, and Connors. They in turn secured the services of the New York City gang members, Red Leary, Billy Porter, Shang Draper, Johnny Irving, and Gilbert Yost. They had all been recommended highly by Leslie as fearless, experienced criminals. They were also all, in some way, indebted to Marm Mandelbaum, which made the likelihood of them double-crossing either Marm or Marm's handpicked protégé, George Leslie, simply out of the question.

There was another much more personal reason Leslie had for recommending Shang Draper and Red Leary for the Northampton bank heist: It would put them both out of New York for a lengthy period of time. Although from all appearances Leslie was a happily married man, he still had an almost unquenchable appetite for women. With Josie Mansfield now out of the picture, he focused his attention on the wives of his two cohorts—Kate Leary and Babe Draper. With both Leary and Draper out of the way in Massachusetts for an extended period of time, Leslie would once again be free to take up his illicit romances with both women, unencumbered by the prospect of being caught by either man. It made perfect sense to Leslie; that is, until the whole bank job fell apart.

—⚏—

Robert Scott and James Dunlap had made their way from Chicago, Illinois, to New York City to set up a new base of operations following the Great Chicago Fire in October 1871. According to legend, the fire had been started by a cow that belonged to an Irishwoman named Catherine O'Leary. She ran a neighborhood milk business from the barn behind her home, and when one of her cows kicked over a kerosene lantern in the barn, it ignited the blaze that ultimately consumed Chicago. The city was devastated in a matter of days. Vital records, deeds, libraries, and museums were all destroyed. The Chicago Federal Building, which housed the post office, lost $100,000 in currency that was burned as the fire swept through the city.

In the days following the blaze, massive looting was reported in the city. Rumors spread like the fire itself that criminals were now breaking into safes and bank vaults, plundering the city. Banks and businesses hired

Pinkerton detectives to protect their buildings and property, and federal troops spread throughout the city to quell riots and looting. The troops arrived under the command of General Phillip Sheridan to assist in maintaining order. Chicago, now a burned-out wasteland, was placed under martial law. It only took four years to rebuild the city, and by 1875, little evidence of the massive destruction remained. But by then, many criminals like Robert Scott and James Dunlap had moved their base of operations to New York City where the country's wealthiest citizens kept their money and jewels stashed in banks. These two hardened criminals ingratiated themselves with the New York City underworld—Marm Mandelbaum especially—by bringing with them thousands of dollars' worth of stolen and smoke-damaged loot, all of which Mandelbaum was happy to fence for them at her usual going rate of ten cents on the dollar.

When Scott and Dunlap told Marm about their plans to rob what appeared to be the lucrative Northampton Bank in Massachusetts, she put them in touch with Leslie, who for his usual and customary fee of $20,000 agreed to mastermind the robbery. Scott and Dunlap offered to cut Leslie in on a share of the robbery if he wanted to come along, but Leslie had other things in mind—most notably, the prospect of getting Red Leary and Shang Draper out of the city for a while so that he could freely pursue Kate and Babe.

Scott, Dunlap, and Connors, along with Leary, Porter, Irving, Draper, and Yost, set up their nefarious operations in the attic of an old school in the quaint New England town in western Massachusetts. From the attic of the Bridge Street School—located next door to the Bridge Street Cemetery, just off the main thoroughfare—they set Leslie's plan into motion. There were no houses on either side, and the hideout could be easily accessed through the cemetery entrance. Leslie's plan called for the gang to use the cemetery as the hiding place for the stolen cash and securities they took from the bank. It was, as always, an ingenious plan by Leslie.

Not far from the school hideout and the cemetery was the town's train station, which Leslie identified as the gang's form of getaway. The Northampton National Bank was on the corner of Main and Center streets, next to the courthouse. The one fly in the ointment was that the third floor of the bank was the private residence of Judge Thomas Forbes, the town's leading jurist and a bank director. Gaining access to the vault from the roof of the building was out of the question, but Leslie surmised that it might be possible to find a bank employee who would offer his services for a small percentage of the loot.

The gang spent several days observing John Whittelsey, a bank cashier. They studied his activities at the Northampton National Bank and followed him after work. Whittelsey left the bank every day at 4:00 P.M. and walked to his nearby Elm Street home. Several inquiries about Whittelsey's loyalties led Scott and Dunlap to the conclusion that Whittelsey could not be bribed into taking part in the robbery. Scott was given explicit instructions from Leslie to telegraph him if the gang was unable to secure another inside man. Scott decided he had come far enough and wasn't about to drop the whole robbery just because they couldn't follow Leslie's instructions to the letter. Scott decided he would find an alternative solution.

The gang continued to follow Whittelsey, finding out everything about him, his family, and their routines. Their reconnaissance paid off. The Northampton National Bank was unattended from the time the guard, Deputy Sheriff Henry Potter, and Whittelsey left at 4:00 P.M. until it was opened the next morning by Whittelsey at 8:00 A.M. Scott and Dunlap came up with a scheme to get into the bank, and now all they needed was to gain access to the vault. That is where William Edson, the corrupt salesman, came in.

Already having a connection with Northampton National Bank, Edson traveled to Northampton to find out what he could about the vault and the combination. The bank manager, Thomas Warriner, allowed Edson to examine the vault as part of what Edson referred to as "routine maintenance" on the safe. Warriner told Edson that the vault keys were a little tight, and Edson said he could fix that easily with Warriner's permission. Warriner had no reason to suspect Edson of anything, so he allowed Edson to remove the locks and take them, along with the keys, back to his private boardinghouse room in Northampton where he could work on them. Alone in his room, Edson made wax impressions of the keys which were subsequently given over to Scott and Dunlap. Edson returned the keys to the bank and suggested to Warriner that a new bank vault combination should be made, and that only one man, notably John Whittelsey, should be responsible for it. Warriner agreed and had the combination changed. Whittelsey, a trusted employee, was the only one besides Warriner who knew the safe's new combination. The combination would be safe with him.

Manhattan's Fifth Avenue was the home to top-notch restaurants like Delmonico's. The wealth of the nation congregated and lived in this luxurious neighborhood, far from the filth and crime that permeated the nearby New York City slums.
Credit: Milstein Division of United States History, Local History & Genealogy, The New York Public Library, Astor, Lenox, and Tilden Foundations

The prices of the famed cuisine at Delmonico's restaurant were sufficiently high to discourage anyone but the very wealthiest from patronizing it. It was New York City's most renowned culinary spot. **Credit: Picture Collection, The Branch Libraries, The New York Public Library, Astor, Lenox, and Tilden Foundations**

THE DINING-ROOM OF THE FIFTH AVENUE HOTEL, ON MADISON SQUARE.

While many of New York City's inhabitants spent day-to-day never knowing if they would eat, the city's wealthiest citizens wined and dined in the most luxurious surroundings such as the main ballroom of the Fifth Avenue Hotel. **Credit: Picture Collection, The Branch Libraries, The New York Public Library, Astor, Lenox, and Tilden Foundations**

FIFTH AVE.HOTEL

The Fifth Avenue Hotel was one of the most lavish and luxurious hotels in New York City and was home to many of the city's wealthiest inhabitants. Built in 1859, the extravagant hotel was not given much chance of success but quickly became the most prominent lodging in the city. **Credit: Picture Collection, The Branch Libraries, The New York Public Library, Astor, Lenox, and Tilden Foundations**

New York City slums were teeming with filth, crime, and disease. Thousands of immigrants were crowded into the tenement housing where families of six to ten people were often forced to live in a single room. **Credit: Picture Collection, The Branch Libraries, The New York Public Library, Astor, Lenox, and Tilden Foundations**

A FIVE POINTS RUM SHOP.

Five Points in New York City's Sixth Ward was a cesspool of poverty, violence, crime, and vice. The neighborhood was home to nearly 300 salons and more than 600 bordellos. Prostitutes openly plied their trade along the streets and in rum shops throughout the area. **Credit: Picture Collection, The Branch Libraries, The New York Public Library, Astor, Lenox, and Tilden Foundations**

A former circus barker from Vermont, "Jubilee" Jim Fisk is one of the most flamboyant and wealthiest Wall Street investors of all time. His penchant for wine, women, and song and his no-holds-barred business tactics, ultimately led to his downfall and untimely death.
Credit: Print Collection, Miriam and Ira D. Wallach Division of Art, Prints and Photographs, The New York Public Library, Astor, Lenox, and Tilden Foundations

Drawn by B. West Clinedinst

"Jubilee" Jim Fisk's Grand Opera House, home to his railroad empire, came under siege after the infamous Black Friday debacle in which investors lost fortunes when Fisk and his partner Jay Gould attempted to manipulate the gold market.

THE LATE COLONEL JAMES FISK, JR.—FROM A PHOTOGRAPH BY BRADY.   EDWARD S. STOKES.

EDWARD S. STOKES.

EDWARD S. STOKES was born in Philadelphia in the year 1841, and is consequently in his thirty-first year. He is five feet nine inches high, and weighs about one hundred and forty pounds. He is slightly built, but very wiry and active on his feet. In conversation he talks quickly and to the point, and hurries his affairs through as rapidly as possible. Stokes is a man of fine appearance, of a dark complexion, with piercing eyes and regular features. His hair, which was jet black a couple of years ago, is now partly gray, and were it not for his active movements he would pass for a man of forty-five years. Mr. Stokes married a lady of good family some ten years ago, and has by her one child.

About two years ago Stokes became interested with Fisk in some business transactions. was by Fisk introduced to Mrs. Mansfield. That person conceived a fondness for him which excited the jealousy of Colonel Fisk. The two men became involved in business difficulties, and Mr. Fisk had Stokes arrested and locked up on a charge of embezzlement. This charge not being sustained, Stokes sued Fisk for false imprisonment. Mrs. Mansfield espoused Stokes's side in the quarrel, and the two waged war against Mr. Fisk.

The legal investigations consequent upon and attending these proceedings have occupied much space in the papers for the past year, and the public is familiar with the details. Stokes accuses Fisk of swindling him out of upward of $200,000. The legal proceedings had nearly exhausted the remainder of Stokes's fortune, and it is asserted that, being unable to further prosecute Colonel Fisk, he determined to murder him.

NEW YORK CITY.—THE DEATH-BED SCENE AT THE GRAND CENTRAL HOTEL—COLONEL FISK, IN HIS LAST MOMENTS, SURROUNDED BY HIS RELATIVES AND FRIENDS.

"Jubilee" Jim Fisk was shot by a disgruntled business partner, Edward "Ned" Stokes, on January 6, 1872, at the Grand Central Hotel on Broadway. Fisk, the circus barker who became the flamboyant terror of Wall Street, died on the morning of January 7, 1872, with his wife and friends at his side. He was only thirty-seven years old. **Credit: Print Collection, Miriam and Ira D. Wallach Division of Art, Prints and Photographs, The New York Public Library, Astor, Lenox, and Tilden Foundations**

Unlike his flamboyant partner, Jim Fisk, Jay Gould was a quiet, dour man. Gould and Fisk together nearly bankrupted the country with their scheme to manipulate the gold market causing the infamous Black Friday financial crisis in 1869. **Credit: Print Collection, Miriam and Ira D. Wallach Division of Art, Prints and Photographs, The New York Public Library, Astor, Lenox, and Tilden Foundations**

Harper's Black and White Prints   From Harper's Magazine. Copyright, 1885, by Harper & Brothers

JAY GOULD
1836–1892

In October, 1872, William Marcy "Boss" Tweed was arraigned on a 220-count indictment for failing to audit claims against the city. The trial ended in a hung jury, but at a retrial in 1873, Tweed was convicted of embezzlement of public funds and sentenced to thirteen years in prison and $12,000 in fines. He escaped and went to Cuba and then to Spain, but was extradited in 1876. He died in prison two years later. **Credit: Picture Collection, The Branch Libraries, The New York Public Library, Astor, Lenox, and Tilden Foundations**

INSPECTOR THOMAS F. BYRNES.

New York City Police detective Thomas Byrnes revolutionized modern detective work and introduced the "third degree" into the annals of crime fighting. He was instrumental in bringing the robbers of the Manhattan Savings Institution to justice.

Credit: Print Collection, Miriam and Ira D. Wallach Division of Art, Prints and Photographs, The New York Public Library, Astor, Lenox, and Tilden Foundations

There was just one more hurdle to overcome as far as Scott and Dunlap were concerned—the night watchman. At first they planned to overpower the watchman to gain access to the vault, but they soon discovered that he took his leave of the unguarded bank at approximately 4:00 every morning. After that hour, they would have clear access to the vault.

The Rufus Gang had arrived in Northampton in September 1875. It was now a cold January 1876. It was time to act. Just after midnight Scott, Dunlap, and the others broke into John Whittelsey's house on Elm Street and rounded up all the sleeping occupants. They all wore masks and long, cotton coats. Their temperament was courteous and businesslike. The gang referred to each other in code, using numbers instead of words or names to communicate. Once the occupants of the house were awakened, they were made to dress, then handcuffed and herded into Whittelsey's room. They were made as comfortable as possible.

At the time, the house was occupied by John Whittelsey and his wife, her niece, Mattie White, and a maid, Kate Nugent. Also staying at the house were friends of the Whittelseys, a man named Cutler, his wife, and an invalid girl named Annie Beaton. The gang stopped all clocks in the house so their victims had no idea what time it was.

Mrs. Whittelsey pleaded with the criminals not to hurt her husband as they led him alone out of the room. With Whittelsey downstairs and handcuffed to a chair, Scott and Dunlap began their interrogation of him, demanding the combination to the bank vault. Dunlap stood over him, threatening him with a pistol. Scott insisted that he give him the numbers without hesitation. Whittelsey attempted to give them false numbers, but when he couldn't repeat the combination accurately they beat him. Finally, Whittelsey gave them the right combination.

Just before 4:00 A.M., the gang bound and gagged everyone in the house and left for the bank. They left two guards behind to watch over the victims. Whittelsey was still handcuffed downstairs out of sight of the other captives.

With the night watchman gone, the gang entered the bank undetected using the key Edson had made for them and gained full access to the contents of the bank vault. Two hours later Scott, Dunlap, Connors, and the rest of the gang left Northampton by train, headed back to New York City.

Within a matter of hours, they had made off with the largest heist of cash and bonds up to that point in American history. The thieves had stolen nearly $1.6 million in cash, bonds, certificates, and other securities that they had hidden beneath a platform at the Bridge Street schoolhouse, where they had been hiding out for months. Weeks later they would return and reclaim their stolen loot.

At 6:30 A.M. someone heard screaming inside the Whittelsey home. Mrs. Whittelsey was at an open window at the front of the house, having freed herself, and was screaming at the top of her lungs. "They've taken my husband and are robbing the bank! They're all at the bank! Please help my husband!" she screamed.

By that time the robbers were long gone, and the robbery of the Northampton, Massachusetts, bank was now history—almost.

—⁓—

THE NORTHAMPTON BANK ROBBERY

BOSTON, Mass., Jan. 27—Later details of the robbery of the Northampton National Bank at Northampton, Tuesday night, by masked robbers, state that the result is something appalling. The table of the securities taken shows a total of $670,000. Of course, much of this is nonnegotiable, so that it is difficult to estimate the real loss to the bank and depositors. The bank officers offer a reward of $25,000 for the return of the property and conviction of the burglars. The loss falls comparatively light upon the bank, the greater part of the securities belonging to special depositors . . .

—*The Brooklyn Daily Eagle* (January 27, 1876)

THE PRESENT CONDITION OF AFFAIRS—LETTER FROM THE NATIONAL BANK EXAMINER

Springfield, Jan. 28—It is certain that the total amount in various securities taken by the burglars from the Northampton National Bank will be quite as great as the $720,000 previously reckoned. The bank authorities do not themselves yet know how much the private securities will foot up as they were not accustomed to examine this property. It seems likely that from $200,000 to $300,000 of nego-tiable private property was stolen, besides the registered bonds and certified stock . . .

There is yet no trace of the burglars, and it seems certain that they have reached New York or Boston or both. It is the opinion of the best bank authorities that the robbers will not attempt to work off their plunder, but are waiting for a compromise . . .

—The New York Times (January 29, 1876)

BOSTON, Jan. 28—A special dispatch to the *Herald* has the fol-lowing additional particulars of the Northampton Bank robbery: It is generally believed at Northampton today that the loss by robbery of the Northampton National Bank has been understated and that the aggregate actually reaches, if it does not exceed, $1,000,000. Many of the losers are silent, still declining to say how much they lost.

—The New York Times (January 29, 1876)

—⟪⟫—

By the time of the Northampton Bank robbery, Boss Tweed was back in prison. In 1875, Tweed had escaped from jail and fled to Cuba. He ulti-mately made his way to Spain, where he was once again apprehended and returned to the United States.

William Marcy Tweed was a huge, barrel-chested, potbellied man who stood nearly six feet tall and weighed close to three hundred pounds. He had a large head with a broad forehead, a bulbous nose, and a rosy complexion. He wore a neatly trimmed brown beard and had sparkling blue eyes. Tweed's appetites were not solely for money and power. He was known to gorge himself on huge expensive meals that he had prepared especially for him.

By all accounts New York City's corrupt boss was devoted to his wife and eight children, although he was known to have kept two mistresses, upon which it was later confirmed he had bestowed nearly $2 million for their upkeep including homes, clothes, jewelry, and other expensive gifts. Not necessarily known for his tastes in high fashion, Tweed was nonetheless fond of expensive jewelry, and always wore a large diamond stickpin on his usually white, starched, high-collared shirts. He was not a well-educated man, having dropped out of school when he was just four-teen years old, and his language was always filled with a smattering of profanity. He didn't smoke, and although he'd once been a big drinker, he'd given it up on the advice of his physician. He was a dog lover and breeder and had an affinity for flowers and caged birds. His offices were filled with fresh flowers each day, and he had dozens of singing canaries housed in elaborate gilded cages.

Tweed, the uneducated son of a New York City chair maker, was the first politician in America to be called "Boss," a title that even today conjures up the image of power, money, greed, and corruption. "The fact is that New York politics were always dishonest long before my time," Tweed aptly acknowledged. "This population is too hopelessly split up into races and factions to govern it under universal suffrage, except by the bribery of patronage or corruption . . ."

There was nothing in Tweed's background to remotely suggest his tal-ent for political corruption. He was a fourth-generation New Yorker, born in 1823 on Cherry Street in the city. Boss was the youngest in a family of five children. He worked in his father's chair-making shop and later became a salesman for a saddle-making factory. When he was older he went into partnership in the chair-making business with his father and one of his older brothers. But young Bill Tweed always had his eye on politics, and although he lost his first try at elective office, he came back from the experience with a vengeance. He rose quickly within the rough-and-tumble world of New York City politics, which, as Tweed had noted himself, had been a corrupt playing field long before he'd joined the game. His base of power was Tammany Hall, where he was elected grand sachem—the leader of the organization. *Tammany Hall* was a general term for the Democratic Party in New York City, as well as the Tammany Society, a social organi-zation, with clubs throughout the city that helped the poor and indigent. Tweed oversaw the workings of both organizations.

His plunder of the New York City coffers went unabated for nearly twenty years. He was too powerful for anyone to stop. On one occasion alone Tweed and his cronies made off with close to $6 million in a single morning's work. At one meeting Tweed and his fellow conspirators autho-rized the payment of an additional $6.3 million for the new courthouse building. Most of this was sheer graft. Of the $6.3 million authorized for the new courthouse, Tweed and his Tammany Ring ended up with a neat $5.5 million in their own pockets. It was all in a day's work for the likes of Boss Tweed.

The good times for Tweed and his cronies ended in 1871 when he was first arrested and tried for corruption, and although he served a year in jail, he was rearrested and faced civil proceedings against him. By then, most of his cohorts had abandoned him. Many fled the country, while others were tried for their own offenses. "Elegant" Oakey, former mayor of New York City, was acquitted after two trials. Tweed's judicial appointments were driven out of office. Judge Barnard was impeached and Judge Cardozo resigned. Connolly, Sweeney, and Garvey were offered a deal not to be prosecuted if they gave back what they had stolen. In the end, after all the trials, resignations, legal wrangling, and deals, the City of New York was only able to recover less than $1 million from the Tammany Ring leaders out of the estimated $200 million stolen from the city's coffers over the years.

Since Tweed was unable to raise the $3 million bail placed on his release, he languished in the Ludlow Street Jail, awaiting trial. He knew the political handwriting on the wall. Somebody had to pay, and it appeared it would have to be him, one way or another. All his property and holdings were attached by the government. All his former friends and associates had deserted him. In October 1875, the State Supreme Court denied his appeal regarding the huge civil suit against him.

In late December 1875 Boss Tweed escaped from the Ludlow jail. While visiting his wife and children at their new home on Madison Avenue, and while accompanied by two guards and a warden of the jail, Tweed excused himself from the dinner table where the family, guards, and warden had all sat down to eat, and went upstairs to freshen up before being returned to his cell. After being gone for an extended time the jailers went upstairs to find him and discovered that Tweed had fled out the back door of the brownstone. Tweed had reportedly paid $60,000 for help in making his escape. He hid out in an isolated farmhouse in New Jersey for several weeks where he altered his appearance by shaving off his beard, wearing a long gray wig, and donning eyeglasses. Going under the assumed name of John Secor, Tweed took a schooner out of New York harbor and landed in Florida, where he hid out for a short time in a shack in the Everglades. From Florida he made his way to Cuba. By the time the authorities had traced his whereabouts to Santiago, Cuba, Tweed had escaped to Spain.

Secretary of State Hamilton Fish requested that the Spanish authorities arrest and extradite Tweed back to New York. Although Spain and the United States had no extradition treaty, Tweed was arrested and held until the United States Navy cruiser *Franklin* arrived to bring him back to the United States. Ironically, the Spanish authorities used a cartoon depicting the likeness of Tweed, drawn by Thomas Nast for *Harper's Weekly*, to identify Tweed. Even in his grand scheme to escape, Tweed could not escape the lasting image of greed and corruption that Thomas Nast had so expertly and forever ascribed to him. By the time of the Northampton bank heist, Tweed was back in jail. Tweed, once the most powerful man in the most powerful city in the world, would never again leave the confines of the Ludlow Street Jail. He died there on April 12, 1878, from severe pneumonia.

—⚬—

Thomas Nast's cartoons in *Harper's Weekly* helped bring about the downfall of the once all powerful Boss Tweed. And although Nast is probably best remembered for his role in bringing down Tweed, his contributions to American culture and society are still predominant today. Nast created and was the first to publish the caricatures for the Republican and Democratic parties—the elephant and the donkey, respectively. Although he didn't create it, Nast did popularize the caricature of Uncle Sam, and he also created the image we now think of as Santa Claus, inspired by the poem "The Night Before Christmas," written by Clement Moore. Ironically, Nast had to have his wife read the poem to him since he could not read or write.

—⚬—

Along with everything else that had transpired in 1876, the downfall of Boss Tweed spelled trouble for Marm Mandelbaum's criminal empire, and that included George Leslie. Tweed had always kept a tight rein on the police and courts, and Mandelbaum had kept a steady grip on Tweed through bribes and payoffs. With Tweed in jail and reformers on the prowl, it wouldn't be long before they turned their attention toward the criminal underpinnings of the city.

And as if matters weren't bad enough, in early September of 1876, Leslie was shocked to read about the James Gang's attempted robbery of the First National Bank in Northfield, Minnesota. More than a hundred members of the town opened fire on the bank robbers, killing three of the James Gang; the Younger brothers, Bob, Cole, and James, were all wounded and captured. Jesse and his brother Frank, Leslie's longtime criminal heroes, were also reportedly wounded, but managed to escape. Jesse James went into hiding following the disastrous Northfield raid.

—⚉—

Leslie had been enjoying the absence of Red Leary and Shang Draper. It gave him the opportunity to discreetly and freely engage in his romantic liaisons with their wives, Kate and Babe. But his romantic frivolity soon came to a screeching halt. Leslie was shocked to read in the newspapers about what had transpired in Northampton. Scott and Dunlap had veered terribly from Leslie's intricate plans by holding Whittelsey's family hostage and torturing Whittelsey, the bank clerk, for the combination to the safe. Leslie had always been adamant that no one was to get hurt in any of his bank heists, and that meant gang members as well as bank customers and employees. It just wasn't good business. As far as Leslie was concerned, bank heists should only hurt those with money to lose, meaning rich businessmen and industrialists who could make their money back. When no one was hurt or killed during a robbery, it was less likely that the police would pursue the matter as vigorously. Ever since the Panic of 1873, one of the worst economic crises in American history, most of the public had maintained a jaundiced view of banks. It had served Leslie well to rely on the public's mistrust of banks—at least, until the Northampton Bank robbery. The break-in of Whittelsey's home and his torture at the hands of Scott and Dunlap changed everything. The gang had even stolen Whittelsey's gold watch, and this—not the millions in cash and securities stolen in the heist—became the focal point of conversation in both the news and among the public. This did not bode well for anyone.

Leslie made contact with Scott and Dunlap and in no uncertain terms told them he wanted nothing further to do with them. He also demanded that they return Whittelsey's gold watch in an effort to take the heat off the investigation. Begrudgingly Scott returned the watch by mail. Leslie advised Mandelbaum to also disassociate herself from the gang, since he believed their actions could only lead to disaster. He was right.

Mandelbaum was not as forthcoming about breaking off her agreement with Scott and Dunlap. Her fear was that they would take their business to her chief rival, John "Traveling Mike" Grady, who was trying to establish himself as the chief fence in New York City. However, it didn't take long for her to see the wisdom in Leslie's advice.

The Pinkerton Detective Agency had been hired by the Northampton bank officials just days after the robbery, and detectives were already hot on the trail of the robbers. Only a month after the robbery, the Pinkertons had developed several good leads in the case. In a ransom note, sent to Northampton bank officials, Scott and Dunlap had included two of the stock certificates stolen during the robbery in order to prove the authenticity of the note. The certificates were private issue, which meant no one except the owners of the certificates could cash them in. Frustrated by Mandelbaum's reluctance to sell the certificates, Scott and Dunlap took matters into their own hands. In the ransom note, Scott and Dunlap offered to sell the certificates back to the bank for $150,000. The bank stalled for months, sending the robbers dubious replies. At one point, Edson, the crooked locksmith, met with bank officials, claiming to be an innocent go-between. The bank offered a $60,000 ransom for the return of the stolen certificates, but Scott and Dunlap demanded the full $150,000 they had originally asked for.

Leslie warned the others—Leary, Draper, Porter, Irving, and Yost—that Scott, Dunlap, and Connors would likely be captured and would probably give them up as part of a plea bargain. They didn't heed his warning.

The bungled Northampton bank heist was too close a call for Leslie, and he vowed never to let another of his plans go awry as it had there. From this point forward, he would personally oversee any bank heists that he planned; it was the only safe way to do it. Had the Rufus Gang used the little joker like Leslie had told them to, none of this would have happened. He wasn't about to let it happen again. There was too much at stake, especially since he was all but ready with his plans to pull off the biggest bank heist in history at the Manhattan Savings Institution—the Fort Knox of New York City banks.

10

THE RUFUS GANG

I have no use for men who fail. The cause of their failure is no business of mine, but I want successful men as my associates.

—JOHN D. ROCKEFELLER (1885)

Following the robbery of the Northampton Bank, Edson, the crooked lock salesman, went to New York, ready to collect his share of the loot. He'd agreed to help the gang in return for $50,000 in cash. Robert Scott, the titular head of the Rufus Gang, had established an elaborate communication scheme. Scott would place advertisements in the classified section of the *New York Herald*. In the advertisement, Edson would receive instructions as to where to meet. Edson and Scott met on the corner of Thirty-fourth Street and Broadway. There, Edson was paid a mere $1,200 in cash. It was a far cry from the $50,000 he had expected, and Edson was livid. Scott explained that much of what they had stolen from the Northampton Bank was nonnegotiable bonds and securities, meaning only the person whose name was on either the bond or security could cash them. Unless they could somehow sell them back to the bank, the bonds and securities were worthless.

Most of the stolen securities were left hidden under a stoop at the Bridge Street School in Northampton. Edson convinced Scott that he could sell the bonds and securities back to the bank for a substantial profit. Scott reluctantly agreed to let him try. Scott, Dunlap, and Connors returned to Northampton to retrieve the hidden securities, but Northampton was still crawling with police and Pinkerton detectives. The trio of robbers decided not to take a chance trying to recover the bonds and securities from where they had stashed them.

While they were in Northampton, Edson took it upon himself to pay a visit to Mr. Warriner, the Northampton Bank manager. There, claiming to be an innocent go-between, he told Warriner that the robbers would be willing to sell the nonnegotiable securities back to the bank for $150,000. Warriner offered him the sum of $60,000 instead, with no questions asked. Edson said he would see what he could do.

By now, Pinkerton detectives were already on the case. Back in New York City, Edson met with Scott, Dunlap, and Connors again, and told them what the bank manager had offered for the return of the securities. Scott became furious and refused the bank's offer. He decided that Edson could no longer be trusted. He had compromised the gang by contacting the bank manager directly. Scott told Edson that their relationship was over and that he would have no further dealings with him. Edson decided he would set his own plans in motion.

After several months, the stolen securities were finally retrieved from their hiding place in Northampton. Scott contacted the bank manager by letter, negotiating the sale of the securities back to the bank. The letter arrived at the Northampton National Bank in late February 1876. As a show of good faith, two certificates of stock owned by private depositors accompanied the letter. Warriner didn't respond to the letter. Instead, he insisted on traveling to New York, where he attempted to contact the gang directly. Scott refused to meet with anyone from the bank.

Edson had no further contact with any of the gang until September of 1876, when he accidentally ran into Scott on a trolley car. The two men argued and Scott vowed that Edson would not receive one red cent from the sale of the securities back to the bank. Scott stormed off the trolley at the first available stop.

Scott sent a second letter in October 1876 to the bank, still maintaining that the securities would be returned for $150,000. The bank still refused to negotiate. Scott sent two more letters to the bank during October, trying to sell back the securities. Bank officials stalled in an effort to buy more time for Pinkerton detectives, who were hot on the trail of the Rufus Gang.

In November, still unable to unload the stolen securities from the Northampton Bank robbery, Scott, Dunlap, and Connors decided to contact Edson. Edson at this point became fearful of the gang's intent. He knew that Scott saw him as a potential threat, and had even accused him of being a snitch. Still, Edson agreed to meet with them. Things within the gang were falling apart. Leslie had predicted the Rufus Gang would dissolve, and he had been right.

Despite the fact that the Rufus Gang had stolen close to $2 million from the bank, most in nonnegotiable bonds and securities, all anyone seemed to care about was the beating inflicted on Whittelsey, the bank cashier, and the gold watch the gang had stolen from him. By breaking into Whittelsey's home, holding his family hostage, and torturing him to get the vault's combination, the Rufus Gang had personalized the heist. Leslie had always relied on the notion that the public didn't care about bank robberies, since it was only the wealthy who suffered. The majority of New Yorkers were too poor to have bank accounts. So public opinion was with Leslie—with all bank robbers—since the wealthy robber barons were despised by the poor and lowly of New York. But the actions of the Rufus Gang turned public sentiment against the thieves. Instead of an image of the little guy robbing from the wealthy big shots, the public was left with the distasteful image of a gang of ruthless criminals terrifying a family, beating and torturing one of their own, and stealing from him a prized possession—his gold watch—perhaps the only thing of worth the poor cashier owned.

Scott, Dunlap, and Connors met with Edson. Edson was adamant that his conversation with the bank manager had solely been focused on selling back the securities for the benefit of the gang, and that he had done nothing to give away the identity of the gang members. Scott angrily called him a liar. Despite their mistrust of each other, since they had been frustrated in their own attempts to sell back the securities, they agreed to let Edson try. Edson would set up a meeting with the bank officials and Connors would negotiate the sale of the securities.

In mid-November 1876, Connors met with the Northampton National Bank president, a meeting facilitated by Edson. The bank president made it clear to Connors that the most the bank would pay for the return of the securities was the $60,000 they had originally offered. Connors left the meeting without a deal.

It became obvious to Scott, Dunlap, and Connors that they might never be able to sell back the securities at the price they wanted, so they decided it was time to pull up stakes and leave New York for Philadelphia.

So far Leslie, as well as Marm Mandelbaum, had managed to steer clear of any connection to the Northampton heist. Although Leslie had warned the other gang members—Red Leary, Shang Draper, Johnny Irving, Jimmy Porter, and Gilbert Yost—to keep a low profile, it didn't matter. Unlike Leslie, who had never had any run-ins with the law, the others were known by both the police and Pinkerton detectives. All of them had at one time or another served time in jail or prison. Leslie's biggest fear was that someone would link him to the Northampton robbery. If it happened, his cover, which he had taken so long to perfect, would be blown. Worse, all his plans to rob the Manhattan Savings Institution would be for naught.

While Scott, Dunlap, and Connors were busy trying to negotiate the sale of the stolen loot back to the bank, the other gang members resumed their former lives. Shang Draper was back behind the bar in his saloon and back with his beautiful wife, Babe. Red Leary was back at his Coney Island hotel with his wife, Kate. Irving and Porter were living together on Clinton Street, and Yost had taken up residency in a small hotel. But Pinkerton detectives and New York City police, notably chief of detectives Thomas Byrnes, were hot on their trail.

While Northampton bank officials stalled for time, Edson, fearing the worst, began to crack under the pressure. He didn't want to go to jail, at least not for the paltry sum of $1,200. Billy Connors showed up at Leslie's Fulton Street home, begging Leslie to help them get rid of the securities. Leslie had given strict orders that no one from the gang should ever visit him at his home. Leslie managed to get rid of Connors fast, letting him know in no uncertain terms that he wasn't to come back or make contact with him ever again. Leslie worried it might be too late. Someone might have followed Connors to the Fulton Street address. Leslie knew the Pinkerton detectives would be smart enough to piece together the puzzle.

In early February 1877, as Scott and Dunlap boarded a train for Philadelphia, two Pinkerton detectives, including Robert Pinkerton himself, arrested the two men. They were carrying with them suitcases containing a variety of burglars' tools. Connors was arrested at a New York City restaurant. Although held in the Ludlow jail, now home to the infamous Boss Tweed, Connors managed to escape. Charges against him were later dropped by police due to insufficient evidence. Rumors circulated that Connors had turned state's evidence as part of a plea bargain and that he'd been released. Although the police rounded up the other gang members, including Leary, Draper, Porter, Yost, and Irving, charges against them were ultimately dropped due to lack of evidence. When New York City Police detectives went to arrest Red Leary for his complicity in the robbery, Leary managed to lead the police on a merry chase. Although he was ultimately rearrested, charges against him in the Northampton robbery were dropped.

William Edson was not prosecuted. Scott and Dunlap were returned to Northampton to face charges in back-to-back trials. The first trial was for the bank robbery, and the second was for breaking and entering Whittelsey's house, attacking Whittelsey and terrorizing his family, and stealing his watch. The second charge carried with it a maximum sentence of life in prison, while the bank robbery charge carried a mere twenty-year sentence. The attack on Whittelsey and his family would cost them both dearly. The first trial lasted only a few days, with the prosecution's whole case based on Edson's testimony. In less than two hours, the jury returned a verdict of guilty. The second trial lasted longer, but the results were the same—guilty on all charges.

Scott and Dunlap were sentenced to a total of twenty years each in the state penitentiary. Connors, who had reportedly escaped from jail after his arrest, was later arrested in Ohio on charges associated with yet another failed bank robbery. He was sentenced to twenty years in an Ohio penitentiary. Ironically, Connors's cellmate was William Sydney Porter, a man who was serving time for bank embezzlement. After he was released from prison, Porter, a former newspaper reporter, adopted the pen name of O. Henry and became one of America's most celebrated short story writers. Some of his stories were based on Billy Connors's exploits, which Connors had shared with Porter while they were in prison together.

Robert Scott eventually had the securities returned to the bank in hopes of gaining some leniency, but he died in prison in 1882. In 1892, Dunlap was pardoned and released. Eight years later, he was arrested again for attempting to rob a bank. The $1.6 million stolen in the Northampton Bank heist would be worth over $26 million by today's currency standards. Everything except the cash, a mere $11,000, was ultimately recovered by authorities. Neither George Leslie nor Marm Mandelbaum was ever implicated in the case.

—m—

THE NORTHAMPTON BANK ROBBERY

SCOTT AND DUNLAP BOUND OVER FOR TRIAL

IN THE SUM OF $500,000 EACH—THE CONNECTION EDSON, THE BANK-LOCK "EXPERT," HAD WITH THE THIEVES

The first two days of the preliminary examination of the Northampton bank robbers, Scott and Dunlap, have given the public its first clear idea of the method by which the rich "old" bank was "cracked." In fact, it wasn't "cracked" at all. Bank-Lock Expert Edson, of New York—who had been employed by the lock company, and had practical supervision of putting in the new vault doors—managed to afterward take a wax impression of three of the vault keys which he turned over to the burglars. They thus had false keys and Edson to direct them how to use them. With these "helps," the Northampton robbery doesn't take high rank as a piece of science . . .

—*The Springfield Republican* (March, 1877)

—m—

The corruption that marred the decade only grew worse. A series of scandals fed the public's disgust for both politicians and the rich. Most viewed bank robbers as Robin Hoods, robbing from the rich and giving to the poor. Even though these criminals kept much of their stolen plunder for themselves, they still spread more of their ill-gotten gains among the poor and less fortunate than did the robber barons or politicians.

The disparity between the country's rich and poor was never at a larger juncture. The rich wore furs and diamonds and lived in palatial luxury while most Americans wore rags. The average yearly family income in 1876 was approximately $1,200. Many more earned much less. Immigrants and farmers whose farms had gone bust flocked to urban areas like New York City, Chicago, and Philadelphia, looking for work. Filthy, ramshackle tenements spread across the urban landscapes. These slums were teeming with crime, filth, and disease.

Andrew Carnegie, John D. Rockefeller, and the Astors celebrated their wealth as never before. In New York City, the theater, opera, lavish dinner parties, and outlandish carousing consumed the robber barons' leisure time. Fifth Avenue above Fiftieth Street had been transformed into millionaires' row. Vast fortunes were poured into the palaces bordering the new Central Park. New Yorkers knew that no other city in the world possessed a street as magnificent as the new Fifth Avenue. The older families of New York high society settled into their huge brownstones, at first disapproving of the showy tastes and public display of the coarse new millionaires. Elegant hotels flourished throughout the city even as most residents lived in dire poverty and filth. Hotels for the rich, like the New Netherland, the Plaza, and the fourteen-story Savoy, were all built at the very heart of the new millionaires' row on Fifth Avenue.

The New York Riding Club shamelessly catered to the whims of the rich by hosting formal dinners on horseback. One prominent wealthy matron, Mrs. Stuyvesant Fish, held a dinner party to honor her dog, giving the mutt a $15,000 diamond collar. There was, according to many, a widespread opinion of conflict and menacing rebellion. For a time violent labor strikes and riots wracked the country. The general public spoke openly of a new rebellion because of the vast corruption in both government and in business among the robber barons.

Although millionaire Andrew Carnegie found the ostentatious living of his business cronies offensive, and the behavior of most New York millionaires reckless, he also believed "that the houses of some should be homes for all that is highest and best in literature and the arts. . . . Without wealth there can be no Maecenas [a rich Roman patron of the arts]." Despite his resentment toward such ostentatious living, Carnegie resided on millionaires' row for thirty years, first in a brownstone adjoining the Vanderbilt Chateau at Fifty-first Street, and later, in his four-story, sixty-four-room mansion at Ninety-first Street.

The robber barons were taking over the country, and they were not about to let bank robbers or crooked politicians like Boss Tweed interfere with their own form of thievery in railroads, oil, steel, and other lucrative businesses. Bank robbers, men like George Leslie, were being replaced by the robber barons and monopolies in the business world. And the robber barons had decided to put an end to the likes of Leslie's crowd. If there was any robbing to be done, they would do it.

Business, industry, and manufacturing were flourishing across the country. Progress had enabled the robber barons to continue growing their empires as they freely engaged in corrupt business practices, stock manipulations, and the establishment of monopolies. With new inventions, and especially new machinery to expedite agricultural procedures, it was cheaper to harvest goods. Farmers throughout the country were displaced and moved to urban areas like New York City and Chicago to find new jobs. By 1877, 2.5 million immigrants had flooded New York City.

The country now had a vast interconnecting railway system that raked in $1 billion with nearly $500 million going right into the greasy open palms of politicians.

Cornelius Vanderbilt, who had run water shipping companies, entered the railroad business and created an integrated rail carrier. He died in 1877, leaving 4,500 miles of railroad track linking New York City to most of the principal cities in the Midwest. The growth of railroads helped the economy grow. Railroads in rural parts of the country helped start new businesses, which meant more money for the rich.

Edwin I. Drake drilled the first oil well in 1859, and this business grew faster than steel, since in this pre-car era, oil was used to provide kerosene for lights. By 1870, oil was being used for a variety of new goods, including gasoline. More crude oil production and innovations in the drilling and manufacturing processes caused prices to drop. This put a premium on refining processes that required big money.

The iron and steel industry grew, with Andrew Carnegie leading the way in this profitable enterprise. Carnegie ultimately sold out his interests in the iron and steel industry to J. P. Morgan for $250 million.

In 1870, the Standard Oil Company of Cleveland was founded by John D. Rockefeller. It became the dominant oil company, using means both fair and foul to buy others out or to obtain their cooperation. By 1877, Rockefeller controlled 90 percent of the nation's oil-refining capacity, as well as oil pipelines and reserves. Rockefeller was worth over $800 million at the time of his death.

The scandals and corruption that permeated the decade reached up to the highest levels of government. During Ulysses S. Grant's presidency, the president and his cabinet were implicated in the Credit Mobilier scandal, the Gold Conspiracy, Black Friday, the Whiskey Ring, and the notorious Salary Grab. From 1869 to 1877, while Grant was president, economic and political corruption ran rampant. Many historians judge Grant's presidency as perhaps the most corrupt in American history.

At the start of 1877, the great railroad strike began as workers walked out on the Baltimore and Ohio Railroad. Railroad unions demanded better working conditions, and protested 10 percent cuts in pay. The strikes spread to other railroads and soon, all large cities from the Atlantic to the Pacific were pulled into the struggle. The strike lasted over two weeks and was finally settled by federal troops sent in by President Rutherford B. Hayes. The train strike ended in late July 1877, and soon the trains were running again between New York, Boston, and up to Maine. This was the first major strike in an industry that had propelled America's industrial revolution, and the first to be broken by the U.S. military. It was also the first nationwide strike, stretching from the Atlantic to the Pacific.

By 1877 there were as many as three million workers unemployed, more than 25 percent of the country's working population. More than 100,000 workers went on strike, and countless unemployed workers in numerous cities joined the strikers in protests against intolerable working conditions. Farmers, who hated the railroad companies and their extortionate practices, fed the strikers. More than half the freight on the nation's 75,000 miles of track stopped moving. By the end of the strike, which lasted nearly a month, more than 100 had died and 1,000 had been thrown in jail.

President Hayes's disputed election didn't help matters. Most voters in 1877 believed their new president had reached the White House through fraud. Most voters had not cast their ballots for Republican Rutherford B.

Hayes the previous year. Democrat Samuel Tilden beat Hayes, the Ohio governor, in the popular vote, but twenty disputed electoral votes from Florida and other states threw the election into House of Representatives. The electoral college granted all twenty of the disputed electoral votes to Hayes, giving him a one-vote majority, 185 to 184.

On March 5, 1877, Rutherford B. Hayes was sworn in publicly as president of the United States. Samuel Tilden, who had gained significant public exposure for his role in destroying the notorious Tweed Ring in New York City and for putting Boss Tweed behind bars, accepted the outcome. At the end of his gubernatorial term, Tilden retired from office and declined to enter the presidential race in 1880 and 1884.

—⁓—

A BOLD STROKE FOR LIBERTY

ESCAPE FROM LUDLOW STREET JAIL

William Connors, One of the Northampton Bank Robbers, Coolly Walks Out—Negligence or Complicity of Keeper McCarty—The Prisoner Supposed To Have Been Provided With Duplicate Keys—$1,000 Reward Offered For His Recapture

The Sheriff's office was the scene of unusual excitement yesterday afternoon in consequence of the escape from Ludlow-Street Jail of William Connors, supposed to have been connected with the celebrated Northampton Bank robbery. The news was received at 1:30 . . . and the District Attorney was at once informed. All available means to secure the recapture and every precaution was taken to prevent him from leaving the City . . .

On Jan. 13 last, "Jim" Dunlap and "Bob" Scott, alias "Rustling Bob," left this city . . . They were arrested in Philadelphia by the Pinkertons, and lodged in jail to await extradition to Massachusetts. The third man, "Billy" Connors, who was known in this City as a gambler and go-between for the better classes of thieves, was arrested the next day by Detectives O'Connor and Field, of the District Attorney's office at Solari's restaurant on University-place . . . When arrested some burglars' tools and a small sum of money were found in his possession . . .

"William" or "Billy" Connors, about 32 years old, 5 feet 6 inches in height, very broad shoulders, large head, wears 7 ½ hat; full, red face with a scar under the right cheek-bone, which makes a red mark; small sunken eyes of a dark blue color—looks black-eyed; shoulders broad and tapering. A good build, looks powerful; legs are very straight, walks with his feet close together, small foot, wears a neat shoe, and when walking has a swinging gate, especially swinging his left hand . . . has a thick red neck, good teeth, and thick lips set close to the teeth. The Police were notified last night that the Sheriff would pay a reward of $1,000 for the recapture of Connor.

—*The New York Times* (June, 1877)

—⟋w⟍—

The public outrage over the Northampton Bank robbery helped lead to the swift apprehension and conviction of the bank robbers, Scott, Dunlap, and Connors. The New York City police department, as well as the Pinkerton Detective Agency, had also developed more sophisticated crime-solving techniques, and the quality and abilities of the men responsible for tracking down underworld criminals were far more professional than they had ever been. The leading figure in this new crime-fighting professionalism was New York City police captain Thomas Byrnes.

When the detective bureau in New York City was first established during the 1850s, detectives were known as "shadows." In 1857, police sergeant Thomas Lefferts was appointed to the command of the detective squad, followed by Captain George W. Walling in 1858. The detective force was divided into squads, with each squad having expertise in a particular type of crime. Their duties were to make themselves systematically acquainted with the methods used by criminals in each and every criminal endeavor, from pickpockets to bank robbers. They were also assigned to infiltrate known gathering places for criminals, whether saloons or whorehouses, to gather information or to arrest known criminals of any kind.

Thomas Byrnes came to America from Ireland as a child. He was self-educated. In the early 1860s, he was appointed as a police patrolman in the Fifteenth Precinct and rapidly rose through the ranks to captain in 1870. Byrnes was widely referred to as the "personification of the police department . . ." Although he would not be appointed chief inspector of New York City Detective Bureau until 1880, Byrnes's personal wealth and his incorruptible nature made him a formidable foe to both criminals and corrupt politicians alike.

Jacob Riis, a police reporter for the *New York Tribune,* a reformer, and author of the popular *How the Other Half Lives,* one of the first photojournalistic endeavors documenting the plight of New York City's poor, called Byrnes "a czar" who "made the detective service great." Riis also described Byrnes as tough, unscrupulous, autocratic, and utterly ruthless. According to Riis, Byrnes believed criminals had no rights. He was a ferocious and imaginative interrogator and is credited with coining the phrase "the third degree" to describe his methods of unscrupulous interrogation and torture used to elicit information from underworld criminals.

Byrnes was widely admired for his intelligence and cunning. He had keen powers of observation, a subtle knowledge of psychology, especially as it related to the criminal mind, and maintained incredible self-control under many trying circumstances. Byrnes's successful exploits as a New York City police detective led to his being a featured character in several books of the period, including Julian Hawthorne's (Nathaniel Hawthorne's son's) *A Tragic Mystery* (1887) and *The Great Bank Robbery* (1887), about the Manhattan Savings Institution robbery. Hawthorne described Byrnes as:

handsome . . . large and powerful in every sense of the word. His head is well shaped, with a compact forehead, strong nose, and resolute mouth and chin, shaded with a heavy moustache . . . His eyes are his most remarkable feature . . . They have in moments of earnestness an extraordinary gaze. His voice is melodious and agreeable, but he often seems to speak between his teeth, and when aroused his utterance acquires an impressive energy.

More and more banks in New York City and elsewhere were being robbed, and most of the heists were masterminded by George Leslie. The job of catching these criminals fell under the purview of men such as

Captain Thomas Byrnes and members of the Pinkerton Detective Agency. It was no small task.

New York City was one of the most problematic cities in the world to protect against the criminal element. Criminals from all over the country, and for that matter, the world, flocked to New York City, bringing with them newer and more sophisticated means of criminal behavior. Scott and Dunlap's sojourn from Chicago to New York was a case in point. When new criminals were introduced to the New York City underworld, they were usually taken under the wing of one of the many leading criminals. In many cases, much like with Scott and Dunlap, the person they turned to first was Marm Mandelbaum. Mandelbaum (and others like her) shielded these criminals from the law, providing them with legal assistance if needed, a place to hide, a base of operations, and, in many instances, a gang of willing thugs to help them in their treacherous endeavors. Mandelbaum and her colleagues provided these services for a percentage of the ill-gotten gains.

Another of the handicaps faced by both the police and the Pinkertons when it came to the New York City underworld was the easy egress criminals had in and out of the city—by boat, train, and thoroughfare. Criminals could come and go as they pleased, which they often did, with impunity. But Thomas Byrnes and his new methods of criminal detection slowly began to put a dent in the criminal operations of Mandelbaum and others like her.

According to testimony given by Byrnes during a police commission hearing in 1880:

[T]here were 1,943 arrests made by the Detective force for the four years previous to my going to that office; they got 505 years of conviction; for the four years that I have been there, ending on the twelfth of last month, there were 3,324 persons arrested, and they got 2,488 years, two months, and three days of conviction; we have recovered nearly 600,000 dollars' worth of property.

Byrnes's personal exploits were numerous and outstanding. He broke up gangs of criminals and sent many of them to prison. He convicted the criminals who robbed Van Tine & Co. silk merchants, and tracked down and arrested Paul E. Law, son of the ex-governor of Maryland, who was trying to escape from New York City to his native state after shooting four men. But of all his cases, Byrnes took the robbery of Manhattan Savings Bank in 1878, which was in his Fifteenth Precinct, as a personal affront. He ultimately tracked down the robbers through detailed and resolute detective work.

Byrnes held bank robbers in special disregard. He identified them as mostly men of education, fine appearance, and good address—the most expert thieves of the criminal class. This was an accurate description of George Leslie.

Byrnes felt that intelligence gathering was a vital part of detective work, insisting that all of his subordinates keep detailed notes. Byrnes also initiated the practice of photographing criminals when they were arrested, establishing a rogues' gallery of photos along with criminal histories of each suspect. Up-to-date records and information of all kinds were kept under lock and key in files stored at police headquarters at 300 Mulberry Street. Byrnes envisioned that criminal statistics would not only show the efficiency of his detective work but also silence critics who found his tactics of mental and physical torture unlawful. Without a doubt, despite his shortcomings and his ruthless pursuit of criminals through his use of the "third degree" (often beating prisoners until they confessed, or using other psychological methods such as placing them in solitary confinement or in locked hot cells), Byrnes modernized the New York City detective bureau. Not all of Inspector Byrnes's methods were new, but he was better at them than most.

Byrnes was a consummate judge of human nature and relied on two maxims, the first being that there was no honor among thieves. Byrnes knew that criminals, when faced with the prospect of a long prison term, would snitch on their cohorts. "I never met a thief in my life, provided he could benefit by peaching [snitching] on his confederates, from whom [I] could not find out anything I was desirous to know. There is no such thing as honor among thieves," Byrnes said. This maxim proved true in the Northampton Bank robbery, as well as the succeeding Dexter, Maine, and Manhattan Savings Institution robberies.

Another maxim of Byrnes's was that one of the best ways to find out about the behavior and activities of known criminals was through their women. According to Byrnes, all criminals had three weaknesses: women, gambling, and drink. He was not far off, especially when it came to the women in George Leslie's case.

In the case of the Northampton Bank robbery, authorities, including Pinkerton detectives, relied on the ever-present notion that someone in the gang would be more than willing to "peach" on his confederates.

Allan Pinkerton, founder of the Pinkerton National Detective Agency, credited perseverance as being supremely important in detective work. "[The detective] must at all times be upon his guard, ever ready to take advantage of the most trifling circumstances, and yet, with an outward demeanor that dispels suspicion and invites the fullest confidence," Pinkerton wrote in his book, *Thirty Years a Detective,* published in 1884. The Pinkerton headquarters were in Chicago. Allan Pinkerton's son Robert was in charge of the New York City headquarters, and was responsible for the apprehension of Scott and Dunlap and the other members of the Rufus Gang. Still, despite the best efforts of crime fighters such as New York City police detective Thomas Byrnes and Allan, Robert, and William Pinkerton and their army of detectives, George Leslie—the king of bank robbers—managed to elude them. Thomas Byrnes was right about one important aspect of Leslie's life, and that was the fact that he had a weakness for women—definitely Leslie's greatest weakness and the cause of his downfall.

—ⱳ—

LEARY'S CAPTURE AND ESCAPE

The Noted Criminal Arrested for the Northampton Bank Robbery—He Speedily Bids His Captors Good-Bye.

It has been known to a few for several days past that the noted John, alias "Red" Leary, thief, burglar, escaped convict, and gambler, had recently been arrested for complicity in the great Northampton Bank robbery, with Robert Scott and James Dunlap, who have just been convicted of the offense . . .

Leary was taken in a hotel on the Fort Hamilton Road, near the fort, patronized by sporting men and questionable persons. He was with his wife, formerly "Red-headed Kate" Gorman, a confidence woman and shoplifter. Six detectives went there with a warrant for Leary . . . He deceived his captors by his apparent willingness to accompany them, and they permitted him to go into an adjoining room, he pretending that he desired to speak to his wife. He darted out of a door into the open air, and then ran to the rear of the house where a horse and buggy were waiting. He jumped in and drove away down the road toward Brooklyn before the officers realized his design. They started in pursuit and fired several shots after him, but he laughed at them and hallooed "Good-bye" to them as he disappeared from view.

—*The New York Times* (August, 1877)

—⁊⊕⊱—

The portrait of Molly Coath Leslie as an unsuspecting wife was false according to the former members of Leslie's gang. She maintained she didn't know anything about her husband's criminal undertakings. In reports given to newspaper reporters by Leslie's criminal associates, Molly Leslie was not as innocent and unknowing as she was always portrayed, even by Leslie himself, who always swore that his wife knew nothing about his double life. According to accounts given to *Brooklyn Daily Eagle* reporters in 1879 by Shang Draper, Billy Porter, and Johnny Irving, Molly Leslie knew about her husband's criminal activities.

Leslie's former cohorts noted that Leslie lavished his wife with anything she desired. Price was no object, and he indulged all of her whims. Molly Leslie always claimed to authorities that she had no idea of her husband's double life. Leslie's co-conspirators disputed her claim. No one knows for certain exactly what Molly Leslie did or did not know about her husband's infamous criminal career.

Three years after the infamous and bungled Northampton, Massachusetts, bank robbery, authorities rounded up Draper, Porter, Irving, Leary, and Yost, charging them with another burglary. While in jail they freely spoke to reporters about Leslie and his wife. She was, according to these men, fully aware of her husband's robberies and knew about his heists from the beginning, when they'd first met in Philadelphia. Her association with criminals, who frequented her mother's boardinghouse just as George Leslie had done years before, made her fully acquainted with criminals of all shapes and sizes. However, if Molly Leslie knew about her husband's secret life, she did not let on to anyone, including her husband.

—⚏—

Leslie's plans to rob the Manhattan Savings Institution, hailed as the most secure bank in all of New York, were put on hold following the bungled Northampton Bank heist. Although he was not able to act immediately on his ingenious plans, he continued to make preparations for the robbery. Mandelbaum let him build a replica of the bank's vault in one of her warehouses. Leslie had already begun sizing up the bank, making deposits of his own money there so he could study the layout of the place, and making friends with many of the bank's officers—all things he had done with former jobs. This robbery, however, was going to be his masterpiece.

While waiting to put his plan into action, Leslie and his usual gang made plans to rob the Dexter Savings Bank in Maine. It was supposed to be a trial run for the Manhattan heist, and should have gone like clockwork for Leslie and his gang of seasoned criminals. It turned out to be just the opposite. The consequences of this failed robbery in late February 1878 proved to be fatal, in more ways than one. It was the beginning of the end for Leslie and his nine-year reign as king of the bank robbers.

Leslie did everything that he always did when planning his bank heists. He studied the inside and outside of the Dexter Bank. He drew up blueprints of the bank and its vault. He uncovered the type of bank safe used. He built a small replica of the bank in another of Mandelbaum's warehouses. Leslie rehearsed each member of his gang on their roles and supplied them with disguises. He bought the finest burglary tools money could buy. Mandelbaum financed the whole operation at a cost of $30,000—peanuts compared to the loot Leslie expected to steal from the Dexter Bank heist. He assured Mandelbaum that based on his always accurate calculations, the Dexter Savings Bank would have close to $800,000 deposited in its vault at the time of the heist. Mandelbaum would be entitled to her usual 50 percent cut. Leslie would receive the lion's share of the remaining cash and securities, and the rest of the gang would divide up the remaining loot evenly among themselves. That was the way things always worked.

Nothing lasts forever.

11

THE MOST SENSATIONAL BANK ROBBERY
IN THE COUNTRY

We are apt to forget that we are only one of a team, that in unity there is strength and that we are strong only as long as each unit in our organization functions with precision.

—SAMUEL TILDEN (1875)

Leslie's gang made their separate ways to Dexter, Maine, in mid-February 1878. Leslie had secured the services of bank employee James Wilson Barron, someone he thought was a reliable inside man. Barron agreed to let Leslie and the others into the bank for a percentage of the take. He harbored a great deal of animosity toward the bank for reasons he did not divulge to Leslie. That wasn't Leslie's concern. All Barron had to do was let them into the bank after it closed and give them the key to the inner bank vault. Leslie would let his little joker do the rest.

Things didn't go as planned.

Johnny Irving, who had been kept sober by Billy Porter, waited in a horse-drawn sleigh along a narrow alleyway leading to the Dexter bank. It was midwinter and the roads were covered with snow, making the sleigh an ideal getaway transport. Once they had the money and securities from the bank, they would conceal them in a series of railway trunks that Porter and Draper would ship back to New York from the Dexter train station. The stolen loot would sit right under the authorities' noses.

For days, Leslie and his gang—Red Leary, Billy Porter, Johnny Irving, Shang Draper, and Gilbert Yost—stayed at various boardinghouses throughout Dexter. They never met together in public. The robbery had been rehearsed enough times so that each man knew what the other was to do. On the cold, wintry night of February 23, 1878, as they had planned, the gang rendezvoused in the alley behind the Dexter Savings Bank. All the men wore workman's coveralls and dusters. Leslie had provided each of them with theatrical disguises collected from the Opera House over the years. Red Leary was given a clown's bald, flesh-colored wig to hide his fiery hair. Draper was given a long beard and a stovepipe hat which made him look like Abe Lincoln. The others wore fake eyeglasses, wigs, mustaches, and beards.

A single knock at the side door would be the signal for Barron to open up. Leslie knocked, but no one came to open the side door. Leslie knocked again and still no one came. Leslie had taken the precaution of shielding the gang from the street using a black theatrical screen. The screen proved invaluable. It managed to prevent a passing Dexter police patrolman out on a nightly stroll from discovering them. To be sure that the police officer would not come back when they had finally entered the bank, Leslie sent Billy Porter out to the sidewalk wearing his coveralls, a fake beard and glasses, and carrying a bucket, rags, and a mop. The ploy worked just as Leslie had planned: Porter, without saying a word, waved a friendly greeting to the Dexter police officer as he made his nightly rounds. Spying what he thought to be a cleaning man for the bank, the police officer casually waved back. Porter leaned against the bank front door as though waiting for someone to let him in to clean the place. Little did the police officer suspect that the gang *had* come to clean the place—to clean it out.

After several more knocks at the side door, and with still no answer from James Barron, Leslie relied on Red Leary's brute strength to open the side door. Leary put his massive shoulder to the door and shoved it open. The men slipped inside. James Barron was waiting for them but he had no intention of helping them rob the bank. He confessed to Leslie that he had reconsidered his involvement with the heist and wanted out. Leslie told him it was too late to back out. Leslie asked Barron for the key to unlock the outer door to the safe. Barron refused. Through the darkened front window of the bank Leslie could see Billy Porter still leaning against the front door, pretending to be a night cleaning man. Leslie knew Porter couldn't stand there forever without drawing suspicion, especially if someone connected with the bank happened by.

Leslie asked Barron to at least unlock the front door and let Porter in. Again Barron refused. Red Leary had a short fuse. Leary and Draper moved toward the cashier. Leslie tried to stop them but he was no match for their combined strength. Barron put up little struggle. Leary threatened to beat the whereabouts of the outer vault keys from Barron. The entire robbery was out of control. Leslie demanded that they escape while they still could. Draper and Leary vowed they weren't leaving without the money. Draper pulled a revolver and pistol-whipped Barron. Barron fell to his knees. It was then that he confessed: It didn't matter if he gave them the key to the outer door of the bank vault; the vault was on a timer and could not be opened until the next morning. There was nothing left to do but flee, but not before Leary and Draper roughed up Barron. They bound his hands behind his back using handcuffs and stuffed a gag inside his mouth. They wedged Barron between the outer and inner doors of the bank vault. Leslie once again tried to stop them, but to no avail. They shoved the doors closed on Barron, leaving him bound, gagged, and stuffed into the small space between the two huge vault doors.

The gang was out the side door and gone in a matter of minutes, running through the snow to the waiting sleigh driven by Johnny Irving. Billy Porter slipped away from the front door of the bank and escaped with them. Vowing not to leave empty-handed, Leary and Draper stole $100 from one of the cash drawers and $500 from Barron's pocketbook.

Leslie wasn't concerned about the bungled job, or the money (or the lack of it). Leslie was more disturbed by the violence. He wasn't used to it, and upbraided his cohorts endlessly as they made their escape. It was bad enough that they hadn't been able to get into the bank, but injuring a cashier like that would only make matters worse, just as it had with the bungled Northampton Bank robbery.

Leary and Draper didn't care. As far as they were concerned, Barron had gotten what he'd deserved for going back on his word.

It was the next day, February 24, 1878, that Leslie learned from reading the newspaper that James W. Barron, the Dexter Savings Bank cashier, had been found by authorities jammed between the outer and inner doors of the vault with his hands bound behind him and a gag in his mouth. Barron died an hour after authorities discovered him. It was reported that the bank robbers had killed Barron because he wouldn't give away the combination to the safe. There were no descriptions of the bank robbers, although the newspaper account reported that the Pinkertons had been contacted to find the culprits who had killed Barron and tried to rob the Dexter Bank.

The news of Barron's death after the ill-fated heist so rattled Leslie that he sent his wife back to Philadelphia and joined her there rather than returning to New York City and their Fulton Street home. Leslie was beside himself. He had never done anything that resulted in someone's death. Leslie also realized that he had done something that might cause his own demise. He was right. He hadn't killed Barron, but now he was an accessory to murder.

After hiding out in Philadelphia for a few weeks shortly after the robbery, hoping the headlines about the Dexter Bank heist and the murder of Barron would die down, Leslie returned to New York where he set up a meeting with Irving, Draper, and Leary at a saloon in Brooklyn. With a murder charge now hanging over their heads, things had changed.

Draper was quick to brand Leslie as a potential "give-away," meaning that if anyone were to snitch to the police about what had happened at the Dexter Bank with James Barron, it would likely be Leslie. He accused Leslie of being a threat to the rest of the gang. Draper and Leslie had a violent quarrel, and Leslie accused Draper of being a threat to the whole operation. If it hadn't been for what Draper and Leary did to Barron, there wouldn't be a murder charge hanging over all their heads. This charge infuriated Draper, who lunged at Leslie. Leslie was not a violent man and never had been, but seeing Draper coming at him, he toppled the table they had been sitting at and drew a small pearl-handled pistol. Leslie was still an expert shot, and everybody in the gang knew it.

Leslie had never before carried a gun, not in all the years he'd been robbing banks, but the fiasco at the Dexter Bank made him decide he needed some form of protection, especially from his own gang. Red Leary tried to smooth things over. He said that he'd had no idea Barron would die. It wasn't what he intended. He just wanted to teach Barron a lesson, not kill him. When things had calmed down, the three men discussed who among them might run to the police in order to save their own hides. Leslie felt that the weakest link was Johnny Irving, because of his drinking. According to Leslie, Irving would most likely be the first to break the code of silence.

Draper would have nothing to do with such a notion. Johnny Irving was his brother-in-law, and Draper believed he would keep his lips tight despite his drinking. Draper had other matters he wanted to discuss. He was sick and tired of the way they had been dividing up the money, with Leslie always getting the largest share. From here on out, Draper said, everything would be split evenly. Leslie disagreed, and another quarrel ensued. Draper threatened to kill Leslie if the spoils weren't divided evenly, saying the others were with him on this. Leslie wasn't about to be intimidated.

The meeting ended with no resolution. When Shang Draper informed Johnny Irving that Leslie viewed him as "leaky," someone out to save his own skin at any price, Irving became furious. He threatened to find Leslie and kill him that day. Draper was able to calm him down, but both vowed that with the murder charge hanging over all their heads, it was a good idea to keep an eye on Leslie, just in case.

This would be harder than they thought. Leslie had one more big job to pull—the Manhattan Savings Institution—and he would do it with or without their help. Mandelbaum cautioned him that Leary and Draper were dangerous men, and although they owed their allegiance to her, she couldn't control them if they thought their own lives were in danger. She came up with an idea that she thought might soothe the hard feelings, especially about dividing the loot fairly among all the members of the gang. Mandelbaum told Leslie that instead of their previous arrangement, she would pay each of the robbers a salary based on what she thought their services were worth. In that way everyone would be satisfied; everyone except Leslie. He wasn't about to take just any measly salary from her. She was nothing without him.

It had taken Leslie nearly three years to plot the Manhattan Savings Institution heist. It would be his last bank robbery, and he predicted it would be his most profitable. If he had to, he would take his plans for the bank job elsewhere. That's exactly what Mandelbaum was afraid of. She couldn't allow that to happen—not with Leslie . . . not with anyone. Marm demanded absolute loyalty. Leslie, growing more bitter and nervous about the murder of James Barron by the day, decided he would pull off the Manhattan robbery job without any of his usual gang, and for the first time, without Mandelbaum's help. In order to do it, Leslie would have to play a treacherous game of cat and mouse with Mandelbaum and his regular gang. Leslie depended on being smarter than them all in order to pull this off.

Leslie knew he would need to be protected from the wrath of his former gang, if they found out he was planning a double-cross, and from Mandelbaum herself. He would also need someone to help finance the robbery and then fence whatever stolen securities, jewels, and other valuables he managed to steal from the Manhattan bank. Leslie knew exactly the man he could turn to: "Traveling Mike" Grady, Mandelbaum's biggest rival. He could cut Grady in for a percentage of the loot and still be left with enough money to retire a very wealthy man.

George Leslie hadn't made many mistakes throughout his criminal career, but all you need is one.

—mv—

THE LATE BANK ROBBERY AND MURDER

DEXTER, Me., Feb. 25—The funeral of J. W. Barron, the murdered Treasurer of the Dexter Savings Bank, was largely attended this afternoon. The inquest was concluded this morning, the verdict being that death was caused by violence at the hands of two or more unknown parties. A team left Dexter on Friday evening, about 6 o'clock, and was driven rapidly to Greenville, and thence on to Moorehead Lake. It contained three men. A strange team was noticed on the outskirts of the village, just before evening, driving very leisurely. The same team has been seen here under suspicious circumstances, previously. . . . The bank Treasurer leaves a wife and one child. His life was insured for $16,000. Detectives from Boston reached Dexter on Sunday morning by special engine.

—*The New York Times* (February 26, 1878)

—⁓—

The New York and Brooklyn newspapers hailed the robbery as "the most sensational in the history of bank robberies in this country."

According to bank examiners and police, the exact amount the robbers stole was $2,747,700, of which $2,500,700 was registered and nonnegotiable. The robbers also took approximately $11,000 in cash. It was an incredible amount in the nineteenth century, and would equal approximately $50 million by today's currency standards. As successful as the heist had been, it had not gone exactly as Leslie had planned; in fact, not at all as Leslie had planned.

Located at Bleecker Street and Broadway, the Manhattan Savings Institution was one of the largest and most imposing banks in the world. It was not merely a bank; it was also a depository for the safekeeping of money, jewelry, securities, and other valuables. It was patronized almost exclusively by the wealthiest citizens of New York City. It held a massive vault made of concrete, stone, and steel, protected by triple steel doors, each locked with a separate combination. It was by all accounts a ponderous labyrinth of bolts, locks, and seemingly impregnable doors.

Leslie's plan to rob the Manhattan Savings Institution began as all his plans did—with his attempt to get an inside man for the heist. The gang bribed a police officer to gain access to the lobby of the bank through the apartment of janitor Louis Werckle. Werckle, his wife, and his mother-in-law were bound, gagged, and held until the robbers had plundered the bank. They left one man behind to guard them while the others went into the vault using hammers and chisels. Within two and a half hours, they had managed to clean the place out and make a clean getaway. Werckle and his family were set free, unharmed.

The robbers used brute force to get into the bank vault. The outside steel doors were pried off their hinges and the vault was forced open, the thick door nearly smashed. While all of this caused a considerable amount of noise, it didn't attract any attention, and even if it had, it would not have mattered. The gang had bribed a local police officer, John Nugent, who was on duty in the area at the time.

Many steel deposit boxes were strewn around the opened bank vault. There were twenty-five of these boxes in the safe; fifteen were opened and ten remained intact. Some of the boxes contained money, bonds, and jewelry, and many of these valuables were taken by the robbers. In their frenzy to open the steel boxes, the gang missed an additional $2 million in cash that was lying in money sacks on the floor.

During the three years spent planning the robbery, Leslie had carefully surveyed the premises of the bank until every inch of the place was familiar to him. A replica of the bank was constructed in one of Marm Mandelbaum's vacant warehouses in Brooklyn, where Leslie rehearsed every detail with his gang, as always. The robbery of the Manhattan Savings Institution was like a massive theatrical production, with him as the producer and director. Leslie had always enjoyed the theater and was an avid theatergoer throughout his life. With laborious practice, the whole enterprise was soon down to split-second timing. All the time Leslie was rehearsing his regular gang, he was making plans to pull off the heist using another gang. He couldn't afford to let his real plans be discovered so he continued working with his original gang so as not to arouse suspicions.

According to his usual routine, Leslie had drawn a series of intricate architectural plans of both the interior and exterior of the bank and had spent months observing its workings. He had ingratiated himself with the bank's higher echelon, including the bank's president, Edward Schell, whom Leslie knew through his many social contacts in high society.

Months before he actually broke into the bank for the first time, Leslie located and bribed a vault maker; from him, he learned how to duplicate the combination lock of the bank safe. He experimented with his duplicate lock for months until he discovered a way to throw the lock's tumblers out of gear. He spent considerable time and money introducing a confederate, Pat Shevlin, into the service of the bank to serve as an inside man on the caper. Through his contacts with the bank president, Leslie was able to get Shevlin hired as a bank guard. It was Shevlin who let Leslie into the bank after hours, where Leslie worked on finding the secret to the vault's tumblers with his little joker. Shevlin's connection with the bank spanned three years, during which time Leslie broke into the bank three times in a series of futile attempts at finding out the combination to the bank's vault.

Despite all his best efforts, Leslie was unable to find the secret to the vault's combination. He tried to align the tumblers using his little joker, but even this proved futile. Through trial and error he discovered that by drilling a hole through the dial indicator, he could slip a small wire into the gears to throw the combination indicators out of gear. On his first break-in,

Leslie worked through the night but was still unable to crack the combination. Just minutes before the bank opened the next morning, Leslie puttied up the hole he had drilled in the vault dial and fled. Because he had damaged the vault dial the night before, bank officials found it impossible to open the vault the next morning. They had no idea that it had been tampered with, and thought only that the tumblers had somehow been corrupted. A new lock and combination was installed and Leslie was forced to start all over again. This made Leslie more determined than ever to discover the combination.

He broke into the bank a second time with Shevlin's help, only to be scared off when a passing police officer happened to peer into the darkened lobby. Although the officer couldn't see what was going on inside, he did spy a cleaning man who waved a feather duster in his direction and gave the officer a thumbs-up signal. It was Red Leary in disguise. The police officer left. He was satisfied that nothing was out of order at the bank and that the janitor was simply going about his nightly duties. Still, it was too close a call, so once again Leslie left without learning the vault's precious combination.

The third time was the charm. Once again Shevlin let Leslie into the bank, and once again Leslie worked furiously on manipulating the vault's combination lock. This time, he brought Gilbert Yost with him, one of the finest safecrackers in the criminal underworld. Leslie trusted Yost implicitly. This time, with Yost's help, Leslie was able to pry the dial knob off the safe and insert his most-sophisticated version of the little joker. He would not have to leave this newest and best version inside the dial, waiting for someone to use the combination the next day. He had so perfected his little joker that now, once inserted within the dial, several expert spins of the knob would reveal the right stops on the tumblers, giving him the vault combination. After inserting the joker into the dial and replacing the knob, he turned the dial once around to the right and then once around to the left. After breaking into the bank three times in early March 1878 and spending over three grueling hours in the darkened bank, Leslie finally came away with the combination—80-9-25. He gave Yost the numbers.

Yost tried the series of possible combination numbers, turning the dial expertly in a series of possibilities until at last he heard the tumblers click inside the lock. With one triumphant tug, he opened Leslie's longtime nemesis. Leslie had cracked the combination to the most sophisticated bank safe in the country. With this job, he had truly earned his title as best of the best. The Manhattan Savings Institution was his for the taking, but Leslie decided he wasn't going to plunder the bank that night. It was March 15, 1878. Leslie needed time to set into motion his double-cross. He managed to convince Yost and the other members of his regular gang that it would be best to hold off robbing the place until the spring, when he would be sure there would be more money and securities locked away in the vault. Leslie had been right all the times before, so his gang, including Shang Draper, agreed to wait. This bought Leslie time to organize another gang to rob the bank with.

—⁂—

Leslie already had a falling out with gang members Leary, Draper, and Irving over the murder of the Dexter, Maine, bank cashier, James Barron. Although Leslie kept in contact with the gang so as not to arouse any suspicions about his intended double-cross, he stayed away from them except for rehearsing the bank job in Mandelbaum's factory. As time went on, the relationship between Leslie and his old gang members worsened. Each of his gang had accused the other of being the weakest link, questioning each other's loyalty to the gang and their operations. Both Shang Draper and Johnny Irving had threatened Leslie outright, warning that they wouldn't hesitate to kill him if it was discovered that he had sold them out to the police or Pinkerton detectives.

Since the aborted Dexter bank robbery, and with his wife Molly now safe in Philadelphia, Leslie had sold off all his furniture and books at his luxurious Fulton Street home. Over late March and April of 1878 he made it a point to never stay in the same place for longer than two nights. He finally settled into a remote cottage at 861 Greene Avenue in Brooklyn, taking on the assumed name of George Herbert. Toward the end of April, before returning to Philadelphia to visit his wife, Leslie contacted Traveling Mike Grady, Mandelbaum's archrival.

What Leslie had done was unthinkable, or so his fellow criminals would have thought if they had discovered his deception. Leslie intended to rob the Manhattan Savings Institution, but not with Leary, Draper, Yost, Porter, and Irving. He needed another gang and Grady could provide him with one.

In late April 1878, Leslie had traveled to Philadelphia to be with his wife, Molly. She had grown anxious and fearful since he had been out of contact with her. He told her that he had decided to retire from the revenue service. Without revealing the real grounds for his decision, he told her that things had become too dangerous. He had made too many enemies— dangerous enemies.

Leslie now told his wife that his most recent undercover assignment as a revenue agent had led him to believe that his enemies might try to assassinate him. Molly, reportedly not knowing the true nature of her husband's dilemma, told him to go to the police or contact the Pinkertons. Leslie told her that he already had, and that the Pinkertons had assigned him a bodyguard. It was another lie, or at least a partial one. Leslie *did* have a bodyguard, but he wasn't with the Pinkertons or any other law enforcement agency. Since he'd made his secret arrangement with Traveling Mike Grady, Leslie was being guarded by one of Grady's top men—Johnny "The Mick" Walsh.

Leslie told his wife that he had one last detail to attend to in New York City, and that he would be back by the end of May. Molly pleaded with him not to go, but Leslie knew that the Manhattan Savings Institution was ripe for the picking. He left Philadelphia secure in the knowledge that with the combination, Grady's backing, and Walsh's protection, he would soon be a very rich man. He and Molly would move west and start a new life.

It was the last time Molly ever saw him.

Mandelbaum was unable to smooth things over between Leslie and the other gang members. She tried to convince them that for the good of the business, they should take back their threats and learn to get along as before. No one had leaked any information to the police, and she was sure that her protégé George Leslie would not stoop to such a thing. But nothing she said would convince Draper and Irving. Besides the tensions that arose because of their business arrangement, there was another, more personal matter that concerned Shang Draper. Draper had heard rumors of his wife's infidelity with Leslie, and although he could not prove it, he was certain that Leslie had a degree of affection for Babe, and had for some time. Just before Leslie had left New York to visit his wife in Philadelphia, Draper had found a camel-hair shawl in Babe's possession, and knowing that he had not bought the expensive gift for his wife, Draper took the shawl to the dry-goods store whose label was sewn into it. There the owner of the shop confirmed that Babe and a very handsome, well-dressed gentleman had come into the store, arm in arm. When Babe had swooned over the shawl, the gentleman had immediately bought it for her. She then smothered him in kisses. The shop owner gave Draper the best description he could of the man who had bought the shawl for his wife, and when he described the ornate pearl stickpin the gentleman was wearing, Draper knew it had been Leslie. Leslie wore that stickpin all the time. The breaking point for Draper came when he discovered that his wife had in her possession a small, double-barreled, pearl-handled pistol. Draper recognized the gun. It belonged to Leslie. Draper had more than just the matter of Barron's murder or the proceeds from the bank heists to settle with Leslie. Now he had a much more personal score to settle with him.

On one of their many secret rendezvous, Babe Draper had come to Leslie's hotel room, her face bruised. She told him that Draper had beaten her and it wasn't the first time. Leslie flew into a rage. He knew there was nothing he could do about it now, not with the Manhattan heist in the works. He couldn't risk doing anything that might jeopardize it. Since secretly hooking up with Traveling Mike Grady, Leslie had seen no need to arm himself. "The Mick" Walsh was always there to protect him. Leslie had given Babe Draper the small two-shot pistol he used to carry, telling her that if her husband ever laid a hand on her again, she should use it on him. She had tearfully agreed.

Traveling Mike Grady was the number-two fence in New York City after Mandelbaum. He was a dour man of considerable girth who was never seen without a black peddler's box slung over his shoulder. The box did not contain the assortment of paraphernalia usually associated with such boxes. Instead, Grady kept jewelry, cash, and bonds inside, all stolen. Grady used the money and other assorted financial collateral in the peddler's box to buy and sell from his criminal clientele. Grady was known throughout the underworld as a frugal, penny-pinching man. Despite being worth an estimated $4 million in stolen merchandise and property, he was content to wear tattered old clothes and burn only a single candle in his small office on Broadway and Houston Street. The area was known widely as the Thieves Exchange, where criminals and fences like Grady and other small-time operators met nightly to squabble over the exchange of a variety of stolen goods. Since Marm Mandelbaum was New York City's premier fence, clients still went directly to her. She never ventured out to the Thieves Exchange, since she felt such a practice was far beneath her exalted position. Grady, on the other hand, would go anywhere to make a deal, and with anyone. But George Leslie was not just anyone; he was the King. Thus, Grady was surprised when Leslie approached him for help.

Marm Mandelbaum knew that Grady, with conniving shrewdness, had slowly begun to chip away at her monopoly on fencing stolen property. Bringing someone as illustrious as George Leslie into his stable of criminal clients would be a crowning achievement for him.

Leslie waited until he uncovered the combination to the bank vault before he approached Grady to help him put together another gang. He knew he wouldn't have time to rehearse the new gang as he had so diligently with his old gang, so having the combination in hand only made the situation all the easier. Leslie had spent much of his criminal career leading a double life. Now he would try living a third life, betraying not only his gang but Mandelbaum as well. He had turned to Grady for both his help in robbing the bank and for his protection against the likes of Shang Draper and Johnny Irving. Grady agreed to supply Leslie with whatever he needed to rob the Manhattan bank and to split the proceeds, sixty-forty, with Leslie getting the larger share. Grady also agreed to pay Leslie's accomplices in the bank robbery out of his share. Based on Leslie's calculations of what would be inside the Manhattan Savings vault, he would become a very rich man—much richer than if he had continued his ongoing relationship with Mandelbaum.

Leslie swore Grady to secrecy and decided he would use members of Grady's gang, even if they hadn't been rehearsed. Leslie never had a chance to use Grady's hand-picked gang. Leslie had the architectural plans, and, more important, he now possessed the combination to the safe. Leslie knew he would have to continue the charade with Mandelbaum and his old gang, but not for long. Grady assured him he would take care of everything, including protecting Leslie's life.

Grady's enforcer, violent criminal Johnny "The Mick" Walsh, was deadly with both a knife and his bare hands. Walsh had his own gang of cutthroats in the Bowery but had thrown in with Grady as a way of expanding his territory. Walsh, a stocky man with an unusually large head, had been jailed a hundred times before he turned twenty-six years old. He was suspected of more than twenty killings but had never been prosecuted for any of them. Since most of the men Walsh was suspected of having killed were other known criminals, the police didn't intervene. They refused to get involved in the gang wars, preferring instead to let the various gang members wipe each other out. Johnny "The Mick" Walsh was contributing his fair share to this situation.

Leslie knew that sooner or later, either the authorities—Byrnes or the Pinkertons—or one of his cohorts—Draper or Irving—would catch up with him. If it was the police or Pinkertons, he would face charges not only for the attempted bank robbery in Dexter, Maine, but also as an accomplice to the murder of bank cashier James Barron. If it was Draper or Irving who made their move against him, then Leslie knew he faced certain death. Walsh was his insurance against his former gang members.

—w—

After Leslie returned from Philadelphia, in early May 1878 he set up housekeeping at his Greene Avenue cottage and went about his daily business. Walsh kept careful watch over him. Mandelbaum pressured him for a date for the Manhattan Savings robbery, but Leslie stalled her while he solidified plans with Grady to pull off the job. He was almost ready.

On the night of May 29, 1878, George Leslie stopped in at Murphy's Saloon in Brooklyn for a drink. He was alone, except for Walsh, his constant shadow. Someone in the saloon approached him and handed him a note. Walsh could see the man meant Leslie no harm and was simply delivering a letter. Leslie opened the envelope and quickly read the note inside. He immediately recognized the handwriting as Babe Draper's. Shang had found out about their affair and was out looking for him. Leslie had to get out of the city fast, before Shang caught up with him. Babe wanted him to take her with him. She would be waiting for him at her Halsey Street house, near Saratoga Avenue. He was to come quickly while Shang was still out. Leslie tore up the note. He asked Walsh to hail him a carriage. He told Walsh not to follow him, assuring his bodyguard that he'd be safe. He told Walsh to meet him back at the Greene Avenue place. Leslie took the carriage and told the driver to head toward Halsey Street. Walsh watched him go.

—⁂—

On June 4, 1878, George Leslie's body was discovered at the foot of Tramp's Rock, in Mott's Woods, three miles from Yonkers. His body was partly decomposed and lying under some bushes. He had been shot twice, once in the heart and once in the head. A pearl-handled, double-barreled pistol was found resting on his body. The gun was later identified as the murder weapon. It was Leslie's own gun, the one he had given Babe Draper to protect herself with. George Leslie was just forty years old.

It was Marm Mandelbaum who later identified Leslie's body. She contacted his wife in Philadelphia and subsequently defrayed the costs of his burial at Cypress Hills cemetery. Draper, Irving, Porter, Yost, Grady, Walsh, and a host of other notorious underworld figures attended the funeral. In the crowd of mourners were Pinkerton agents and New York City police detective Thomas Byrnes. Molly Leslie fainted and had to be carried from the service. There had been no form of identification found on the body. His wallet, rings, and jewelry had all been taken. The only things that authorities found in the pocket of his coat were two small crystal salt and pepper shakers.

—⁂—

The murder of George Leslie was never officially solved, although police investigators and Pinkerton detectives accepted the theory that Leslie had been killed by one or several of his criminal associates who lived in fear that Leslie would sooner or later reveal their connection to the murder of bank cashier James Barron during the attempted robbery of the Dexter Savings Bank in Maine. Based on the police investigation, it was surmised that Leslie had been killed elsewhere and his body left at Tramp's Rock to make it look like a suicide. There were no bloodstains on the body, and his clothing had been meticulously arranged. Whoever shot Leslie had killed him at another location and then transported his body by wagon, perhaps concealed under hay or straw, dumping the body at Tramp's Rock.

Detectives were able to locate a witness who remembered that a wagon drawn by a single horse was in the Tramp's Rock vicinity around the time police thought Leslie had been killed. According to the witness, who could not recall the identity or description of the driver of the wagon, or any other distinguishing details, did recall that there were wisps of straw sticking out of the bed of the wagon and that there appeared to be something covered with straw on its bed.

The authorities, piecing together what little circumstantial evidence they had gathered, believed that Leslie might have been killed not only because of his cohorts' fears that Leslie would go to the police with the names of those responsible for Barron's murder, but also because some of his associates held a grudge about the way their spoils were being divided up. Detectives uncovered evidence revealing that a few weeks before Leslie had been murdered, there had been a quarrel between Leslie and various parties at a Brooklyn saloon over the division of proceeds from various robberies. Police were able to identify the men Leslie quarreled with as Shang Draper, Johnny Irving, and Red Leary. Police brought most of them in for questioning. Through Byrnes's effective use of the third degree, authorities uncovered another potential motive for Leslie's murder—jealousy. According to one of the men brought in for questioning, Shang Draper was jealous of Leslie's attentions to his wife, Babe. Draper vehemently denied this, telling police that the notion he was jealous of Leslie was absurd. When confronted with evidence that Leslie had recently bought an expensive camel-hair shawl for his wife at a dry-goods store, and that Leslie had been seen in her company before, Draper laughed at his accusers, challenging them to prove it by getting the dry-goods store owner who purportedly sold the shawl to Leslie to testify. Draper was confident that the store proprietor wouldn't dare testify; both a bribe and the threat of harm to him and his family would keep him from talking. Shang Draper maintained that he and Leslie had always been the best of friends.

More police work on the case led authorities to believe that in all probability, Leslie was lured to his death after having received a letter in Murphy's Saloon the night of his disappearance. Based on an anonymous tip, probably provided to police by Johnny "The Mick" Walsh, who was the only one with Leslie on the night he'd disappeared, police learned that Leslie was decoyed to Brooklyn that night by what appeared to have been an amorous note from one of Leslie's many lovers. Leslie had gone off, police assumed, in the expectation of a tryst. Since questioning of the carriage driver who drove Leslie that evening revealed that Leslie had been dropped off in Brooklyn near Halsey Street, police surmised that the woman in question must have been Babe Draper.

More detective work by the police led them to conclude that Leslie was murdered either in or somewhere near Shang Draper's home on Halsey Street, and that the body was then taken and dumped at Tramp's Rock. Police were also relatively sure, based on the near-hysterical condition of Babe Draper when she was questioned, that she had been forced to write the note that had lured Leslie to his death. The case was based purely on speculation and circumstantial evidence. No one was ever charged in Leslie's murder. The King of Bank Robbers, the man responsible for robbing or masterminding the robbery of millions of dollars, was killed and buried in a $10 plot in Cypress Hill Cemetery.

—〰—

FUNERAL OF THE VICTIM—HIS WIFE PRESENT —WHAT THE POLICE SAY

The funeral of George Howard [Leslie], the burglar, who was found murdered in Mott's Woods, on Palmer-avenue, Yonkers, took place at noon yesterday from the establishment of J. J. Diehl, undertaker. . . . The publication of the fact that the funeral would take place from Diehl's drew a large crowd of curious spectators to the neighborhood. Detective King said last night that he had not succeeded in discovering the whereabouts of the woman "Lizzie," the mistress of Howard, but had obtained information which he declined to make public, but which he said would lead to her discovery within the next 24 hours, if not sooner . . . Howard's [Leslie's] wife in Philadelphia has telegraphed that she is destitute of means to pay her fare to this City.

Notwithstanding this excuse, however, and in spite of the assertion made by the undertaker Diehl, that there were no women at the funeral of Leslie, it was learned late last night, positively, that Howard's [Leslie's] widow was there . . . An elderly woman and two young women were also present. These with four young men were the only persons who were permitted to enter the undertaker's shop. The elderly woman is well known to the Police, but her name is withheld by them. She was visibly affected while looking upon the features of the dead burglar. . . . Two of the young men were professional thieves, another was a respectable man who had known Howard [Leslie] while alive, but was ignorant of his true character, and the fourth was a casual acquaintance . . . Mrs. Howard [Leslie] and her brother, and a number of others who had waited outside, followed the remains to the grave . . .

—The New York Times (June 10, 1878)

GEO L. HOWARD [LESLIE]

How the Bank Burglar is Said to Have Been Killed
A Series of Clues that Seems to Lead to the Belief that Shang Draper, Billy Porter, Johnny Irving, and Others were Implicated
An alleged history of the circumstances leading to the tragic death of George L. Howard [Leslie], the noted bank burglar, who was murdered on the night of May 29, 1878, has been given to the public. If the alleged clues are true, it would seem that Shang Draper, Billy Porter, Johnny Irving, John Dobbs, and a burglar named Perris are all implicated in his death, although it is not stated which one of them, if any, fired the fatal shot . . . The alleged facts condensed are that George Leonidas Howard [Leslie] was a well known bank burglar, a man of refinement and culture, a skillful mechanic so far as the machinery of bank locks and safe combinations are concerned, and a man who for this reason was a most useful and valuable person to men who had conspired to rob a vault or safe. It appears that his aid and advice was always secured in every one of the larger robberies that have been committed for the last ten or twelve years . . . He always essayed large jobs, and was generally successful, so that he was enabled to live with almost princely extravagance. On February 23 of last year the Dexter (Maine) Savings Bank was robbed. James W. Barron, the cashier, was found jammed between the outer and inner door of the safe, and in addition a cord had been tied around his neck so tightly that his skin was cut. The burglars are believed to have done this because he would not give away the combination. Only $100 was stolen and $500 from the pocketbook of Mr. Barron. An

hour after Barron was found in the position described, he died. From the description of those seen lurking about the bank, Detective Wiggin, of Boston, is satisfied that the murder was committed by Worcester Sam, Johnny Dobbs, Howard [Leslie], and an unknown man with black whiskers. . . . the case was prosecuted under the instructions and information given by Mrs. Howard [Leslie], who was the daughter of an aristocratic boardinghouse keeper in Philadelphia, and who for a long time did not discover her husband's business, but believed him to be an Internal Revenue detective . . .

—*Brooklyn Daily Eagle* (March 10, 1879)

—⋙—

With George Leslie dead, Shang Draper took over as the leader of the gang.

On October 27, 1878, five months after Leslie's death, Leslie's old gang broke in and robbed the Manhattan Savings Institution, getting away with nearly $3 million in cash and securities. The heist was made easier since Gilbert Yost was in possession of the vault combination that Leslie had previously uncovered. The heist that Leslie had planned for three years was pulled off without him. The gang used Pat Shevlin, the confederate that Leslie managed to have placed inside the bank, and they found a crooked police officer in John Nugent to look the other way during the robbery. The gang broke through the bank's fortress-like security. It was just as Leslie had predicted—the vault was loaded. What the gang didn't know at the time was that most of the securities they managed to steal were useless to them. The majority of the nearly $3 million they stole was in the form of registered bonds, registered in the owner's name and could not be transferred. Had Leslie still been alive and orchestrating the heist, he would have discarded the registered bonds and gone straight for the bags of cash that were lying around the vault. Without Leslie to lead them the gang was not as sophisticated when it came to the contents of the bank vault. The gang took what they could but despite the apparent magnitude of the haul, the real net worth of the robbery turned out to be about $12,000.

Early on the morning of October 28, 1878, the day after the heist, crowds of people gathered in the vicinity of the Manhattan Savings Institution on Broadway and Bleecker Street. The throng of people had come to find out if their money had been stolen, and if so, if there was a possibility of getting it back. A battalion of police officers was stationed around the bank. The doors to the bank were locked and guarded by police. Spectators jostled and shoved, trying to get a look inside the bank in hopes of seeing the vault from which the money and securities had been stolen the night before. A notice was posted on the front door of the bank:

THE MANHATTAN SAVINGS INSTITUTION WAS ON THE MORNING OF SUNDAY, OCTOBER 27, ROBBED OF SECURITIES TO THE AMOUNT OF $2,747,700, OF WHICH $2,500,700 WERE REGISTERED AND NOT NEGOTIABLE. FOR THE PURPOSE OF PREVENTING LOSS TO DEPOSITORS IT IS ORDERED THAT NO PAYMENTS WITHOUT 60 DAYS' NOTICE SHALL BE MADE, AS PROVIDED BY THE BYLAWS OF THE INSTITUTION. THE SURPLUS OF THE BANK IS MORE THAN SUFFICIENT TO COVER ANY PROBABLE LOSS THAT MAY BE SUSTAINED BY REASON OF THE ROBBERY.

The notice was signed by Edward Schell, the president of the bank and the bank's secretary. Louis Werckle, the bank's janitor who had been bound and gagged by the robbers, along with the night watchman (who also lived in the building), had been taken into custody, questioned, and released. Bank officials assured the public and police that no expense had been spared in the construction of the bank vault, and that every possible step had been taken to ensure the bank's security. The robbery was the work of an extremely sophisticated band of professionals.

According to the police, owing to the large space between the door of the bank vault and the vault itself, it was not unusual that the robbers were able to carry on their operations without being heard. The solid foundation of the walls would have prevented any sounds of their sledgehammers from being heard outside.

—m—

THE RESPONSIBILITY FOR YESTERDAY'S BANK ROBBERY

The daring robbery of the Manhattan Savings Institution, situated at the corner of Bleecker Street and Broadway, N.Y., yesterday morning, will probably be remembered as the most sensational in the history of bank robberies in this country. The sum of money represented by the securities stolen, namely $73,000 in negotiable and $2,506,700 in registered securities, together with $11,000 cash, makes this haul the largest yet recorded . . .

—Brooklyn Daily Eagle (October 28, 1878)

THE ROBBERY

The Vanished Millions of the Manhattan Savings Institution Excitement Created by the Discovery—No Trace of the Robbers Yet Found—The Watchman and the Janitor Released. Depositors Clamoring for Their Money. Belief that the Bank Will be Able to Meet all demands—The Combination of the Safe—Action of the Police—Searching Various Dens of the City. A Talk with Superintendent Campbell. What He Says about Bank Robbers. No Notification Sent to the Police of Brooklyn.
The robbery was almost the sole topic of conversation in financial circles to-day. Early this morning crowds of people assembled in the vicinity of the bank building at Broadway and Bleecker Street. In the throng were many depositors who had come there to ascertain what possibility there was of getting their money . . .

The Manhattan Savings Institution was on the morning of Sunday, October 27, robbed of securities to the amount of $2,747,700, of which $2,506,700 are registered and not negotiable . . . Werckle was at the bank to-day. He is a small, sickly looking German with weak features and a manner that denotes indecision. He told the story of the robbery substantially as it has been published. The combination of the door of the outer vault which he gave the thieves and by which they opened it was 80-9-25. The combination was changed to-day . . . Mr. Alvord, Secretary of the Bank, assured an EAGLE reporter to-day that the loss in any event would not exceed $85,000, and it would, in all probability, fall below that figure. Some inconvenience would be caused by the loss of the bonds, but they would either be speedily recovered or a new issue would be made . . . the work of the burglars, indicate their expressed opinion that the case is without its rival in the annals of the force, and that the whole sagacity and shrewdness of the force will necessarily be called into play to effect the capture of the burglars. Pinkerton detectives have received instructions to go to work on the case and they are now very busy. . .

—*Brooklyn Daily Eagle* (October 29, 1878)

—⁓—

Several thousand circulars were printed and distributed by the bank. The circular described the numbers, amounts, and other important details about the stolen bonds. The circulars were distributed to banks and security brokers across the country, warning them against buying or negotiating for any of the described stolen bonds. Police detective Byrnes worked the case day and night but was forced to admit that his search for clues had proved unsuccessful. For weeks, no arrests were made in the case. The police and Pinkerton detectives knew all the most notorious bank robbers in the city, including Draper, Porter, Irving, and others, but were unable to uncover any clues linking any of them to the robbery. George Leslie, the architect from Cincinnati, had pulled off the biggest bank heist in history, but he never lived to see it. Easy money was harder to come by than he'd thought.

MEMENTO MORI

See now how things fall out.

–JACOB A. RIIS, *HOW THE OTHER HALF LIVES* (1890)

Byrnes and police superintendent George Walling had assured the public that New York City detectives were on the right track, and that some—if not all—of the perpetrators of the bold Manhattan Savings Institution robbery would be hunted down, captured, and convicted. He and Byrnes were not far off. After months of detective work, Byrnes was finally able to break open the case. The moment came after months spent interrogating Pat Shevlin, the night watchman. Byrnes's reputation as a detective was pure and simple: He would buy you—or break you—but he would get what he was after. Byrnes used a little of both with Pat Shevlin.

Shevlin had been promised $250,000 for his involvement in the robbery. After Leslie's death, the new gang paid him merely $1,200 for all the work he had done. Unlike the others associated with the robbery, Shevlin was an amateur. Byrnes pressured Shevlin with his now-famous third-degree form of interrogation. Shevlin was isolated for several days in a small, darkened room where he endured periodic beatings at the hands of Byrnes and others. Finally, Byrnes made Shevlin a promise: He would see to it that Shevlin did only a short prison term for his part in the crime. All of this finally led Shevlin to confess.

Armed with Shevlin's confession, Byrnes quickly apprehended most of the Manhattan bank robbers and their accomplices. The only one he was not able to apprehend was Marm Mandelbaum. With Leslie dead, there was no way to connect Mandelbaum to the heist. Byrnes was able to arrest and convict Jimmy Hope, William Kelly, and Banjo Pete Emerson, all of whom had taken part in the Manhattan Saving Institution robbery. Although Leary, Draper, Irving, Porter, and Yost had all taken part in the robbery, Byrnes had no need to arrest them. They had already been apprehended on other burglary charges. Johnny Dobbs, who had also been in on the Manhattan job, managed to elude police but was later caught and sent to prison. Dobbs, who had had a lengthy criminal career, died in the alcoholic ward of Bellevue Hospital in New York City. Hope, Kelly, Emerson, and Dobbs had all been added to the gang after Leslie's murder.

The police officer that the gang had bribed, John Nugent, went to trial but was not convicted. It was reported that Nugent managed to bribe one of the jurors in his trial. Nugent was later arrested and convicted of a highway robbery and sent to the state penitentiary. Pat Shevlin was also put behind bars as an accomplice in the heist.

The original members of Leslie's gang—Leary, Draper, Irving, Porter, and Yost—were arrested by police detective Thomas Murphy and New York City police captain Thomas Dunn in December 1878 on an unrelated charge—the burglary of a feed store on Graham Avenue in Brooklyn. The safe in the feed store had been forced open and approximately $600 in cash and silver was stolen.

A city detective assigned to tail Billy Porter had seen him enter a hardware store and buy a hammer. The detective knew Porter's reputation as a burglar, and also his reported involvement in the Manhattan heist. Porter, knowing he was being followed, gave the detective the slip. But when the burglary of the grain store on Graham Avenue was reported to police, detectives found the hammer that Porter had purchased lying near the opened safe. It was easy enough to trace the hammer back to Porter.

The gang had been under surveillance for weeks since moving into Porter and Irving's house on Patchen Avenue. Police surrounded and raided the house after discovering that Porter lived there, arriving in the early morning of December 19, 1878, and capturing Billy Porter and Johnny Irving, who were both inside. Police also found Shang Draper hiding in an outhouse behind the raided home. Gilbert Yost, who had been out for an early-morning constitutional, wandered into the middle of the raid and was immediately arrested. Porter and Irving were both neatly dressed and had the appearance of gentlemen. Draper was literally caught with his pants down, still wearing his nightshirt; he was identified as one of the Northampton, Massachusetts, bank robbers. Immediate plans for his extradition to Massachusetts to stand trial began shortly following his arrest at the Patchen Avenue home. Draper, along with Red Leary, was finally handed over to Massachusetts authorities to stand trial in connection with the Northampton bank robbery.

Red Leary, who was apprehended in late 1879 for his involvement in the Northampton heist, escaped from the Ludlow Street Jail with the help of his wife Kate, who, with help from cohorts, tunneled through the wall of the jailhouse and freed her husband. Leary managed to elude police for nearly two years before finally being recaptured by Robert Pinkerton, director of the New York City arm of the Pinkerton Detective Agency and the son of the agency's founder. Robert Pinkerton had been on Leary's trail in connection with the Northampton bank robbery and his subsequent escape from the Ludlow Street Jail since the Northampton robbery in 1876.

Leary was finally captured in February of 1881 at Fort Hamilton while driving a sleigh on his way to see his wife at their Coney Island hotel, The Red Light. Leary was sent to Massachusetts to stand trial in connection with the Northampton Bank robbery, along with Shang Draper. Both men were subsequently acquitted because of lack of evidence.

Billy Porter and Johnny Irving, both rounded up during the 1878 raid on their Patchen Avenue house following the robbery of the Graham Avenue grain store, were sent to the Raymond Street Jail to be held for trial. Porter was tried first, but the jury failed to agree on a verdict. At his second trial Porter was convicted and sentenced to five years in prison. Johnny Irving was also convicted and sentenced to five years. Both men were never officially charged in the Manhattan Savings Institution robbery.

While Porter and Irving were waiting to go to prison, they escaped. Porter was recaptured almost immediately and served his full sentence. He was released from prison in 1883, and was not associated with any crimes following his release.

Irving managed to elude police for nearly a year. He was finally arrested in Philadelphia during a failed robbery attempt and sentenced to four years in prison. After he completed his sentence, he was returned to New York to face his sentence there, but was discharged by the courts on time served and good behavior.

Gilbert Yost, who was being held at the Raymond Street Jail along with Porter, Irving, Draper, and Leary, saw his fellow prisoners depart from the miserable jail quarters. It wasn't until he saw his good friend and confidant, Shang Draper, finally sent to Massachusetts to stand trial that Yost began to break down. He became despondent, going whole days without speaking or eating. Authorities were afraid Yost might attempt suicide, so a jailer was placed in his cell day and night. After attacking a guard, Yost was placed in solitary confinement with a guard posted outside his cell. Ranting and raving, Yost was ultimately declared insane and sent to an asylum in Auburn, New York. He was finally discharged from the asylum after a period of five years. He later committed a burglary out west and was sent to prison, where he spent his final days.

After Shang Draper was acquitted of the charges against him in Massachusetts, he renounced his former criminal life and vowed to leave it behind. He resumed his duties as the owner and proprietor of his saloon on Sixth Avenue. Draper continued to operate his saloon until 1883, and later operated a successful sporting goods business.

By the end of 1879, the Manhattan Savings Institution case was closed. George Leslie was dead. Gilbert Yost was in an insane asylum. Red Leary and Shang Draper were acquitted of charges associated with their involvement in the Northampton Bank robbery and never charged in the Manhattan Savings Institution heist. Billy Porter and Johnny Irving both served prison sentences on other charges. Johnny Dobbs, Jimmy Hope, Banjo Pete Emerson, Patrick Shevlin, and William Kelly were apprehended, successfully prosecuted, and sent to prison for their involvement in the Manhattan heist.

The Manhattan Savings Institution was robbed of an estimated $3.5 million in cash and securities. Most of the securities stolen in the heist were nonnegotiable and police recovered most of the bonds and cash from the burglars. According to a *New York Times* report in October 1879, "The other securities stolen by the burglars have value now only as waste paper."

—w—

A NIGHT-WATCHMAN'S TALE

HOW THE MANHATTAN BANK WAS ROBBED

PATRICK SHEVLIN, ONE OF THE WATCHMEN, CONFESSING HIS GUILT—ARREST OF THREE MORE SUSPECTED PERSONS—A CURIOUS YARN OF BURGLARIES PLANNED FORMERLY

The mystery that has for so many months surrounded the Manhattan Bank burglary is at last to be cleared up, as one of the robbers has made a full confession. This thief is no other than the bank's night watchman, Patrick Shevlin. He is at present under lock and key, and his confession not only will convict himself, but it is thought will also cause the conviction of William Kelly, whose arrest is brought about, and that of "Johnny" Dobbs and "Jimmy" Hope, who have been for some time under arrest for the crime. Shevlin's story was forced from him . . .

—*The New York Times* (June, 1879)

BANK BURGLARS CAPTURED—TWO OF THE MANHATTAN BANK ROBBERS ARRESTED IN PHILADELPHIA

Peter Ellis, alias Luthey, alias "Long Pete," alias "Banjo Pete," and Abraham Coakley, alias John Hennessey, both of whom are charged with complicity in the Manhattan Savings Bank robbery, were arrested Wednesday evening in Philadelphia by Inspector Byrnes, Sergt. Meakim, and Detective Reilly, of this City, assisted by a Philadelphia officer, after a desperate struggle . . . It is said that at the moment Coakley and Luthey were arrested they were within a few hundred feet of where Samuel Perris, alias "Worcester Sam," and Jimmy Hope were waiting to meet the prisoners, and that Perris and Hope escaped

... They associated with such cracksmen as George Leonidas Leslie, alias George Howard, who, in the Spring of 1878, was murdered by comrades, who hid his body at Tramp's Rock, near Yonkers ...

Coakley and Hope were arrested and lay in jail awaiting funds which were to be advanced by one Grady, in New York. Grady could not or would not give sufficient money, and it is said that to release them, Dobbs, Perris, George Howard [Leslie], and Tom Draper, planned a coup on the Dexter (Me.) Savings Bank, and that in executing it the Cashier, James W. Barron, was killed on Feb. 22, 1878. One of the theories in regard to the murder of Howard [Leslie] was that he had no hand in the murder, but that, unnerved by it, he told more than he should have done, and was made away with ... Hope and Coakley, after some delay, secured their liberty ...

—The New York Times (April 30, 1880)

THE GREAT BANK ROBBERY

FORTUNES OF THE MEN WHO TOOK PART IN THE CRIME

Capt. Byrnes Goes to Philadelphia—Career of Cannon, the Recently Arrested Agent of Jimmy Hope
The Case Soon to Be Closed—Story of the Robbery with Hitherto Suppressed Facts

... As it is officially admitted that this great case will soon be closed, and as hitherto suppressed facts in relation to it have just come to light, a review of the circumstances under which the crime was planned and committed, and of the admirable detective work done by Capt. Byrnes and his assistants, will be interesting ... Many inaccurate statements have appeared about the recovery of the United States coupon bonds stolen from the bank ...

—The New York Times (October 6, 1879)

—⚍—

The late 1800s and early 1900s ushered in an era of reform for the Gilded Age. The loosely aligned gangs of criminals like the ones operated by the likes of George Leslie and Marm Mandelbaum slowly disappeared. Many of those involved were either sent to prison or died violent deaths. Another more sophisticated and organized criminal element emerged from the ashes of these early criminal gangs—the mafia.

It was also during this period that many writers turned their attention toward corruption, social reform, and exploitation by big business. These "muckrakers," a term coined by Theodore Roosevelt referring to the writers' ability to uncover "dirt," helped make significant and lasting changes to the social landscape of the Gilded Age.

Jacob Riis exposed life in New York City's tenement slums in his book, *How the Other Half Lives*, published in 1890. Henry Demarest Lloyd published *Wealth against Commonwealth* in 1894, attacking the business practices of the Standard Oil Company. Ida Tarbell also exposed the Standard Oil monopoly in a series of articles in *McClure's Magazine* in 1902. Lincoln Steffens's *The Shame of the Cities* (1904) exposed the plight of the inner-city poor. Big business, crime, and municipal corruption were all under attack, and no one could escape from it.

—m—

George Leslie was murdered in May 1878, nearly six months *before* the famous Manhattan Savings Institution heist ever happened. Many legitimate resources, including *The Encyclopedia of Crime,* incorrectly indicate that Leslie died in 1884. This erroneous information has been perpetuated in other research documents. According to published reports,

> . . . George Leonidas Leslie, alias "Howard," alias "Western George," was killed in Brooklyn in May 1878, and his body was discovered at Tramp's Rock near Yonkers on June 4 of that year. He had been treacherously shot in the back of the head. Leslie was a burglar, but he had become infatuated with a woman, and the gang to which he belonged thought he was telling too many secrets and he was made away with. Porter and Irving were suspected of this crime, but the police could not fasten it upon them and they were never tried for it.

> —*The New York Times* (October, 1883)

—〰—

Johnny Irving was killed in 1883 during a shootout at Shang Draper's saloon on Sixth Avenue. Johnny "The Mick" Walsh was drinking at Draper's saloon when Irving and Billy Porter showed up. Walsh had some old scores to settle with Irving, going back to the incident involving Black Lena, as well as Irving's involvement in the murder of George Leslie. Walsh had been assigned by Traveling Mike Grady as a bodyguard for Leslie. It was Irving or Draper who were suspected of luring Leslie to his death. Walsh confronted the drunken Irving. A fight ensued. Walsh drew a revolver and shot Irving dead. Reportedly, Billy Porter then shot and killed Johnny "The Mick" Walsh. Although Porter was taken in for questioning, he was never prosecuted for the murder of Walsh. The police reported that Irving and Walsh killed each other at the same time. Porter disappeared after the incident. Shang Draper was never implicated in either of their murders.

AN EARLY MORNING TRAGEDY IN "SHANG" DRAPER'S BAR-ROOM

JOHN IRVING'S PURSUIT OF JOHN WALSH RESULTING IN THE MURDER OF BOTH—A SINGULAR STORY OF CRIME

Four criminals stood in a group in front of the bar in Tom, alias "Shang" Draper's saloon at No. 466 Sixth Avenue a few minutes before 2 o'clock yesterday morning. After gulping down some liquor they began to converse. Just then the side door leading to the saloon from the adjoining entry was suddenly opened and a man rushed in holding a revolver in his right hand. Without saying a word to anybody he began firing at John Walsh, professionally known as "Johnny the Mick," who was one of the group of drinkers. Walsh's companions, who recognized the intruder as "Johnny" Irving, a well-known thief, became panic stricken at the first report of the pistol and made for the door to escape from the place. Walsh backed along the counter toward the rear of the room with his right hand in his overcoat pocket, where he carried his pistol, and Irving followed him closely, pointing his revolver at him.

There are no living witnesses of what followed. The reports of pistols fired in rapid succession were almost immediately heard, and when a number of men, attracted by the noise, rushed into the place they found Walsh and Irving lying dead on the floor of the billiard-room, which is just behind the bar-room of the saloon . . . A man was running diagonally across the avenue toward Twenty-eighth Street and toward him Leary pointed, shouting; "Arrest that man—he's one of 'em." The detective ran ahead and overtook the fugitive in the middle of the roadway. The man made no resistance. Hickey thrust his hand into the man's overcoat and from the pocket on the right hand side drew a revolver. Then he led him along into the bar-room, where the prisoner was recognized as Billy Porter, a bosom friend of Irving . . . Coroner Martin discharged Draper and "Red" Leary, because it was proved that they were not in the saloon when the shooting occurred . . . Porter was turned over to the custody of Capt. Williams . . . Both the men killed in the shooting were notorious thieves and their death was the result of a feud of long standing between them. Irving and Porter were members of the same gang and Walsh was supposed by them to have divulged their secrets to the police. . . .

—*The New York Times* (October 17, 1883)

—⋙—

Shang Draper later gave up his life of crime and established a sporting goods store where he managed to live a legitimate existence. His store later failed and due to extensive gambling debts, Draper died destitute in 1907.

"SHANG" DRAPER DYING

Noted Crook and Gambler Said to Have Little Money

MEMPHIS, Tenn., July 21—"Shang" Draper, a leading light of New York's underworld for a generation, is dying at Mountain Valley, a health resort near Hot Springs, Ark., where he has been treated for enough diseases to have killed three ordinary men.

Draper is best remembered through his connection with the big Northampton and Manhattan Bank robberies made by "Red" Leary, "Jimmy" Hope, "Johnny" Irving and other notorious crooks. He had a gambling place on West Twenty-eighth Street, New York, where he made a fortune, which he afterward dissipated largely in helping broken gamblers and crooks in trouble. Now it is doubtful whether Draper has enough money to pay for a decent funeral.

—*The New York Times* (July, 1907)

—⚍—

Babe (Irving) Draper sought out the help of Traveling Mike Grady after her husband's arrest and subsequent extradition to Massachusetts to stand trial for his involvement in the Northampton Bank robbery. Grady supplied her with money and a train ticket to Cleveland, Ohio, where she had family. She never made it out of New York City. Her body was found floating in Silver Lake three months after her husband's arrest. She had been strangled.

—⚍—

Traveling Mike Grady was ultimately able to put Marm Mandelbaum out of business by offering higher prices for stolen goods than she could. He became the head of the most dominant fencing operation in New York City. Grady died in 1880 of cardiac congestion following a bout with pneumonia.

—⚍—

Red Leary died in a New York City Hospital in 1888 after being hit on the head with a brick by William Train, a criminal associate, during an argument. Leary died of a fractured skull.

—⚍—

Kate Leary, one of the city's most gifted shoplifters and pickpockets, died in 1896 from alcoholism. She was fifty years old. After her husband's death she sold off their Coney Island hotel and saloon, The Red Light. Although she lived at the hotel, she had become infirm during her last few years, the effects of alcohol having taken their toll.

—⁂—

James W. Barron, the cashier murdered during the bungled Dexter, Maine, bank heist, was accused after his death of systematically embezzling money from the Dexter bank by altering figures in his books. According to published reports, the embezzlement was prompted by his addiction to morphine. Barron reportedly was a drug addict who had been stealing money to pay for his habit. After the bungled heist, police and bank investigators discovered that they were unable to account for nearly $4,000 in Barron's ledger. It was also surmised by investigators that Barron had decided to kill himself rather than face arrest. According to detectives, Barron was concerned that his wife would not receive his life insurance if he committed suicide, so he made his death appear to be murder at the hands of the bank robbers. None of this was ever proven to be true.

BARRON'S CASE

**The Pros and Cons of the Murder and the Suicide Theories
Why and How the Cashier May Have Killed Himself so as to
Create the Belief that He had Been Cut off by Robbers**

BOSTON, February 8—The startling developments in relation to the Dexter Savings Bank at Dexter, Maine, which have been made public from time to time within a week, have been more or less warmly discussed in every household in this city . . . On the evening of February 22nd, 1878, nearly one year ago, James Wilson Barron was found, insensible, with a rope over his shoulder, handcuffed, and a gag in his mouth, lying on the floor between the outer and inner doors of the money vault of the Dexter Savings Bank, of which institution he was at the time cashier. He expired the next morning at 5:45, never having returned to consciousness, and the general belief of the citizens of the town was that burglars had entered the bank to rob it, and that Barron, by refusing to divulge the secret of the combination of the safe lock, had been murdered by the criminals . . .

[D]etectives of this city were next put to work on the case, and the first thing that astonished them was that the burglars left no tools behind them. Then they found that the money was not taken from the cash drawer in the counter; that Barron's pocketbook had not been stolen; that his clothes were not torn; that the dust of the floor of the rear room gave no appearance of a scuffle; that no tracks were seen in the snow under the open window; that the gag used . . . would not have prevented Barron from making out cries; and further, that it was not such a gag as burglars use . . . They were quick to perceive that there was no combination to give away, for the inner safe had a time lock . . . So the delusion that he died in trying to protect the inner safe was at once dispelled . . .

On interviewing the medical men the detectives learned that there was air space in the vault sufficient to support respiration [for] twenty-four hours, and that Barron had but slight wounds, not sufficient [in and] of themselves to cause death, and that he had died having all the symptoms of opium poisoning . . . He also held insurance on his life to the amount of $13,000 . . . He had strong motive to make the suicide appear like murder, for if the former were suspected, it would be difficult for his widow to collect the insurance . . .

—Brooklyn Daily Eagle (February 10, 1879)

DAY OF THE BARRON MURDER

The Prosecution Opens the Great Trial—Damaging Testimony against the Two Accused Men—Buying Crackers and Cheese
DEXTER, Me., October 22—County Attorney F. H. Appleton opened the Barron murder case for the prosecution this morning. He spoke about the Stain gang in Medfield and said the Government would prove the allegations . . . Elmer A. Brewster, of Dexter, testified that he noticed the two prisoners in the court one week ago to-day. He had

seen them before. On the day Barron was murdered, a few minutes after noon, a man came in the witness's store and bought crackers and cheese. He did not stop to have the paper around them . . .

—*Brooklyn Daily Eagle* (October 23, 1887)

—⟋⟍—

Jay Gould gained control of the Union Pacific Railroad in 1883. By then he was in control of more than 10,000 miles of railway throughout the country. He acquired controlling interest in the Western Union Telegraph Company, and by the time he died in 1892, he had amassed a fortune totaling approximately $72 million. He left his entire fortune to his family.

—⟋⟍—

Josie Mansfield died at the age of seventy-eight in 1931 from complications suffered from a fall in a Paris department store. Following the murder of Jubilee Jim Fisk, Mansfield moved to Europe, finally settling in Paris, France, where she married a wealthy New York City lawyer, Robert Livingston Reade, in 1891. In 1897 Reade was declared insane from excessive drink and use of chloral hydrate. Mansfield inherited his fortune and lived out the rest of her life in substantial comfort.

—⟋⟍—

Edward S. Stokes died in November 1901 at the home of his sister, Mrs. Mary McNutt, 73 St. Nicholas Avenue in New York City. He was sixty years old. After selling his interest in the Hoffman House in 1897, Stokes retired from any active business enterprises. He suffered from a series of debilitating diseases at the end of his life, including Bright's disease.

EDWARD S. STOKES DEAD

Long Period of Unconsciousness Unbroken to the End

HE HAD BEEN ILL FOR YEARS

The Dead Man's Career Was Filled with Storm and Trouble— His Connection With James Fisk Jr., Whom He Killed

. . . His old nonchalance had left him forever when he was released. His manner was often described as that of a haunted man. He feared assassination and sometimes said he would "die in his boots."

—The New York Times (November 3, 1901)

—〰—

Ulysses S. Grant died in 1885. Although his presidency was marred by endless scandals—which made many of those in his administration rich—Grant himself left office virtually penniless. After his presidency, he became a partner in a financial firm that later went bankrupt. Diagnosed with throat cancer, he began writing his memoirs in hopes of raising enough money to pay off his debts and to provide for his family after his death. Grant's *Personal Memoirs* was completed shortly before his death and published by Charles L. Webster and Company, the publishing company started by author and humorist Mark Twain. The book by Grant ultimately earned nearly $400,000 ($8 million by today's standards), and is considered by many literary historians the best book ever written by an American president.

—〰—

Samuel Tilden, the man who helped put the infamous Boss Tweed behind bars, governor of New York, and the Democratic presidential candidate who lost the disputed 1876 election, died on August 4, 1886. He left most of his large book collection and much of his $6 million estate to help establish the New York Public Library. Forty years after his death a commemorative statue was erected in his honor. It now stands along Riverside Drive. Ironically, the inscription on the statue's pedestal is I TRUST THE PEOPLE.

—∞—

Thomas Byrnes successfully apprehended the robbers of the Manhattan Savings Institution. He became famous for introducing the criminal interrogation process known as "the third degree" into the lexicon of criminal justice. He created a criminal identification system for the New York City detective bureau and was appointed chief inspector in 1888, making him the second-highest-ranking police officer in the city. Despite all his accolades, even Byrnes fell under the microscope of reformists—most notably Theodore Roosevelt. In 1895, Byrnes, who was at the peak of his powers, appeared before the Lenox Committee, made up of four police commissioners, including Commissioner Roosevelt. The Committee was probing police corruption in the city. Byrnes was publicly humiliated by Roosevelt after admitting that he had accumulated nearly $400,000 in cash and property on his $5,000 a year salary. Before the committee could act to remove Byrnes, he resigned. Byrnes claimed that his weakness as a police officer was due to being ensnared in a tainted system of crime and vice. He opened his own detective agency that catered to financial institutions. He died in 1910.

—∞—

Fredericka "Marm" Mandelbaum, the most notorious receiver of stolen goods in the country, could not escape from the significant reforms that swept through the Gilded Age. In 1884, New York County district attorney Peter Olney, a man of unwavering honesty, knew that Mandelbaum's bribes to both Tammany Hall politicians and police had kept her immune from prosecution. He turned to Pinkerton detectives to help him apprehend the elusive Mandelbaum. After several months of undercover work, one of the Pinkerton detectives, posing as a thief, gained her confidence. Working for Mandelbaum, the undercover detective stole a supply of silk and attached identifying marks to it so that it could be traced. It was—straight back to her. In July 1884 police raided one of Mandelbaum's warehouses where the marked bolts of silk were being kept and arrested both Mandelbaum and her son Julius at home. It was the first and only night in her entire criminal career that she spent in jail.

Although she had always been confident that her many political connections and bribes of judges and police officers would keep her in good stead, it was relayed to Mandelbaum, through her attorneys, that nothing could be done to protect her anymore. Reformers were keeping a watchful eye on every level of government, especially the police and judicial system. She was informed that her days were numbered. Just before her case was scheduled to go to trial in December 1884, Mandelbaum gathered together close to $1 million in cash and fled to Canada.

Mandelbaum had been released on $15,000 bail and remained in her home on Rivington Street. Although she was being watched closely by Pinkerton detectives after making bail, she still managed to elude them by having one of her servants, who was the same height and size, dress up in her clothes and bonnet, with her face covered by a veil. She sent the decoy out of the house on an extended errand in the city. The Pinkerton detectives followed the decoy, thinking it was Mandelbaum.

According to newspaper accounts, the servant led the Pinkertons on "a wild goose chase." Once the coast was clear, Mandelbaum, her son Julius, and her clerk and bodyguard, Herman Stroude, boarded a waiting carriage and made their getaway, racing to the New Rochelle train station and safely boarding the train. Mandelbaum and the others exited the train at Chatham Four Corners in New York, and from there took another carriage over the border into Canada. No one stopped her, and the Pinkerton detectives were left far behind, scratching their heads. All efforts to extradite her failed. She secretly reentered the country only once after her flight to the safety of Canada, when her daughter died in 1881. Mandelbaum crossed the border to attend the funeral and then slipped safely back over the border.

Although Pinkerton detectives eventually located her, living in luxury in Toronto, under the extradition laws between the United States and Canada at that time, she could not be forced to return. She lived out her remaining days in Canada.

Fredericka "Marm" Mandelbaum died in February 1894 at the age of seventy-six. Her body was returned to New York City for burial. A huge crowd of mourners turned out for her funeral. Several mourners reported to police that their pockets had been picked during the graveside service.

"MARM" MANDELBAUM ARRESTED

CAUGHT IN A HOTEL IN HAMLITON, CANADA, BY LOCAL POLICE

TOTONTO, Dec. 8—For some days past the detectives here have been endeavoring to locate Mme. Mandelbaum, her son Julius, and Herman Stroude, her confidential clerk. It had been ascertained that the party came to Toronto about a week ago and registered at the Rossin House, one of the leading hotels. . . . They took furnished rooms on Simcoe Street, an aristocratic quarter of the city, and lived quietly, taking their meals at one of the city restaurants. Their presence in Toronto having been published in all the papers, with a full description of her appearance, Mme. Mandelbaum remained very closely in her apartments, completely changing her style of costume and carefully disguising herself . . . This morning Chief Stewart and Detective Castell surprised Mrs. Mandelbaum and her son in the ladies' parlor by saluting them by their proper names. . . . When shown their pictures, the fugitives acknowledged their identity, and offered to pay for their release. They will be arraigned before the police magistrate upon a charge of bringing stolen property into Canada.

—The New York Times (December 9, 1884)

MANDELBAUM WANTS THE JEWELRY

HAMILTON, Ontario, Dec. 24—Mother Mandelbaum still remains here waiting the decision of the customs authorities, who seized her jewelry and diamonds for non-payment of duty. Lawyer Steele has the case in hand and has gone to Ottawa to lay the papers before the Commissioner. He feels confident that the property will be returned to the Madame. The Chief of Police has had circulars printed containing a list and description of the jewelry and has mailed copies to the Police Departments of all the principal cities in the United States and Canada. This may possibly lead to the identification of the goods, if they were stolen.

—*The New York Times* (December 25, 1884)

MRS. MANDELBAUM'S VISIT

HER FAVORITE DAUGHTER'S DEATH BRINGS HER HERE

Visiting the Body at Night with Her Son Julius—Tired of Canada, But on Her Way Back There

"Mother" Mandelbaum, the noted receiver of stolen goods, and her son Julius, over whom indictments are hanging, have been in this city for the past two days, and they left for Canada yesterday afternoon, without having been detected by police. The cause that led the mother and son to risk their liberty was the death of Annie, the 18-year-old daughter of the "fence." Annie was in Hamilton, Ontario, with her mother, brother, and youngest sister, Lulu. She left there a few weeks ago to pay a visit to some friends in this city, and while here she contracted a severe cold which finally developed into pleuro-pneumonia . . . Last week the girl's case assumed a serious aspect and she died on Sunday evening. Word was at once sent to the mother. As soon as Mrs. Mandelbaum received word of the death of her daughter she started in company with Julius to Buffalo . . .

. . . She claimed that she was a persecuted woman, but said before long she would have matters righted.

"Will you ever return to New York for good?" asked one of her friends.

"I don't know," she answered. "I've often thought of coming back, delivering myself up, and standing trial. I am sorry that I ever left New-York. I should have faced the music."

"Have any overtures ever been made to you by police officials?"

"That's a question I don't like to answer," she responded. "But I will say that if I spent $10,000 I could come back to New York and be a free woman."

"How did this strike you?" was the next query put to the woman.

"It didn't strike me at all. I'm sick and tired of putting up money to square things, and I don't intend to do it anymore. The more money you produce the more they want. If I hadn't been so free with my money I wouldn't have got in this scrape."

"How do you like Canada?"

"The name of the place is enough to sicken me. I'm tired of it. I long to get back to New-York, and don't be surprised to see me come back someday to stand trial."

At this point Julius notified his mother that the carriage was in readiness, and the two started at once for the train.

—*The New York Times* (November 12, 1885)

OLD "MOTHER" MANDELBAUM IS DEAD

She Was a Famous "Fence" Well Known to
the Police of This City

HAMILTON, Ontario, Feb. 26—Mrs. Fredericka Mandelbaum, known in New York City as a notorious "fence" and who did a profitable business there in that line for a number of years, died here this morning. She came here about ten years ago when the New York authorities began proceedings against her and her convictions seemed probable. A legal fight ensued for her extradition, but with the assistance of Howe & Hummel, the criminal lawyers of New York, she was enabled to remain in Canada . . . Her body will be taken to New York tomorrow afternoon for interment there Wednesday morning . . .

For nearly a quarter of a century she prospered. Her success was in a great measure due to her friendship for and her loyalty to the thieves with whom she did business. She never betrayed her clients, and when they got into trouble she procured bail for them and befriended them to the extent of her power . . .

It is said that professional jealousy of her success as a receiver of stolen goods, and a quarrel with a clique of detectives who had long been her friends, led to her downfall. Pinkerton detectives were employed to secure her arrest. A trap was laid for her, and the shrewd woman was caught. This happened in July, 1884, when several pieces of black silk, which had been marked, were taken by a "stool pigeon" from a Broadway dry-goods store and sold to Mrs. Mandelbaum.

—*The New York Times* (February 27, 1894)

—ɷ—

New York City has remained resilient. Despite the crime, corruption, and political and financial tribulations, the city has survived in all its glory.

On September 11, 2001, New York City was attacked by terrorists. One of its most prominent symbols of financial power, the Twin Towers, was destroyed. Nearly 3,000 people were killed.

In March 2008, New York governor Eliot Spitzer was forced to resign amid accusations that linked him to money laundering and a prostitution ring. *The New York Times* criticized Spitzer for remaining in seclusion in his Fifth Avenue apartment.

According to the AFL-CIO's Executive PayWatch, "[T]he *average* CEO made 42 times the average blue-collar worker's pay in 1980, 85 times in 1990, and a staggering 531 times in 2000."

Some things never change.

Bibliography

Books

Adams, Charles F., Jr., and Henry Adams. *Chapters of Erie and Other Essays*. Boston: James R. Osgood & Co., 1871.

Albion, R. G. *Rise of New York Port, 1815–1860*. New York: Charles Scribner's Sons, 1939.

Alexander, De Alva Stanwood. *A Political History of the State of New York* (3 vols.). New York: Henry Holt and Company, 1909.

Allen, Frederick Lewis. *The Vanderbilt Legend.* New York: Harcourt, Brace and Company, 1941.

Anonymous. *James Fisk, Jr. The Life of a Green Mountain Boy.* Philadelphia, 1872.

Anonymous. *The Life and Assassination of James Fisk, Jr.* Philadelphia,1872.

Asbury, Herbert. *The Gangs of New York.* New York, 1927.

Atkins, Gordon. *Health, Housing and Poverty in New York City, 1865–1898.* Ann Arbor, Michigan: Edwards Brothers, 1947.

Balsan, Consuelo Vanderbilt. *The Glitter and the Gold.* New York: Harper, 1952.

Barnes, David. *The Draft Riots in New York.* New York: Baker & Godwin, 1863.

Beebe, Lucius Morris. *The Big Spenders.* Garden City, New York: Doubleday, 1966.

Bigelow, John, ed. *Letters and Literary Memorials of Samuel J. Tilden.* New York: Harper & Brothers, 1908.

———. *The Writings and Speeches of Samuel J. Tilden* (2 vols.). New York: Harper & Brothers, 1885.

Blake, E. Vale. *History of the Tammany Society.* New York: Souvenir Publishing, 1901.

Bowen, Croswell. *The Elegant Oakey.* New York: Oxford University Press, 1956.

Browne, Julius Henri. *The Great Metropolis: A Mirror of New York. A Complete History of Metropolitan Life and Society, with Sketches of Prominent Places, Persons and Things in the City as they Actually Exist.* Hartford, Connecticut: American Publishing Company, 1869.

Burnham, Alan, ed. *New York Landmarks.* Middletown, Connecticut: Wesleyan University Press, 1963.

Burrows, G. Edwin and Mike Wallace. *Gotham: A History of New York City to 1898.* New York: Oxford University Press, 1999.

Caldwell, L. K. *The Government and Administration of New York.* New York, 1954.

Churchill, Allen. *The Improper Bohemians.* New York: Dutton, 1959.

———. *The Upper Crust.* Englewood Cliffs, New Jersey: Prentice-Hall, 1970.

Clinton, H. L. *Celebrated Trials.* New York: Harper & Brothers, 1897.

Coleman, Charles H. *The Election of 1868: The Democratic Effort to Regain Control.* New York, 1933.

Costello, Augustine E. *Our Police Protectors: History of the New York Police from the Earliest Period to the Present Time.* New York: A. Costello, 1885.

De Leeuw, Rudolph M., compiler. *Both Sides of Broadway, from Bowling Green to Central Park.* New York: De Leeuw Riehl Publishing, 1910.

Dickens, Charles. *American Notes for General Circulation.* London: Chapman and Hall, 1842.

Eliot, Elizabeth. *Heiresses and Coronets.* New York: McDowell, Obolensky, 1959.

Ellis, David M., James A. Frost, Harold C. Syrett, Harry J. Carman. *A Short History of New York State.* Ithaca, New York: Cornell University Press, 1957.

Ernst, Robert. *Immigrant Life in New York City.* New York: King's Crown, 1949.

Fairfield, Francis Gerry. *The Clubs of New York.* New York: H. L. Hinton, 1873.

Fiske, Stephen. *Off-hand Portraits of Prominent New Yorkers.* New York: G. R. Lockwood & Son, 1884.

Flick, Alexander Clarence. *Samuel Jones Tilden.* New York: Dodd, Mead, 1939.

Franklin, Allan, and Thomas Nast (illustrator). *The Trail of the Tiger, being an account of Tammany from 1789; The Organization and Sway of the Bosses.* New York, 1928.

Genung, Abram Polhemus. *The Frauds of the New York City Government Exposed: Sketches of the Members of the Ring and Their Confederates.* New York, 1871.

Gold Panic Investigation. 41st Congress, 2nd Session, H. of R. Report No. 31. Washington, 1870.

Goldstone, Harmon H., and Martha Dalrymple. *History Preserved: A Guide to New York City Landmarks and Historic Districts.* New York: Simon and Schuster, 1974.

Grodinsky, Julius. *Jay Gould: His Business Career, 1867–1892.* Philadelphia: University of Pennsylvania Press, 1957.

Holbrook, Stewart Hall. *The Age of the Moguls.* Garden City, New York: Doubleday & Co., 1953.

Hoyt, Edwin P. *The Goulds: A Social History.* New York: Weybright & Talley, 1969.

Hudson, W. C. *Random Recollections of an Old Political Reporter.* New York, 1911.

Jones, Willoughby. *The Life of James Fisk, Jr., Including the Great Frauds of the Tammany Ring.* Chicago: Union Publishing Company, 1872.

Josephson, Matthew. *The Robber Barons.* New York: Harcourt, Brace and Company, 1934.

Kilroe, Edwin P. *Saint Tammany and the Origin of the Society of Tammany or Columbian Order in the City of New York.* New York: Private Printing, 1913.

Lening, Gustav. *The Dark Side of New York, and Its Criminal Classes from Fifth Avenue down to the Five Points. A Complete Narrative of the Mysteries of New York.* New York, 1873.

Lundberg, Ferdinand. *America's Sixty Families.* New York: Vanguard Press, 1937.

Lynch, Denis Tilden. *Boss Tweed: The Story of a Grim Generation.* New York: Boni and Liveright, 1927.

Maher, James T. *The Twilight of Splendor.* Boston: Little, Brown, 1975.

Mandelbaum, Seymour. *Boss Tweed's New York.* New York: John Wiley and Sons, 1965.

Maurice, Arthur B. *Fifth Avenue.* New York: Dodd, Mead & Co., 1918.

Mayer, Grace M. *Once Upon a City: New York from 1890 to 1910.* New York: Macmillan, 1958.

Morris, Lloyd R. *Incredible New York*. New York: Random House, 1951.

Myers, Gustavus. *The History of Tammany Hall*. New York: Boni and Liveright, 1917.

Nast, Thomas. *Miss Columbia's Public School, or Will It Blow Over?* New York: Francis B. Felt & Co., 1871.

Newton, Michael. *The Encyclopedia of Robberies, Heists, and Capers*. New York: Facts on File, 2002.

O'Connor, Richard. *Hell's Kitchen: The Roaring Days of New York's Wild West Side*. New York: J. B. Lippincott, 1958.

O'Conor, Charles. *Peculation Triumphant: Being the Record of a Five Years' Campaign against Official Malverism AD 1871–75*. New York, 1875.

Osofsky, Gilbert. *Harlem: The Making of a Ghetto: Negro New York, 1890–1930*. New York: Harper & Row, 1966.

Paine, Albert Bigelow. *Thomas Nast: His Period and His Pictures*. New York: Macmillan, 1904.

Patton, Clifford W. *The Battle for Municipal Reform: Mobilization and Attack, 1875–1900*. New York, 1940.

Pember, Arthur ("A.P."). *Mysteries and Miseries of the Great Metropolis*. New York: D. Appleton, 1874.

Richmond, Rev. J. F. *New York and Its Institutions, 1609–1873*. New York, 1873.

Riordan, William L. *Plunkitt of Tammany Hall*. New York: Alfred A. Knopf, 1948.

Ross, Ishbel. *Charmers and Cranks: Twelve Famous American Women Who Defied the Conventions*. New York: Alfred A. Knopf, 1961.

Rovere, Richard. *Howe and Hummel: Their True and Scandalous History*. New York: Farrar, Straus, 1947.

Saarinen, Aline B. *The Proud Possessors*. New York: Random House, 1958.

Shaw, Frederick. *The History of the New York City Legislature*. New York: Columbia University Press, 1957.

Smith, Matthew Hale. *Sunshine and Shadow in New York*. Hartford, Connecticut: J. B. Burr & Co., 1869.

Stone, William L. *History of New York City*. New York: Virtue & Yorston, 1872.

Strong, George Templeton. *The Diary of George Templeton Strong, 1835–1875*. Edited by Allan Nevins and Milton Halsey Thomas. New York: Macmillan, 1952.

Sullivan, James. *History of the State of New York 1523–1927* (6 vols.). New York: Lewis Historical Publishing Co., 1927.

Swierczynski, Duane. *This Here's A Stick-Up: The Big Bad Book of American Bank Robbery.* Indianapolis: Alpha Books, 2002.

Tilden, Samuel. *The New York City "Ring," Its Origin, Maturity and Fall.* New York: Press of John Polhemus, 1873.

Tompkins, Calvin. *Merchants and Masterpieces.* New York: Dutton, 1973.

Walling, George Washington. *Recollections of a New York Chief of Police.* New York: Caxton Book Concern, 1887.

Warshow, Robert Irving. *Jay Gould: The Story of a Fortune.* New York: Greenberg, 1928.

Wecter, Dixon. *The Saga of American Society: A Record of Social Aspiration 1607–1937.* New York: Scribner, 1937.

Werner, M. R. *Tammany Hall.* New York: Doubleday, Doran, 1928.

Wheeler, Everett P. *Sixty Years of American Life: Taylor to Roosevelt, 1850–1910.* New York: E. P. Dutton & Co., 1917.

White, Bouck. *The Book of Daniel Drew: A Glimpse of the Fisk-Gould-Tweed Regime from the Inside.* New York: Doubleday, Page and Company, 1910.

NEWSPAPERS AND MAGAZINES

Brattleboro Vermont Journal
Brooklyn Daily Eagle
Harper's Weekly
The Nation
New York Herald
The New York Times
New York Tribune

INDEX

ABOUT THE AUTHOR

J. North Conway (Jack Conway) is the author of eleven books, including *American Literacy: Fifty Books That Define Our Culture and Ourselves* and *The Cape Cod Canal: Breaking Through the Bared and Bended Arm.* An accomplished poet, his poems have appeared in many journals and anthologies, including *Poetry, The Antioch Review, The Columbia Review,* and *The Norton Book of Light Verse.* He is a former newspaper and magazine editor and he currently teaches English at the University of Massachusetts in Dartmouth and Bristol Community College in Fall River. He lives in Assonet, Massachusetts.